Molly and Me

Molly and Me

GERTRUDE BERG

WITH CHERNEY BERG

McGRAW-HILL BOOK COMPANY, INC.
New York   Toronto   London

To Lewis

Contents

A Foreword to the Wise

I have lived and am still living a very happy life. Such a remark, I know, is a hopelessly unfashionable beginning for a modern autobiography, and I apologize.

But in my life there are all kinds of things that haven't happened to me. I have absolutely no scarlet admissions to make about a weekend on a movie star's yacht in the Bay of Naples. I can't write about how I divorced three husbands, became a drug addict, and finally, after years of searching, found the real meaning of Life in a spoonful of mescalin. And, if all those things and more had happened to me, I'm not so sure I'd want to write about them. Even when I go to a doctor, I don't tell him everything, because it seems to me that there are some things—my weight and age, if you want a for-instance—that should remain personal.

The reason I'm not the confessing type is probably my parents' fault. My mother and father brought me up to feel that there were some things you talked about and some you didn't. And, as a child, whenever I had a story to tell about a friend my father would always say, "Don't be a monitor!" This advice left an impression, but not a scar.

Sometimes I get the feeling that Dr. Freud invented mothers and fathers for their children to hate. If I had ever met the gentleman, I'm afraid psychoanalysis would have been set back fifty years. I adored my parents. On the other hand, I don't feel I have to make a production of it.

Certainly I have faults, but why should I torture myself? I know that I'm addicted to soda water, that I try every new diet I hear about, that department stores are my downfall, and that I'm very weak when it comes to noodle soup (with lots of noodles). I also like to eavesdrop on other people's conversations and I have a total recall for everybody else's mistakes. Aside from that I'm normal—normal enough not to want to write a confession. Anyway, it would be on the dull side; you're not missing a thing.

The best I can do is start at the beginning and hope. But starting at the beginning isn't always that easy. People don't just appear, they come from someplace. Everybody has ancestors and everybody is descended. I must have come from a long line but the furthest back I can remember is my father's father, Mordecai Edelstein. So I start with Grandpa for two reasons: because he would have liked it and because he was the first one of us all to come to America. He started us here in the New World. It was his discovery and he was our link to the past on the other side. And he was the one who could always say "Before your time this was" when he told stories. So, for me, in the beginning there was Grandpa. . . .

PART ONE

THE CITY

1 *Ah, Columbus!*

Grandpa Mordecai was a man I could talk to—if he felt like talking. If he didn't, I could sit with him in a room for hours, and he wouldn't say a word. But when he did talk he had something to say. He came from Lublin, Poland, and I liked to talk to him about the Old Country, and if it was a good day he would answer my questions. The Old Country fascinated me, and I wanted to know all about it. But Grandpa didn't like to talk about the old days. When I asked him why, he would just say, "Because!" And the "Because" was that he wanted to talk about New York.

To Grandpa New York was more than a city. It wasn't that the United States ended where Yonkers began. He knew the names of all the states, their capitals, their chief products. To him the compass was divided into three points—uptown, downtown, and crosstown. Uptown took you to "Chicagy," downtown went to "Angelnd in Eurp," and if you wanted to go to "Californy," you had to go crosstown.

Grandpa acted about the city as if he was one of the original settlers, an Indian. And as far as the family was concerned, he was the pioneer, the man who went west and found the New World. He wouldn't accept the honor. It belonged to Christopher Columbus—the greatest man who ever lived. He felt so close to Columbus that sometimes he called him by his first name. Every once in a while when he was thinking quietly about America and New York City he would sigh and say, "Columbus! Ah, Columbus!"

Let anyone say a word against America and Grandpa would

3

get insulted. He took it as a personal reflection on his hero and he would say "A klug zu Columbus!" which can be translated roughly as "What a curse on Columbus—that such a pimple should insult such a man!" The Yiddish is shorter and the words have to be said to the accompaniment of a glare in the eye, a look to heaven for justice, then a long, sad shake of the head.

Grandpa's memories always started with Castle Garden at the foot of the Battery, where he met and fell in love with the New World at first sight. This great hall packed with arriving immigrants was to him the seven wonders of the world under one roof. When I asked him what it actually looked like, he could only say, with a faraway look in his eyes, "Big! big!"; and when I asked him what happened there, he would say, "Questions."; and when I asked him what kind of questions, he would shrug, smooth out his mustache, and rattle off what he could remember: "Who am I? I'm Mordecai Edelstein. Where was I born? In Lublin. What kind of work do I do? Tinsmith." Then he was quiet, turned his hands palm up, looked at his long, strong, calloused fingers, repeat "Tinsmith!" and start talking again: "Such a lot of people came off the boat; laughing ones, crying ones, hugging ones. I was alone, and I could watch them. I told myself, 'It won't be long; I'll have my own family coming off the boat; we'll be crying, laughing, hugging. Why not?' I told myself. 'Look where I am. Me! Mordecai Edelstein from Lublin. I am in America! And not only in America, I am off that boat!'"

"A boat!" Grandpa added, shaking his head at me. He seemed to look somewhere beyond me, not even seeing me. "They gave it a name, *Atlantic*. A boat! a captain! Only my enemies should go on such a boat. But, listen, for fifteen dollars who expected a palace? But, also, who expected a barn? In every room—room? A closet. They put twelve men, one

on top of another, like wood. A window? A little hole. If you
opened it, God forbid, the ocean came in for company. Food?
If you were hungry and you were strong, they put a pot upstairs on deck two times a day. For what they cooked two
time was plenty. But why complain? I wouldn't be on it forever. Two weeks. How many people in steerage? Every place
there was a person. It looked like the boat was made of people,
and if somebody wanted to take a deep breath, everybody
else had to stop and take turns, so crowded it was.

"And it wasn't only people; they took their beds with them.
Everybody brought a feather bed. In America you want a bed,
you buy a bed. In Lublin you wanted a bed, you made it or
you waited for somebody to die. You weren't a person until
you had a feather bed—that's why everybody took theirs along
when they left. Who knew you could buy a bed in New York?
So the boat was crowded with people, imagine what it was with
mattresses. A mattress came from a father, and where did he
get it, from his father, and where did he get it, from his
father. Where else? A store? Ay, in America, but how could
you know?"

I asked Grandpa how he felt when he saw the Statue of
Liberty for the first time from the boat. "You don't read books
in school? When I came there wasn't a statue," he said im-
pressively. "Did Columbus see a statue?" he went on. "Did
I see a statue? Did I need a statue? I wasn't in Poland, I
wasn't in Russia, the Tsar wasn't chasing me around any
longer, I didn't live in a ghetto—that was *my* Statue of
Liberty. When the people got off the boat, you know they
kissed the ground. You, an American girl, don't know, and I
don't want you should ever have to know, God forbid! Ah,
Columbus! A smart man you were!"

Grandpa Mordecai was very concerned with progress. When
his friends talked about the Good Old Days, Grandpa didn't

want to hear. He had no use for the Good Old Days—it was tomorrow that interested him. Sometimes taking a walk with him and listening to his remarks was like a tour of Old New York the way it used to be. As we went along Houston Street, he pointed out a fire hydrant and told me he remembered when they first put it in, how water was sold from wagons or drawn from wells. Walking up Third Avenue, he would talk about the "El" and how they used to have steam engines pulling the cars. He would point out food markets and tell me all about the prices they used to charge when he first came over—beef was ten cents a pound, twenty cents for the better cuts. There were free lunch counters for those who had the price of a glass of beer—five cents. A man could make ten dollars a week if he worked hard. There were traffic jams with horses and wagons and it was just as hard to cross Broadway then as it is today. But Grandpa did not resent time passing. There had to be changes, according to him, and he looked at change like a philosopher. "It's like it always was," he would say, "only today people are wearing different hats, that's all, that's the whole thing." He took things as they came. If he liked what was happening, he called it progress. If he didn't he would call on Columbus to see what a mess was being made out of his discovery.

What bothered Grandpa most was that people didn't seem to be as friendly as they used to be. He was always talking about how it used to be on the Lower East Side, and to hear him you'd think there was a party going on every night of the week. As he got older and a little crankier, the number of parties seemed to increase but it was always the same story and the same party and it was always summertime on the roof. Everybody in the building he lived in would congregate on the roof where it was also hot but where there was, at least, a breeze. Some of the neighbors would bring up accordions, maybe a harmonica or two; there was a man who played the violin, and on a hot summer's night everyone would sit around enjoying what little breeze there was and singing songs from "The Old Countries." The German of "Muss I'Denn" mixed with the Russian "Fireflies," the French "J'ai du bon Tabac," and the Yiddish "Auf dem Pripichek"—and if the songs didn't always mingle in the New York air above the roof, the singers mingled below. Grandpa would tell about the youngsters who sat behind the chimneys and held hands and he could even name some that got married later on. Since his apartment was on the top floor he supplied the water for drinking and a little fruit for a "pitnik."

It was always the same party in these stories about a happier New York, but he would argue all night just to prove it was not. He'd even change the address of the building but it was the exact same party every time. It was fun for me to argue with him because that was one of the ways to get him to tell me stories.

"It's your America," Grandpa would say to me. What he meant was, I was lucky and didn't know it, and he'd prove it to me with another story.

Grandpa had the right kind of voice for telling stories. It was deep, it was soft, and in a room full of people, all talking, it played bass. Grandpa was the kind of man to go with his voice. He had a big head with hair that curled down over the back like pictures of Buffalo Bill. He had blue eyes that would turn black when he got mad. And when I looked at him from the side he had the look of an American eagle just about to tell a joke. Grandpa was a tall man. So tall that when I was a very little girl I thought he was a giant come for a visit. I called him Mr. Grandpa or Uncle Grandpa until one day it dawned on me that Grandpa wasn't a name. And when I found out that Grandpa was my father's father he stopped being a piece of furniture with knees for me to sit on and became a great big toy that told stories.

Grandma Rudisel, Grandpa's wife, died young and I never knew her. My image of her comes from a single story I heard more than once when I was a child. With five boys, two girls, and a husband like Grandpa in a small apartment, Grandma Rudisel didn't have to worry about what to do with her leisure time. More than once Grandpa came back to the apartment with what he considered his special treat for his wife—a fancy dress covered with spangles. But Rudisel had nowhere to wear it—except between the stove and the dishpan and the washtub. Yet she would receive the dress with tears of appreciation in her eyes and wear it around the apartment when she could. His children used to laugh in later years when the story was told. Grandpa would nod at whoever recounted the story, look at the laughers, and say, "You have a lot to learn—a whole lot— believe me!"

Grandpa spoke with an accent. In my parents' home that wasn't unusual. Almost every grownup I knew spoke not the King's English but the Tsar's or the Kaiser's. Grandpa could speak Russian, Polish, and German. But he insisted on speaking English all the time because he was an American and Americans spoke only English. Grandpa also spoke Yiddish but only when he had something to say that a child shouldn't hear. Russian or Polish, the languages he was born into, were used only when he couldn't help himself: when he had to add or measure or find out how many square feet of tin he'd need to make a new roof. He excused this lapse by saying that English had hard numbers.

Grandpa was too stubborn to be beaten by English numbers. He memorized what he needed. Sometimes, I remember, I would hear him mumbling over a boiling pot of solder. It sounded like he was saying an incantation: "Twelve inches makes a foots. Three foots is a yard. So if there's thirty-six inches into one yard, what good'll it do me?" And then "what good'll it do me" would start him off: He'd say it faster and faster until it made no sense at all and became a song. The song would have a slightly Russian lilt and before he even knew it, he'd be reciting a table of lengths in his native language—and then he'd be happy until he remembered he was now an American and he'd have to think in "twelve inches makes a foots."

How Grandpa ever got to America he never said. All I knew was that as a young man he got into trouble in Lublin, then a part of Russian Poland. He was already working as a tinsmith, and he was tall, powerfully built, and beneath his good nature and kindness there was a terrible temper. The Jews in Poland were taxed way beyond their means. Things were always bad and only got worse—never better. One day young Mordecai, Mordche for short and Max in English, heard the Tsar's tax collector read a proclamation that taxes were being raised again and if they weren't paid, everybody's household goods would be confiscated. The people were scared but Grandpa was furious. He ran out of the crowd and hit the tax collector. There was a saying in the Lublin ghetto: "Where Mordche hits, the grass never grows again."

The people hid Mordche from the police, and next day there was no trace of him. For six months his family thought he was dead. The next thing his family heard from him was through a letter he wrote a friend saying he was in America. He had been afraid to write his family because the police opened letters, and he wanted to protect them. He asked his friend to tell them he was going to send for them as soon as he could.

All I know of his route to freedom was that he walked to Hamburg, worked there long enough to earn his fare, and took a boat to America. Whenever he spoke about it, it sounded like an overnight trip to Chicago on the Twentieth Century.

A tinsmith in New York was a master mechanic, and Grandpa quickly got a job at nine dollars a week making tin cans for tea, coffee, and cookies. He found a flat at 166 Norfolk Street on the Lower East Side. It didn't have heat, and it didn't have running water. There was a pump in the hall and the toilet was in the backyard. But soon Mordecai had built himself a galvanized tin bathtub and little by little bought furniture for the day when he could send for his family.

By 1891 Mordecai had enough money saved to buy seven steerage tickets at fifteen dollars a head, and sent them to Lublin and waited. At three o'clock one morning the boat with Mordecai's family arrived at Castle Garden. Grandpa's family, frightened, alone, confused, waited for their names to be called. When "Edelstein" was called, they looked around for Mordche. When he came over to the little knot of relatives, they didn't recognize him. They saw a well-dressed man with a hat, no beard, but a mustache. The only way they recognized him was by his voice, the only thing about him that hadn't been Americanized. He had brought along a banana for each of the children. They had never seen one before, and he had to show them how to peel and eat it. As his own English was largely confined to the word "Pickles," a word he knew from making pickle barrels, Mordecai brought a few "landsmen" along to help him to get his family through immigration. My father always said that everytime he ate a banana he remembered Castle Garden—he was four years old at the time.

At 166 Norfolk Street, on the top floor, a party was waiting for Grandpa's family. For once there was enough of everything—meat, bread, drink. If you wanted you could have as much every day—this was the way Americans lived!

One of Mordche's friends who could speak English almost

like a native welcomed the family with a speech. "This is a New World," he said. "You'll all be citizens, Americans! But first you have to have American names." He lined the children up and gave each one a hundred per cent American name. Sura became Sarah, Yussel turned into Joe, Gitell became Mary, Selig was Jake, Yankov was called Johnny, and Lieble got to be Louie. All this was done by pointing a finger and announcing the new name, while Grandpa looked on watching a dream come true. This was what he had brought them over for—to become Americans.

The family liked Norfolk Street. It was like a little town, everybody knew everybody, one man's family was everyone's business, and whenever Mordecai talked about moving away from Norfolk Street, the children would set up a howl. Grandpa compromised—in five years they moved four times, from 166 to 184, from 184 to 175 and then to 171, all Norfolk Street. Each move was to another apartment on the top floor. Mordecai said the air was better up there. Besides, in summer all the neighbors would come up to the roof to sleep, and that meant a party every night. He loved company.

Mordecai had lots of friends, some he had made in America and some from Lublin. A friend from Lublin who was very important to him was a man who had renamed himself Mr. Petersburg. He worked for the Erie Railroad in New Jersey. He convinced Grandpa that working for a railroad was a good thing, and he said he could arrange for a job if Grandpa wanted it. But he would have to call himself Petersburg and make believe he was a brother. Grandpa agreed, and he got a job as a metalsmith in the North Patterson shops of the Erie.

The job was good—both for Mordecai and the railroad. He could fix anything made of metal, and soon he was a trouble shooter for the Erie. He was sent up and down the line fixing passenger cars. He became indispensable, so much so that during the summer when everyone in the shop was laid off, he was kept on. They didn't want to lose him.

Mordecai prospered, and in spite of his family's objections he moved them to Jersey City. He was a railroad man now, and it was the kind of life that suited him. He liked the people he worked with and he liked the work. He was an American among Americans, and he took on their habits, with little added touches of his own. When he saw that the men brought their lunch to the shop, he did the same. But he brought his raw and cooked it in a solder pot over a blowtorch. He liked a hot meal. His favorite lunch was mushrooms and barley, and as soon as he came to work he would put it on to simmer. Nobody minded. To be different then wasn't such a sin.

One day the head of the division dropped in for an inspection. He got a whiff of the cooking food. The foremen tried not to notice the smell and to steer the man away from Grandpa. But the inspector followed his nose and ended up at Mordecai's bench. When he wanted to know what was going on, Mordecai took the lid off the pot and showed him. He invited the head of the division to have lunch with him, and he did. Grandpa told me he was a very nice man, but he ate like a bird.

A few months later, during the summer layoff period, the Erie hired an efficiency expert. The expert took a look at the payrolls and when he came to Mordecai's name—he was still Mr. Petersburg—he wanted to know why that man was being kept on when everyone else was being laid off. The explanation that he was a valuable man wasn't enough, so Mordecai was laid off.

Grandpa never said whether or not he was annoyed. He just opened his own shop. To hear him tell it, it was as simple as that. But one thing he took pride in telling was that when the shops reopened, the foreman came to him and asked him to come back to work. Grandpa's version of his answer was told with a theatrical flourish. "Sir," he said, "I am not for hire. And if you should wish to inquire, I happen to be a business-man."

Grandpa's shop was in the front room of his house in Jersey City. He liked it that way. He wanted to be near his family because, after all, what's a family for if not to be near? And if any of them didn't like the noises he made banging on tin and hammering rivets they could always leave. The world was a big place and there must be plenty of quiet spots for people with sensitive ears. Nobody objected. Nobody dared. But Grandpa liked to store up arguments for just in case.

It wasn't too long before he was doing pretty well with his own tinsmithing business. But pretty well wasn't good enough. That he happened to be the best tinsmith in the country he knew, his friends knew, his family knew, but strangers on the street didn't know. So he had to tell them. Grandpa used to tell me the story with motions and with the introduction that took the place of "Once upon a time." He would start with "Before your time this was" and the tone of voice would always make me think it was so long ago it was before The Flood. He would start out telling me how he built a boat, a five-foot model of a steamship and all of tin. He would hold his hands out in front of him five feet apart and I could almost feel the weight of the boat. There were three funnels, lifeboats, masts, and two little anchors. There were portholes and hatches and little ladders. According to Mordche the model was pretty good. Translated, because Mordche was a hard man to please, that meant the model was perfect and he was very proud of it.

Grandpa put the ship model in his front window. A few people came to look, but not enough. So he built another display, a squirrel cage with a wheel inside. He put a squirrel in the cage and when it ran the wheel turned and people came to look—lots of people.

Grandpa wasn't too much of a philosopher. He liked people too much to worry about what was wrong with them. But the story about the boat and the squirrel cage had a moral and he would apply it to everything. If there was a bank robbery in Detroit the moral worked and if there was a flood in China the moral also worked. The moral was simple. Grandpa worked hard to make a boat that he was proud of. It was practically a masterpiece but what did people come to see? A squirrel running around in a cage! So what was the lesson? The lesson was, you can't join them, you can't beat them, you can't even understand them, so don't bother. Hope for the best and maybe somebody'll come in who'll appreciate the boat. Meanwhile feed the squirrel, it's not his fault.

Mordecai's reputation as a man who could do anything with metal traveled all the way back to Lublin. Every immigrant from there came to see Mordche Blecher, which means The Tinsmith, sooner or later. His home became a clearinghouse for all former Lubliners. They would come, stay for a few days, and then leave for the jobs Grandpa somehow found for them. A few of them even got jobs with the Erie by saying they were relatives of Mr. Petersburg.

One Lubliner who came and stayed was a pugnacious man called Lieple. He was also a tinsmith, and if he had one thing in his favor, in Grandpa's opinion, it was that he said out loud that Mordche was a better tinsmith than he ever could be. Grandpa needed a helper, so naturally he hired an admirer. But before Lieple took the job he joined a union. Unions were new then, and Mordecai thought they were foolishness. A man worked, he got paid. Did he need somebody to tell him that? But, if Lieple wanted to join a union, so let him. Before

Grandpa knew what was happening, he was running a one-man union shop.

Lieple slept on a cot in the back of the shop. Every morning Grandpa would come in, take the ashes out of the stove and start a new fire. Lieple slept through it all. It began to get Grandpa mad. He took to rattling the grate as loud as he could and passing Lieple's bed and bumping into it. The noise and the bump would wake Lieple up. His first words every morning were, "What's the time?" Grandpa would apologize elaborately, as only he knew how. "Sleep," he would say sarcastically, "sleep, I'm not a union man, but you are." Lieple always got up.

Grandpa would tell me about Lieple at least once a year. By the time I was six he was practically an acquaintance. From the way Grandpa talked I always thought Lieple had died but it turned out that he had only gone to Detroit to make automobiles "for Henry Ford." I never thought I would ever see Lieple but one day years later he finally showed up. I was married then and Mordche was a retired gentleman living in a bachelor apartment on the Lower East Side of New York. I had come for a visit and we were talking about the family as usual. There was a knock on the door and when Mordche opened it he let a tall, broad man into the room. Mordche was big too, but he had to look up at his visitor. The visitor looked down and the two of them stood that way for a little bit. The man looked like a gentle wrestler dressed for a Sunday walk. His arms seemed to be falling out of his coat sleeves and the buttons on his jacket must have been sewn on with wires because they looked as though they never could hold the bulk of such a man inside the plain cloth jacket otherwise. The face looked like it had been pressed out of rubber so that it could have a permanent smile. On the lapel of his suit jacket the man wore a small white pin with blue writing on it. From where I sat I couldn't see what it said but it was an election year and I think it must have had some candidate's name on it. He looked like a Roosevelt man not a Hoover man. And besides he had to be a Democrat if he was a friend of Grandpa's. He couldn't be anything else because all of Mordche's Republican friends remove their pins before knocking on Mordche's door. The two-party system worked everyplace in the United States but Mordche's apartment.

The man spoke and after not seeing Mordche for almost twenty years he said, "Nu, Mordche?"

And Mordche, also after almost twenty years said, "So!" He pointed to the button in Lieple's jacket. "Still with the union button?"

And that was Lieple!

Lieple grinned a bigger grin and said, "So! Still a boss?" and they finally shook hands. "You got older, Mordche."

Mordche shrugged and smiled. "What then? I got younger?" He pointed to a chair for Lieple. "A drink, union man? The union says you can take a little schnapps or there's a rule maybe you shouldn't?"

"If you'll have, I'll have."

"I wouldn't have?" Grandpa turned to me. "This is Lieple," he said. Then he turned to Lieple and introduced me. Lieple got up out of the chair, walked over to shake my hand very formally and very gently and then backed himself across the room and into the chair.

From all of Mordche's stories I thought that Lieple would be a little man who could say nothing but yes. But Lieple was big enough to say no if he wanted to. And as I watched these two old men, I could see he let Mordche be the boss because he liked him. Besides, Mordche had an air, a certain something, that made people put question marks at the end of a statement. Friends would say, "It's a nice day, Mordche" but the words came out, "It's a nice day, Mordche?" And if he agreed that it was, the matter was settled. If he didn't answer, his friends would look up for rain clouds.

In his own home everybody knew that Mordecai was the boss. Even the doctors who came to see what was wrong with any member of the family had Mordecai's diagnosis to contend with. It was his family? All right, they had what he said they had. If the doctor was smart, he would agree and keep his opinions to himself. Fathers know best, and Mordecai was the father.

2 *The Retired Gentlemen*

Grandpa Mordecai had been drinking schnapps since he was ten years old. By the time he was eleven it was a habit. He needed his few drinks a day just as some people need their coffee. It wasn't that he was addicted. I suppose he could have done without it if he wanted to—but he didn't want to. He took four drinks a day; that was his ration. As he got older the doctors told him to stop; his wife begged him to stop; and after she died the government took over. They declared prohibition.

Grandpa was a great believer in the law. If the government said you couldn't buy schnapps, so all right, you couldn't buy it. But! Where was it written that you couldn't make it? If you showed him in black and white that there was a law against making liquor, he wouldn't believe you anyway. The government had better things to do than to torment him.

Grandpa's retirement and the Eighteenth Amendment came at about the same time. The retirement left him with lots of time on his hands. And prohibition gave him a hobby, a cause, a project, to amuse him in his old age. At that time his children had all grown up and got married. He was seventy and a grandfather many times. So he moved from the empty house in Jersey City and took a small apartment on the Lower East Side, near Norfolk Street. The apartment was on the first floor. He didn't like to admit that he was getting old. He had a tacit understanding with age: he paid no attention to it and hoped maybe it would go away. But four flights of stairs was a little too much even for him. Also, the apartment he took had a nice large closet.

Grandpa took some bits of copper pipe, his tools, his imagination, and his thirst and built a still. He made his own schnapps from everything and anything that sounded good: potatoes, raisins, grapes, prunes. If it could ferment, it went into the still. The still worked, and he liked what came out of it.

There was always a fragrance about Grandpa's apartment when he was in the process of making a new supply for himself. Sometimes I would visit him in the middle of one of these operations. I loved to tease him about what was going on in his closet.

"What are you cooking, Grandpa?" I would say to him when I came in.

"Cooking? A little prunds for stewing."

"They smell very good."

"For prunds they're all right. Roses they're not."

"Prunes they're not, either."

"A couple there are."

"For schnapps?"

"What do you think? Soda water?"

And then, very carefully so as not to disturb what he called "the works," he would open the closet door and let me look. There, on the upper closet shelf, was a hot plate. On top of the plate was a copper kettle he built. Attached to the kettle was a shiny coil of copper tubing that looked very scientific. The tubes coiled downward to the lower shelf and the end of the tube was fitted into a glass jug where a colorless liquid dripped slowly. The only sound was a constant faint "plop, plop" as the schnapps filled the jug.

"A little drink maybe?" he asked, knowing that I wasn't that brave. I always said, "No," and he always said, "A young girl like you shouldn't drink anyhow." No matter how old I got I was always a young girl to Mordche and that saved me from hurting his feelings and gave me the excuse I needed to refuse his very special four-star product.

Grandpa was a sociable man and he didn't like to drink alone. Everybody who knew him knew that and it saved Grandpa the trouble of inviting people to his apartment. People just dropped in. Because of all the comings and goings it didn't take long for everybody on the block to know that Mordche was making his own schnapps. Even the landlord found out that Mr. Edelstein was using the premises not as per the words in the lease and he came storming in to put a stop to it. The landlord, a Mr. Stone, was a little man with a big sense of responsibility for other people's business. If he was a little late with the heat in the morning, that was all right. If someone was a little late with the rent, that was not so all right. He knocked on Grandpa's door and as soon as the door opened Mr. Stone became a moralist.

"Mr. Edelstein," he said, "I'm surprised at you!"

"Mr. Stone," Grandpa said, "come in. You'll catch a draft in the cold hall. What's the surprise?"

"There's a still in this apartment!"

"That's the surprise? For that you're huffing and puffing?"

"It's against the law, Mr. Edelstein!"

"Have a little drink, Mr. Stone?"

"How could you do such a thing?"

"Mr. Stone, I'll ask you a question? You have a little drink sometimes?"

Mr. Stone said he took a little drink once in a while, but just to be sociable.

"So where does the drink come from, Mr. Stone?" Grandpa asked him and answered for him. "From bootleggers, from gangsters, from public enemies, no?" Mr. Stone couldn't disagree so Grandpa became the moralist. "Shame yourself, Mr. Stone," Grandpa told him. "I'm surprised," and he shook a finger at the poor little accused man, and the more Mr. Stone tried to point out that a still wasn't legal, the more Grandpa accused him of dealing with gangsters. It wasn't more than five minutes before Mr. Stone was practically an uncle to a rum runner. Grandpa, according to Grandpa, was doing his patriotic duty by having a still in his closet and once he got Mr. Stone to agree that having a little drink every once in a while was part of human nature he also got him to agree that making whisky was better than buying from crooks. Grandpa's version was that Mr. Stone had a drink and then apologized.

Being a retired gentleman, Grandpa spent his winters in Daytona Beach with his sister and her family. During prohibition this winter trip was something of a problem for him. His sister, Channa Beana, Channa for Anna and Beana for Beatrice, was a very strict lady. To her, when the government made a law, it was a law. There was no drinking in her house.

Within the same family you couldn't have found two more different people than Grandpa and his sister. He was tall, broad, and by now in his sixties he was beginning to look like Mark Twain with a full, white mustache, flowing white hair, bushy eyebrows, and, in the summer, a Panama hat. Channa Beana was tiny, delicate, like a good-natured but very busy bird. She drank tea. Before prohibition she didn't mind when the men of the family had a little drink. But now the government had said, "No." To her there was no place even for a little "Yes."

Channa Beana knew her brother. She was positive that Mordche was getting his daily drink from someplace. When letters came from up North telling her about the still, she was impressed by his ingenuity but shocked by his nerve. She called it *chutzpa*, which is more than nerve; it's closer to having a hole in the character than just being brave. Channa Beana wrote her brother a letter before he was due for his visit.

Dear Mordche,

You are very welcome to come for the winter and to stay with me and mine. Stay as long as you like. Don't bring the still. I am very good friends with all the people in Daytona Beach. You know what I am talking about.

Your loving sister,
Channa Beana.

Grandpa wrote back:

Dear Sister,

Thank you for the invitation. I'll be very happy to come. I will not bring the still.

Your loving brother,
Mordche.

Grandpa loved his sister. He would never tell her an un-truth. He said he wouldn't bring the still, so he wouldn't. But love or no love, he couldn't change the habits of a lifetime just one, two, three. Of course, there was no harm in promising not to bring the still—it was too big anyway. But there must be another way, and if there was, Grandpa would find it. He thought about the problem, and then he found the solution. He took an old leather valise and lined it with copper. It wasn't an easy job, but it was a labor of love. When the valise was filled with his latest vintage, he was ready for his vacation. Grandpa and his schnapps went south.

Channa Beana never found out about the contents of the suitcase. Grandpa wouldn't have hurt her for the world. So he kept his secret and the suitcase to himself. For a sociable man that must have been very hard. It meant that he had to have his four drinks a day alone. Luckily his room had a mirror. The way Grandpa told the story, when he took a drink he could look at himself in the mirror, raise his glass, say "La-chaim," and have a little company. The drink made him feel like a new man. So he had to toast the new man with another *lachaim*. And that's the way the winter passed, with plenty of company.

When prohibition was finally repealed, Grandpa put the suitcase back in the closet. His still was taken apart and stored, just in case. What had happened once could always happen again. Mordecai prided himself on always learning by experience.

If Grandpa was ever alone, it was when he was walking from one man's house to another's. Even when he lived by himself in later years there was always somebody to talk to or to have a little drink with. If it wasn't a friend, it was a parrot, a cat, a dog, or a fish. The names he gave his animal friends were the result of a simple logic. The parrot he called "Polly," the dog he called "Dog," the cat was called "Cat," and the fish, two of them, were called "Ike" and "Mike." He always used both names, Ike Fish and Mike Fish.

The parrot never learned to talk, but it got to be very good at listening. Grandpa would tell Polly stories about what had happened to him during the day. The bird's main use, however, was as a third person, a judge who was supposed to arbitrate Grandpa's arguments with his friends.

One of Grandpa's favorite people to argue with was Joe Shuster. Grandpa had known Mr. Shuster since they were both children and the two of them had been arguing since the cradle. There were two things Grandpa found to argue about with Mr. Shuster. The first was that Shuster had changed his name. In Lublin the family was known as Shuister and when they came to America Joe dropped the "i" and picked up a fight with Mordche. The second thing that Grandpa didn't like was that Joe Shuster kept saying he was younger than he really was. Instead of saying he was seventy he said he was sixty-eight and Mordche resented it. Mordche's whole object was to make Joe Shuster say he was seventy. It was a matter of honor and Grandpa finally did it with the parrot and a little subtlety. Mordche's idea of being subtle was to invite Mr. Shuster to his apartment, give him a drink, make him comfortable, and then ignore him. He talked only to the parrot and the way Grandpa told it the parrot was the Supreme Court and he was Emile Zola.

"Polly," he said he said, "how many years do I know this man?"

Mr. Shuster saw what was going to be. "Don't start, Mordche," he said.

"To you I'll talk later, Shuster," Grandpa said and kept on talking to the bird. "I know him already seventy years, Polly," and he held up seven fingers so that the parrot would be able to understand.

"Mordche, please! The bird has to know everything? She's a stranger!"

"You're ashamed yourself, Shuster?"

"What's to be ashamed?"

"Listen, Polly, when does a boy become a man?"

"Mordche! How should a bird in a cage know such things!"

"Don't worry. A boy becomes a man when he has a *bar mitzvah*. You had a *bar mitzvah*, Shuster?"

"Of course."

"You know where, Polly?"

"The bird knows geography?"

"In Lublin, Polly. . . ."

"Some smart bird, Mordche. So far I haven't heard one word."

"Polly, you know when I had my *bar mitzvah?* No? When I was thirteen."

"What do you want from life, Mordche?"

"You know who was with me when I was *bar mitzvahed?* Shuster! So how old were you, Shuster?"

"Ask the bird."

"Thirteen, no?"

"So?"

"So! Polly if I was thirteen and he was thirteen and today I'm seventy, so how old is Shuster?"

"The bird is Einstein, he can add?"

"Better than you. . . ."

"Mordche, please. . . ."

"Joe Shuster, me you can tell, and believe me, the bird wouldn't say one word."

Mr. Shuster finally said he was seventy and the only other people in the whole world besides Mordche and Polly who knew were my mother, my father, and myself. Mordche had to have somebody to talk to about his victory. After all, how much can you say to a parrot?

Grandpa had his differences with everyone he knew. Sooner or later somebody was bound to do or say something he didn't like. And then Polly, and sometimes myself, would hear about it.

Many times members of the family borrowed money from Mordecai. He was always willing to lend, the only condition he ever placed on a loan being that it should be repaid, and in a family this can lead to some terrible resentments. One particular relative took his time about repaying a loan, and Mordecai got mad. Since I had a husband by that time and should know a little about life, he would talk it over with me and ask my advice, which he didn't need because he had already decided what to do: He was going to court and let the law decide who was in the right. He would describe to me exactly what he was going to wear to court—his working clothes, his overalls. In this role of a poor working man he was going to walk right up to the bench and say: "Judge, Your Honor, sir, look at me. I'm a poor old man. Out of the goodness of my heart I loaned this man money. You tell me, you are a judge of people, it this right or is this wrong? Should he or should he not pay me back? Last week he bought his wife a fur coat while I haven't even an overcoat to wear in the winter months. Tell me, Judge, Your Honor, do I need a lawyer to plead my case?"

He was positive that there was no judge or court in the land that could resist his dramatic plea for justice. Probably he could have won his case, but he never went to court with it. Once a year, at least, he would rehearse his courtroom drama for me, and then decide to forget it for another year. The relative never paid him back. I think it would have spoiled Grandpa's fun if he had.

One case did get to court. Grandpa retinned a whole roof on the house of a lady-in-law. He repaired the ventilators too and fixed the cornices. When he finished he handed in his bill. She refused to pay. She said it wasn't a good job. That was the last thing in the world to say to Mordche, the Tinsmith. Maybe you didn't like him, maybe you just postponed paying him, but you never said he did a bad job. He sued. First the case was taken up before each member of the family, but Grandpa absolutely refused to have it settled out of court. He prepared his case without a lawyer by making two models, each about three feet high and exact replicas of the house he had fixed. One model was before, and the other after. When the case was tried, Grandpa showed the two models to the judge and made him a speech. He told the judge among other things that if he didn't believe him it was a good job, he should go up to 97th Street and Lexington Avenue and take a look at the building himself.

Grandpa won his case, without the judge going up to Lexington Avenue and 97th Street to take a look at his craftsmanship. He was vindicated. He told Polly all about his triumph. Then he solemnly swore to her that he would never fix that woman's house again—not that it would ever need fixing, because, he assured Polly, when Mordche Blecher fixed something, it stayed fixed.

3 *Forget the Logic*

My father Jake was Mordecai's son; he was more than just a chip—he was the whole block. The only difference between them was their age, and if you counted the years between them it wasn't so much. At a very early age, Mordecai had become the father of two girls and four boys. Jake was the next to the youngest of the boys and the only one who repeated his father, bone for bone and idea for idea.

They were both handsome men, tall, the kind of men that had strong hands that looked capable of doing what had to be done. They were not the sort one thought of as Junior and Senior. They were more like people looking at each other in a mirror that separated them by twenty years. The same blue-gray eyes looked at each other; the same smile smiled back at itself; and the same wrinkles framed the look of something always going on behind the identical innocent expression that fooled everybody but each other.

They were both born bosses with minds of their own—people who never asked advice from anyone except when things went wrong, and then it wasn't advice they wanted, it was someone to blame for not warning them. Since they never told anyone what they were doing, who could tell them what they were doing wrong? Of course, that never could be part of the argument, it made too much sense. And when Mordecai and Jake argued against anyone they were like an Olympic team playing a game that had one rule: forget the logic, get to the point. Anyone who had the bad luck to be pitted against these two in an argument would never get out, would never win, and would never be allowed to forget that he once had the nerve to take on the champions of *non sequitur*.

I remember once my father invited a friend over to the house for a cup of coffee when Mordecai was visiting. My father was an expert coffee cooker but he had one fault. When he talked he lost all track of time. The coffee was perking and he was talking. About fifteen minutes later Mordecai reminded his son about the coffee.

"Jake," he said, "you think maybe the coffee is finished?"

My father looked at his watch, making believe he was timing the process. "Another minute maybe."

The friend, unsuspecting, said that his wife perks coffee three minutes exactly which was according to the directions she wrote away for to the Home Economics Department of Cornell University.

That's all the debate team had to hear. It was like a starting whistle. Mordecai inquired gently, "A college knows from coffee?"

The friend assured him that this was so and that it was all very scientifically worked out.

"They drink it or they test it?" my father asked.

"They must test it," the friend told him.

"A mouse knows from coffee?" Mordecai wanted to know.

"Who said a mouse?"

"So a monkey," my father said.

"I didn't say monkeys."

"You said 'test,' " Mordche told him in case he forgot.

"And," Jake added, "a scientific test is with monkeys **or** mice."

"Sometimes guinea pigs," the friend told them.

"A guinea pig knows from coffee?" Mordche asked.

"Did I say guinea pigs?" the friend wanted to know.

"When it comes to animals," Jake said, "I wouldn't trust them. A headwaiter, yes, but not animals."

"They use professors," the friend told them hoping that would stop the argument. After all, who knows more than a professor?

"That's work for a man who went to college?" Mordche wanted to know.

"Who makes the coffee for them?" Jake asked.

"Another professor," the friend said, piling up protection.

"And where did he learn to make coffee?" Jake asked, getting up and turning off the coffeepot at last. "If you want to know about coffee, taste," and he poured the brew, thick and black as oil, into cups.

The friend's candid verdict was that the coffee was too strong and absolutely undrinkable.

"See how much you know," Jake told him. "This is coffee!"

"The best," Mordecai added. "Just right!"

And the father and son sat there drinking while Jake's friend pushed away his cup and asked for a glass of water. Neither Jake nor Mordecai would admit the coffee had perked too long and between the two of them they drank the whole pot.

They never admitted that the coffee was bad and from that time on Jake's friend was saddled with the reputation of a man who didn't know good coffee when he tasted it. Forever after the poor man was known in our house as "Mr. Coffee Man," his children were called "Coffee's Beans," and his wife was referred to as "How Could She Marry Such a Man?"

Jake had been trained by Mordecai in the mind-of-your-own business, and when he made up his mind to do something, he just did it. For instance, at eighteen he decided that time was passing and he had better get married. He wasn't even eighteen and a half when he had a wife.

Jake's wife was called Dinah. She was my mother. She was a little woman, very pretty, with big black eyes and black hair that she wore in a bun. She looked like a doll you wanted to put in your pocket and take home. That's exactly what my father did when he first met her, put her in his pocket and brought her home. As I understand it, she didn't have much to say in the matter.

Jake's mother and father approved. It wouldn't have made any difference if they hadn't, so it was lucky that they did. On the other side of the fence, my mother's parents weren't so sure. After all, what prospects did this young eighteen-year-old have? What kind of a job and what kind of a future? That was absolutely no sort of a question to put to Jake, because he told them. He was, he said, a diamond setter. He wasn't, but it sounded good, so that's the part he acted until he married Dinah. After that, there was nothing they could say or do about it.

I always wanted to know how my mother and father had met. They enjoyed telling me so much that every time I asked I got a different answer. For my father just meeting and falling in love wasn't a story. It had to be a real-life true romance.

When I was very young my mother and father met in Wyoming where my father just happened to be selling eyeglasses to the Indians. My mother was living in a log cabin on the shores of Lake Twillum. I spent a long time looking for Lake Twillum on all the maps of the West. I couldn't find it but when I got a little older what I did find was that *tvillim* are the phylacteries, the prayer bands that Orthodox Jews put on their foreheads and wind around the arm. No matter. Twillum

was and always will be a lake somewhere in Wyoming and it
was very lucky that my father happened to be near it when the
Indians attacked my mother's cabin. My father, a brave man,
went to the rescue with his wagon full of eyeglasses and his
four horses. He was outnumbered and captured and when the
chief of the Indians saw him he gave orders to set him free. It
just so happened that my father, also a scout for the U.S. Cavalry during the slack season, had once rescued the chief from
a grizzly bear. But Jake refused to be set free unless the girl
the Indians had just captured was also set free—and this the
chief wouldn't do. He wanted to marry the pretty paleface
himself.

Now my mother and father were in real trouble, especially
my father because he had to find a way to rescue my mother
and finish the story and get me to bed. The rescue came about
because of the honest trade he practiced. The chief had a son
who was a very bad hunter. He was nearsighted. My father
made a bargain with the chief. He would cure his son if the
chief let the girl and himself go free. Now, even an Indian
is a father and to such a proposition could a father say no?
No! The boy got his glasses, my father got a wife, I got to
bed, and everybody lived happily ever after.

My father's Western stories were really Middle European
Easterns taken from stories he had heard in Poland and
Russia. For Cavalry read Cossaks, for Indians read Peasants,
but still there was enough reality in the telling so that even
today I have visions of Apaches and Sioux surrounding a fort
—all wearing eyeglasses courtesy of Jacob Edelstein, Indian
scout and trader in spectacles.

My mother never contradicted my father when he told a
story. They were like children together and once they decided
on a story, no one, not even their own child, could make them
change it. If I wanted to know how they really met I found

that I had to make up my own stories—something that would satisfy me—and let it go at that. I would have liked it if they had met each other at an Embassy Ball where manners and chivalry were quite the thing. The closest story to that was the one my father liked to tell in the spring when it was raining. He said he put his overcoat on a mud puddle so that my mother wouldn't get her feet wet—and for that story I read Sir Walter for Sir Jake—and when I told him that I had read it somewhere he wasn't the least bit surprised—it was a very famous story, he said, it had been in all the papers.

4 *The Transatlantic Tailor*

Jake's in-laws were gentle people like their daughter, not argument-winners like the Edelsteins. My mother's father, Harris Goldstein, was a big man, strong, almost as strong as Mordecai the Tinsmith, and he was always happy about something—and if there was nothing to be happy about he'd be thankful there was nothing for him to be sad about.

Harris became a world traveler, almost a professional commuter. He was born in a little town in Russia, left home to become a student in Moscow. There he learned enough to know that he wanted to go to London where he had an older brother who was a tailor and become a tailor too. But Harris had a second brother, also a tailor, who lived in Philadelphia and after working in London for a few years he decided to go to his American brother and help him in his Philadelphia store. By this time Harris had a wife, Czerna.

For nine years Harris and Czerna traveled back and forth between tailor shops in Philadelphia and London, and in the nine years of traveling, Harris and Czerna had nine children. Five were Americans born in Philadelphia and four were English born in London, so that every time Harris took a trip he had immigration problems.

Harris finally made up his mind between being a clothier in London or a tailor in Philadelphia. He settled in New York City. According to Harris the real reason for his final move was a very practical one. He wanted to be in business for himself and in New York the demand for coats and pants was growing along with the population, in London it wasn't. Life in those good old days could be just as simple as that. Also he would explain that he couldn't face the idea of rocking about on board ship for two weeks with nine children. He loved children but on dry land.

I remember my grandfather Harris as a man who would let me and other children take more liberties with him than we would think of taking with anybody else. With Harris you could comb his hair whenever and as often as you felt like it and he stood for it like a big, friendly bear. He would even lie on the floor and let you walk on him if you wanted to. Harris would rather put in a seam crooked than refuse a child anything. He would sit still and let me, a babe in arms, practically, shave him: greater love there isn't.

So Harris opened a business of his own in New York City. Before he knew it he was running a small factory. He became a contractor, a man who made suits that one sold under somebody else's label. He would make one hundred herringbone suits for one company, twenty-five jackets with belts in the back for another, and one hundred and fifty blue serge double-breasteds for somebody else. And on and off, if the season was a good one, he'd do very well.

Every once in a while Harris would think back to the old days in London and wonder how in the world he got himself into such a mess: seasons, lay-offs, changing styles. But he knew the answer without too much thinking: it was better to be in his own business, to be his own boss, instead of having to wear a cutaway and a top hat, bow from the waist and say, "Sir," to every customer. He liked to explain that in London he was a tailor, and he was very careful to pronounce the word with a small t, while in America he was a Tailor. The difference wasn't only in the spelling, he always said. It was in how you could walk down the street, a tailor or a Tailor. That is the real reason he settled finally in America.

Harris's wife, Czerna, my mother's mother, was full of love for everybody and especially for her son-in-law and my father, Jake. She was sedate and well brought up, and I think my father was a relief for her. Jake would do and say things she wouldn't even dream of, but when Jake did them and said them, not only did she think they were funny, but she also thought he was right. As far as she was concerned, Jake could hardly do any wrong, and as far as Jake was concerned, Czerna was perfect.

Czerna means black in Russian and it was a good name for my mother's mother. Her hair was black, so black that I could almost see lights reflected from it. Her eyes, also, were black, like great ripe olives. And her complexion was what I always thought Carmen's would be: lightly tanned, the kind of skin that looks beautiful in bright clothes. She was a little woman with a lovely figure and she was about half the size of all the other grownups I knew. By the time I was ten I was as tall as she was. The men in my father's family teased her, especially when she ate. A half a sandwich would fill her up and my father used to say that if she read a menu in a restaurant, for her that would be a full meal. She may have been small but she worked hard enough for two full-sized people and I never once heard her say that she was tired.

Czerna had ideas about how a woman should look. She was always neat, always clean, and always dressed as though she was just going out. Added to that wonderful sense of knowing she was a woman was a shyness. It was natural with her, not made up or cultivated. Shyness was as much part of her as her tiny feet. It was lovely but it could be aggravating, especially when she refused to speak English in front of strangers. It wasn't that she didn't speak well, it was only because she had an accent and didn't speak quite like other Americans.

Czerna was a little woman men always thought they had to protect. She didn't need it but she was a lady and gave in gracefully. When my father married into Harris's family, he and all his brothers and Mordche became Czerna's bodyguard. To outsiders it must have looked like the Purple Gang had decided to make their headquarters in a lady's garden club. Czerna was a woman who knew right from wrong; the Edelsteins also knew but they liked to stretch a point. And if they did something that Czerna thought was wrong, like drinking tea in the European manner with a spoon in the glass, she told them and they listened to her. They had never listened to anyone before without arguing, but for Czerna they kept still. They just didn't want to hurt her feelings.

My mother was eighteen and my father nineteen when I was born. I wasn't a baby, I was almost a contemporary. Harris, Czerna, and Mordche became grandparents before their time. The whole world seemed young. The neighborhood I was born into, East Harlem on Lexington Avenue and 116th Street, seemed to be growing up with me. The horsedrawn streetcars became electric, the telephone lines went underground, and the policeman in his little traffic booth became a red and green light on a pole. The street, Lexington Avenue, was all of cobblestones and the outside noises of metal-rimmed wagon wheels banging on the stone were gradually replaced by the softer noise of metal on tar. The only time the street was ever really quiet was when the snow fell. I can remember my mother holding me up to the window so that I could see the horses in the street below us pulling their wagons quietly for once and puffing their breath into the cold air. I would make her hold me up for the longest time so that I could scratch pictures into the frost on the windowpanes and make little holes through which I could see the street.

What I didn't know then was how special it was to have a family that made the world into a wonderful, warm, and happy place. I thought all families were the same. I didn't know how lucky I was.

5 *Friday Nights*

My memories of Czerna revolve around Friday nights, the areaway between her apartment and ours, Passover, and her nickname, Bubeshu, or Little Grandma.

I was close to her not only because I loved her but also because she lived just around the corner. Our two houses on Lexington Avenue were separated in the rear by an areaway. From my bedroom window I could look out and down and see her living-room window. That was more fun than the telephone. Every morning when I was going to school, I used to lean out of my window and call to her, "Yoohoo, Bubeshu, *vif'l a zeyger iz es?*" "Grandma, what time is it?" I could have looked at the alarm clock, but it was more fun to ask her. She always came to the window, looked up at me, with her happy face, and told me it was time to get dressed.

I would run over to her house on the way to school, for no reason except to see her, say hello and good-bye. She never said good-bye back, only asked me if I was coming over later. She knew I would, but she understood how much I liked the ritual.

Friday visits, morning and afternoon, to her house were the best. In the morning I would walk right into her kitchen full of confusion. The whole room was a mixture of dough drying for noodles, pots boiling, and the wooden kitchen table sprinkled all over with flour. It was like a rehearsal in a theater. The stage was being set, the props arranged, and the acts run through for this Friday night supper that was ten or eleven hours away and would be the finished performance. The only thing in the whole kitchen that wasn't in a mess was Bubeshu.

38

And when I came back from school and walked into Grandma's kitchen for the second time that day, it was like walking into another set. The place shone. It was as if nothing had gone on the whole day except polishing pots and waxing furniture. How such a frail little woman could do so much was something I tried hard to understand. On those rare days when I stayed home from school and watched her, I began to get the idea: it was continuous, calm, unhurried, well-organized, hard work. Staying home from school was a pleasure— especially on a Friday. If I could convince my mother that I was just a little sick and didn't have a temperature, I could run over to my grandmother's to watch and help.

Preparations for the Friday night dinner began so early in the morning that by the time I was up and dressed and had gotten to Bubeshu's the shopping was already done. The fish had been bought and cleaned, the chicken was plucked, and the dough for the noodles was rolled out and drying. There were no ready mixes in those days and few other time-saving conveniences or machinery. What you did, you did yourself, with some help from your whole family.

Grandma was busy filleting pounds of carp, pike, whitefish, and a species called "buffle." (I never did find out what kind of fish "buffle" was. There must be a definition someplace, but where?) These were the ingredients of gefillte fish that were chopped by hand in a wooden bowl that made a sound like music, then mixed, seasoned, and very slowly cooked by Bubeshu. She was also tending to the noodles for the soup and making the soup too. I loved to watch her little, plump, hands fold the dough, pat it down, and then cut it up into noodles with those quick little slicings that only a really professional cook can manage.

While everything was quietly cooking, that's when the house cleaning began. There was nothing that didn't get picked up, dusted, cleaned, or polished. The sinks in the kitchen and even the bare pipes were all given new pleated calico skirts to hide them, as if they were going out in public. Even the quarter meter for the gas had a little skirt. By four on Friday afternoon the table was set, the house was spotless, and the food was ready, simmering or cooling.

Grandma never complained about her eighteen-hour working day. She acted as if it was her pleasure instead of her chore. The only time she seemed tired was when she would sit down, put her head up against her hand and lean on the kitchen table for a few moments. She always told me that this was the sweetest time of the day for her.

Friday night at sundown is the beginning of the Sabbath, the day of rest. My grandmother lit the candles on the table and said a blessing for the house and all the people in it. It had to be a strong blessing because we were a lot of people: there was my mother, my father, and myself, my grandmother, my grandfather, my aunt Aida, my aunt Bessie and her family. And then came the uncles: Jack, Henry, Sol, Benny—and his family. If my aunt Aida invited a friend, Jack would have to ask a friend—and if Jack asked, then Henry and Sol could also ask; so that by the time sundown came, the table often had twenty-five people squeezed around it.

For Czerna, in spite of the rushing and the cooking and the cleaning, it meant the beginning of twenty-four hours of freedom from worry. Czerna was a very religious woman and to her the Sabbath meant honoring her God and her religion. As soon as she lit the candles on the table, said a blessing and a prayer for her family, the traditional duty of the mother who always welcomes the Sabbath first, she could begin to relax. God, she said, gave women the Sabbath so that they could rest up from the worries of their husbands. No matter what troubles Harris had in his business, as soon as the Sabbath started Czerna asked him to forget them for twenty-four hours. The Sabbath was the day God rested from his labors, and according to Czerna if God could rest, so could Harris.

All those Friday nights of my childhood seem lumped together into one evening. The candles and the yellow lights seemed to brighten the room and make the white tablecloth even whiter. Everything looked new—even the people around the table.

I don't think Czerna ever sat through a whole meal. One minute she was at the table and the next she was gone. I don't know how many miles she traveled going from the table to the kitchen. There was always someone who wanted more soup or another piece of challah, the traditional twisted loaf of white bread, and then one course had to be cleared away and the next one brought in.

There was always enough to feed the twenty-five and whoever else was passing by and who just happened to knock on the door. My grandmother always said a table full of people solved the leftover problem and on Friday nights the problem never existed—the only thing that was left over was the plates. And with enough women in the house that wasn't a problem either.

These Friday nights were like bright spots of color in the routine of the week. The family was on its best behavior and they looked forward to the next Friday even before the first one was finished.

When I was a young girl, my favorite holiday of all the holidays was Passover and especially the week before. There was something inexpressible, an excitement, a rushing, that led up to Passover.

First of all Passover meant new clothes. Part of the meaning of the holiday is the celebration of the coming of spring. And celebrating spring meant that everything had to be new and clean. By my father's definition that included children. I spent the night before Passover waiting for the morning so that I could open the box with my new dress and try on my new shoes. I loved the shoes better than almost anything else. They had buttons all the way up the side and the tops had little black bows. The patent leather always shone. I never wanted to wear them because I knew they would get old and cracked but I always gave in to my vainer self who said I would look well in them. I could hardly wait for the evening to come and for the Seder to begin so that I could get all dressed up.

To a child the Passover celebration meant a party with the whole family together, laughing and singing songs and staying up late.

The grownups were very serious, though. They acted as though they were going to spoil the party. I spent the day going from my apartment to my grandmother's looking for some assurance that I was going to have fun.

Everybody was busy, a little too busy for me. My grandmother was in her kitchen cooking. My mother was upstairs in hers, cooking. The Seders, always held at my grandmother's, were too much for her four-burner stove, which couldn't cope with maybe twenty or twenty-five people. That meant that my mother was upstairs in her kitchen busy, too, so there were eight burners and two ovens going all day.

Without warning, a part of the day came when everything stopped. The table was ready, waiting for the family. The men, my father and my grandfather Harris, dressed in blue suits, had nothing to do but wait. My mother and grandmother left their kitchens and started to get dressed, and I knew that in a few minutes the lights would be turned on and the family would come from all over the city and then, at last, the party could start.

The first guest to arrive was always Mordche and Harris

didn't have to open the door to know who was knocking. After Mordche came the rest of the family. The Brooklyn chapter, the Bronx chapter, and the New Jersey chapter arrived in bunches one after the other and little by little my grandmother's quiet house filled up with people and talk. I knew that the celebration was almost ready to start when my grandfather Harris put the two cut-glass decanters filled with sweet red wine on the table.

Mordche and Harris were the patriarchs of the family and on Passover, as on all the holidays, their word on ritual was practically law. Harris was a very religious man and Mordche was a little bit less so. But if there were differences they disappeared on the first night of Passover. The two elders made themselves responsible for the youngest member of the family. The supper itself is called the Seder. And Seder means order or procedure and part of the order is that the youngest child in the family asks four traditional questions of the head of the house. Mordche and Harris would take the youngest child into a corner of the room. They were both men who remembered when they had been children and they remembered that it's not an easy thing to get up, even in front of your own family, and recite a part of a ceremony. Kindly and gently, prompting here and there, they would listen to the child ask the questions.

I was the youngest once and I asked the questions of my two grandfathers. They heard me in the corner, patted me on the head, and even said I did very well. I said the right words but I'm sure I didn't know what I was saying. It was like reciting "Iwanderedlonelyasacloud" at school. It meant nothing and I had to get older before I could slow the words down into sense. I see now that the questions weren't asked for the benefit of the child but for the grownups who wanted the reassurance that a tradition was being handed on from generation to generation. The Four Questions, because of that, were the heart of the Seder service.

The child says: "How different is this night from all other nights!" And then asks, "Why on this night do we eat matzoh? Why on this night must we taste bitter greens? Why must we dip greens twice, the salad greens and the bitter herbs? On all other nights we may eat either sitting upright or at ease; why on this night are we all at ease?"

And Mordche or Harris would answer: "We celebrate tonight because we were Pharaoh's slaves in Egypt. But the Lord rescued us, with a mighty hand, an outstretched arm. If He had not brought our forefathers out of Egypt, then we and our children and our children's children might still be enslaved to Pharaoh in Egypt. Therefore, even if all of us were men of learning and understanding, ripe in age and wisdom, it would still be our duty each year to repeat the story of the exodus from Egypt."

When Mordche and Harris had finished with the youngest we knew it was time to begin. Harris, at the head of the table, would wait while we all arranged ourselves at the table and when the room was quiet he would raise his wine cup ready to bless the ceremony by saying the kiddush, the traditional prayer of thanks to God for this festival of freedom: "Baruch ahtoh adonai elohaynu melech holem borai prehagofen... Praised art Thou, O Lord our God, Ruler of the universe, Creator of the fruit of the vine..."

There was one Seder that I thought I was going to miss. I had diphtheria and I was too sick to insist that I was well. Not only did I have a fever, I had a broken heart. I couldn't go to the Seder and I couldn't wear my new clothes and I felt that I must have done something terrible to be punished in that way. Medicine was too slow to make me well by evening, so I asked God to help me. I even promised I'd try to like school but He couldn't do anything for me for a few weeks. My grandmother could. She moved her dining-room table next to her window and then she made my mother move my bed next to my window. And then when the Seder started in my grandmother's house Harris read the service loud enough so that I could hear them upstairs in my bed.

That was a small but wonderful thing that they did for me. It was the first time, I think, that I really knew what it meant to be thankful . . . and I remember it came to me that I wasn't just a child, a daughter, a granddaughter, a relative—I belonged to people in the same way that I wanted them to belong to me. I was part of everyone in the apartment across the areaway, not only because I was born to them but because they wanted me to belong for myself—with my faults, with my temper, and with my germs.

That feeling of being loved and loving will always be part of the Seder memory for me. Passover, even now, is a service to be read across an areaway. That's the way that I hear it— and that's the way the sounds of the prayers come to me— with a little echo from brick walls and softened by white curtains in an open window.

6 *Claire, My Anti-School Friend*

I should probably say that I liked school—it sounds better. But the whole truth is, I didn't. I wasn't interested and there was always something I would rather be doing than sitting in a classroom, like, for instance, sitting at home. Besides, I was scared. It wasn't psychological, it was just the way the school looked.

The school was known by a number. P.S. (for Public School 103. It was built out of depressing reddish blocks that my father insisted were probably made by the brother of some city official. The building was big and ugly. When I first went to it at the age of six it was new, but it looked old and somebody had carefully designed it to look like a prison. The windows on the first floor were all barred and I thought that was to keep the students from escaping. When I went into the building I was sure I was right. There were two entrances, one for boys and one for girls. When I got inside I saw I wasn't the only one being accused. Both sexes were lined up by class and marched off to their rooms.

Marching through the halls at nine in the morning was like tramping through a cloudy day. I learned things, though, like the physical law that says the smaller a light bulb is, the less light it gives. The walls were painted gray except where the blackboards broke the monotony and the whole effect was of a place in which no one was going to smile, not even me. Not even when it finally came my turn to have what I thought was one of the best jobs in the class, using the long pole to open and shut the big classroom windows. Whenever I was in charge of the windows I suddenly became very careful about drafts. Five minutes after I had opened the windows I was up and out of my seat closing them. Then, of course, the room got too hot, so I had to get up again and open them just a little bit. I really made use of my turn when it came around about once every twenty-five days. On the other days I wasn't too eager to be a schoolgirl.

Every morning when I woke up I would hope for rain or snow or maybe a flood because if the weather was bad enough I could always talk my mother into letting me stay home. She was afraid of colds. I was a healthy child but as soon as I saw a cloud in the sky I began to talk through my nose. I became very good at sniffling.

The school wasn't too far from home, a few blocks, and as I walked I would see people doing all sorts of things that looked like more fun than what I was going to be doing. The grocer would be in front of his store carrying in supplies of milk and fruit; there would be a van in front of the butcher's and the driver would be lugging in a huge side of beef; the hardware-store man would be unlocking his store—the whole world looked busy and I was the only one who didn't have anything to do but go to school.

I could always talk to my parents about almost any problem but school was one exception. There were two reasons: First, I knew I was being foolish and it wasn't such a terrible problem; I could put up with it. Second, my parents had ambitions for me; they wanted me to go to school and I didn't feel I could disappoint them. At least not right away.

My attitude about school had something to do with the few friends I made. I didn't like children who liked school and it seemed to me that I was in a class of teacher's pets. But there was one girl, Claire, who shared my sour attitude about going to school. Claire and I met, became friends when we were ten, and have been friends ever since.

The first thing that showed me that Claire and I were soulmates was her love of being a monitor. To me being a monitor was the best part of going to school. Maybe I was born to boss because I enjoyed that first little taste of authority.

I felt very responsible in that job and I shushed my classmates for the sheer joy of shushing. And so did Claire. From the minute I saw her bossing her side of the room I knew we would be friends.

The second thing that attracted me to Claire was her clothes. She always wore knee-length gingham dresses, patent leather shoes that buttoned up the side, and a corset. It was the corset that did it. Claire was a big girl for her age and you don't find a ten-year-old girl with the figure of a woman every day. I always tried to get close to Claire so that I could see what made her go in here and out there. Poor Claire must have suffered agonies, because those were the days when the flat-chested figure was the rage and she just wasn't the type, even in the fourth grade.

There was one more thing that made Claire my friend: I was very bad at arithmetic but good at English; Claire was very bad at English and very good at arithmetic. So the solution was obvious: Claire did my numbers and I did her compositions, and together we managed a B average.

One day Claire just happened to take a composition of mine home with her. She showed it to her father, who was a doctor and a very scientific man. He wouldn't believe that anyone in Claire's class could have written it. Claire argued with him so loud and long that, to prove he was right, he told Claire to bring me home.

I should have been flattered but I was nervous. To me a

doctor was next to God and before you called one the house was cleaned, the linen was changed and not only in the sickroom, the furniture was dusted, and the bathroom shone like an operating room. Being sick was just a side issue. Diagnostically speaking, a clean house meant that the patient wasn't so badly off.

When I got to Claire's house—a handsome private brownstone in the very fashionable neighborhood of Madison Avenue and 119th Street—I was good and scared. I was introduced to the doctor, who didn't say much but asked me to go into his office and told Claire to wait outside. That didn't exactly put me at my ease. He asked me, in very medical tones, if I had written the composition. He had it on his desk and he waved it in front of me. I told him that I had written it. He looked at me as though I had a loathesome disease. The diagnosis was clear. I was a liar. He handed me a paper and pencil and told me to write something.

I wrote. I don't remember what I wrote but it must have satisfied his scientific soul because he let me out of the office and told me I could play with Claire—upstairs in her room where we wouldn't disturb the patients.

The house that Claire lived in was the most beautiful I had ever seen and it was the first private house in New York City that I had ever been in. It reminded me of a furniture store— every floor was a showplace. The kitchen was in the basement and it was big enough to hold two apartments like the one I lived in. The front room, on the first floor, was decorated with red damask and the furniture was all of heavy carved wood, the kind with lion's heads and taloned feet. The rugs were thick and it felt so good to walk on them that I was sure it was the wrong thing to do. The second floor was a parlor and the furniture there was all gold and petit point; there were

Oriental rugs on the floor and oil paintings on the walls, all
with little lights attached to make sure you could see they were
the real thing.

The higher we climbed the more ornate things became.
Claire's room was on the third floor and I expected to be taken
into a princess' fairyland. Claire opened the door of her
room—to a white iron bed, a chest of drawers, a throw rug
on the floor. Not even one picture broke up the eggshell walls.
I had expected flounces and frills, dolls and toys, lace curtains
and bright pictures. What I saw was a child's Siberia—a room
that could have been part of an orphanage or a hospital. It
no more belonged to Claire than I belonged in her house.

The finishing touch to my visit was Claire's grandmother.
Right out of a Russian novel she was—tall, stately, white-
haired, and absolutely confirmed in her opinion that she was
a member of the intelligentsia. She spoke correctly, in measured tones, and acted as though the Tsar was waiting for her
in the next room. She popped into Claire's room—one minute
she wasn't there, the next minute there she was. I was raised
to be polite so I stood up. She didn't pay any attention to me
but walked over to Claire, felt her forehead, and decided that
her granddaughter had a fever. "Clairitchke," she said, "you
have a temperature. I think you had better send your friend
home." She did notice me after all. She uttered her ukase and
left the room—she popped out. I never forgot that moment.
After all, I was in the room too. She could have insulted me
to my face.

I went home. I could hardly wait to get there and to hug
my mother and kiss my father. Here was one place in the
world that I was wanted. It wasn't such a fancy home but what
we lacked in furniture we made up in love. I looked around
my home and I saw the Grand Rapids couch, the checkered
tablecloth in the kitchen, the pencil sketch of who knew what

relative on the wall. I walked on a rug that wasn't Persian or Oriental but plain New England and worn in places, and I looked at my room—the nicest room, the room that had the most attention—and saw what I should have seen at Claire's— a brass bed, white curtains, dolls and toys, pictures on the walls, a room that showed the affection and warmth of those who planned it for me. I looked at what had been given me with new eyes and I saw that somebody loved me.

7 *The Dumbwaiter and the* *Laundress*

Home was an apartment, on the fourth floor of a house you would call an apartment house if you wanted to be fancy and a tenement if you wanted to be depressing. Ours was a "walk-up," but nobody minded. In those days, elevators were few and far between, no matter where you lived in New York. The new office buildings, soon to be called skyscrapers —like the Flatiron Building, the marvel of our time—had elevators and we regarded them with awe and suspicion. For almost everyone else the dumbwaiter was the only labor-saving device the landlord provided, and that was an invention!

The dumbwaiter not only helped with the heavy things from the store, carried up ice and brought down garbage, but it also provided a short history of each tenant in the building to all the other tenants. The dumbwaiter shaft made together-ness vertical and banished loneliness—all you had to do was open a shaft door. Everything that was talked about in the building—divorce, marriage, stomach complaints, bankruptcy —and everybody's menu for the week came up or down the dumbwaiter party line. There were no secrets. When a neighbor was in trouble, every family on the shaft knew and talked about it.

For instance, every winter some of the many young children in the house would get sick and the disease would be diagnosed at long distance by the more experienced parents. As soon as a child began to cough all the neighbors would hear the worried parents say, "Stick out your tongue!" or, "Let me feel your forehead," and then the volunteer medical corps would go into action. Heads would pop inside the dumbwaiter shaft and sure cures would be shouted to the worried parents. One apartment swore by cold baths—another by hot. The lady on the first floor cured everything with a spoonful of honey and the man on the top floor did the same with Seidlitz powders. When the doctor finally came, his medical opinion was discussed by everyone on the shaft but hardly anyone would be satisfied with the diagnosis or the suggested medication—usually an aspirin four times a day. As soon as the door closed behind the departing doctor, the advice would start again with variations and additions such as a mustard plaster or a red flannel soaked in goose grease. The parents of the child would always do what the doctor told them to do. And there were no hard feelings on the part of the neighbors. As a token of their concern each apartment sent up a pot of chicken soup. That, at least, every parent knew was good for a sick child. And should have been prescribed by the doctor in the first place.

Another advantage of dumbwaiter living was that if a neighbor came for help or advice a lot of time was saved. There would be no need to go into long-winded explanations because the problem was already in the public domain and thoughtful discussions in various apartments had no doubt solved it. Anyway the fellow with the problem didn't mind because he knew as much about you as you knew about him.

My father was a special fan of the dumbwaiter and when radio was invented, he gave up the shaftway only because of the better coverage. But until that time it was through the dumbwaiter that he got to know everybody, not by their names, but by their locations. He predicted divorce for Mr. and Mrs. 5-D because of their nightly arguments; he knew that Mrs. 3-A's son was going to leave home before even Mrs.

3-A. It didn't take second sight; all it took was a good ear and a comfortable chair near the dumbwaiter door.

My mother, a well-reared gentlewoman, didn't think listening was polite, and she would beg my father to behave himself. He wouldn't. He said he was studying human nature, and to illustrate his lessons he would tell mother that Mr. 4-B was boasting again to Mrs. about the day's "deals" and that Mrs. 4-B was answering, as always: "Julius, you'll end up in a jail!" In spite of herself my mother also began to study human nature.

People in the house must have tried to listen in on us, too. We had our problems like all the other tenants but whenever they were discussed my mother would say to my father, "Jake, shut the dumbwaiter door." As soon as that was done the discussion could start. We seldom had anything to say that other people couldn't have heard but my mother felt that, whatever it was, it wasn't for publication. My father didn't care who heard because it wouldn't make any sense to them anyway. My mother, he said, spoke in riddles that only a member of the family could solve. She would start telling a story about someone in the family and, because of the dumbwaiter, even with its closed door, she never mentioned names. It was always "You know who I mean."

My father would look at me and then say, "I don't know. Who?"

"A first cousin," my mother would say.

"Which one?"

Then my mother would look at him as though he had just lost all his marbles. "I'll tell you later," she would say and my father would take her by the arm and lead her into the living room where she could talk in privacy. "There are other rooms," he'd say. "Nobody made a law for the whole world to talk in a kitchen." When the story was finally out in the open, my father would come back, open the dumbwaiter door, sit down and spill the beans. "You couldn't tell me out loud that Joe's boy skipped school three days in a row? It's such a secret?"

My mother would look at him, then at the open dumbwaiter, put her hands on her hips, and say, "Jake!"

My father would point at the dumbwaiter and tell her, "They don't even know Joe." Then, I suppose because he felt like it, he would go over to the dumbwaiter and shout into it, "Joe is my brother."

When I learned in school that Gaul was divided into three parts I remember thinking of my mother. My mother was divided into three parts. Or, even worse, she was three people —a wife, a worker, and a mother. I'm a wife, I'm a mother, and I'm also a worker but at least I have washing machines— one for the dishes and one for the clothes. To be a wife and a mother is a pleasure—to be a worker around the house I can do without. You want to know why? Because it never stops! If it's not the dishes, it's the beds, after the beds it's the floors, and then the windows, then the furniture, then the clothes. And when you stop it's only to rest up so you can start all over again in the morning. If that sounds like complaining, it is.

Just cleaning the apartment wasn't easy for my mother. The furniture of those pre-World War One days was designed especially to catch dust. Every chair in the apartment had carved designs in the wood that had to be dusted out every day. The Tiffany lamps were magnets for lint and the upright piano in the living room had a fine, flat top of dark polished wood that showed every speck that came in through the open windows. Keeping a home clean in the city wasn't easy. It was work that had to be done every day. It was a constant fight to keep the outside where it belonged. In our neighborhood there were mostly apartment houses, with a sprinkling of brownstones here and there. It was a residential section but it was also a busy place, a cluttered place. Every building burned soft coal. The smoke didn't rise, it settled. It fell on the streets, on the window sills, and every little breeze brought some of it into the house. My mother didn't have a vacuum cleaner. There were commercial models being sold, but they were too big and too expensive for private citizens. Instead she had a feather duster and a fluffy dust mop and she used them like a virtuoso. Nothing, not a stick of furniture or an ash tray, was left untouched. She dusted around, behind, and under everything and when she was finished the apartment was spotless. All the dust was in the air and everybody was sneezing.

It seemed to me that my mother was always moving. When she sat down to rest she peeled potatoes or snipped the ends off the string beans; and if she took a cup of coffee and her hands and feet were still, her mind would be listing what to do next. I think that she could cook a meal with one hand and darn socks with the other.

But for her time my mother was a modern woman. What she had was the ability, the wisdom, to be able to change with the times. In her little life she saw changes that not even a fortuneteller would have dreamed of. She had to get used to the telephone, electric lights, the horseless carriage, people flying around in the air, movies silent and then talking, and women voting. Imagine! But no matter how much progress there was outside, inside, the house still had to be cleaned and the dishes had to be washed. Progress was for everybody except housewives.

My father sympathized. He knew all about housework and about how much there was to do. He understood the problem, and because he did he insisted that when times were good my mother should take advantage of a modern convenience—a laundress. Thereby began a long, if not great, debate.

My mother had other ideas. She felt that when times were good some money should be saved for when times got bad. We lived like an Aesop story about the grasshopper and the ant: my father thought like the grasshopper and my mother thought like an ant. Just to confuse the animal analogy, my father called my mother's idea living like a squirrel. My mother let him talk. She acted. During the good times she would buy clothes for us, not one suit for my father but three, not one dress for me but four of different sizes. She laid in supplies of stockings and slips and shoes, and when things did get bad we always dressed like they were still good. The money for the laundress was something she wanted to put away. But finally my father wouldn't hear of it. There was going to be a laundress!

So, every Monday morning there was a laundress. She was a colored lady who spoke only when she had something to say, and when she said it, it was with dignity and without nonsense. She was, maybe, five feet tall and that's exaggerating. She was young, in her thirties, but when you looked at the pink palms of her hands, she had the calluses of a woman who was much older. Her name was Clara, and she was very well acquainted with work. You could see that the minute she walked into the house. From her handbag she'd pop out a red bandanna and wind it around her head, and then she'd change from street shoes to a pair of slippers that must have worked as hard as she. Then she would put two big kettles on the stove and begin to boil water. My mother would keep trying to make her sit down and have a cup of coffee but she wouldn't. She wouldn't even stop to gossip, not even a little.

All the time she worked, Clara would be singing, and my mother would be asking her questions to which there were never any answers: "How's your family, Clara?" Clara would keep humming her little song, interrupting herself just long enough to say, "Just fine, thanks." Then she'd pick up her humming where she'd left off. Sometimes their conversations sounded like two parts from different plays being read at the same time:

"Clara? How's your father?"

"I can't find the bleach, Mrs. Edelstein."

"Is he still living in Georgia?"

"Here it is. Clothesline is getting frayed."

"How are the crops this year on the farm, Clara?"

"Where'd I put that old stick?"

And that's the way it would go. My mother appreciated having Clara and all the work she did but still she wasn't happy about the extravagance of it all. But there was nothing she could do about it.

My mother was helpless because my father was the manager of the Murray Hill Lyceum at this time and he worked all night and slept almost the whole day. The bedroom happened to be right off the entrance hall, and he liked to sleep with the door open just a little so that he could know who was coming in or going out. Even asleep he liked company—noise didn't bother him, but silence made him nervous. To him the normal noises of the house were like a lullaby: the doorbell, the pots clanking, the dishes rattling, and footsteps up and down in the kitchen all made him at peace with the world. Every once in a while he would open an eye and peer out to see my mother or myself, or, on Monday, Clara. And if there was no Clara he would know about it. First of all he'd know because he'd miss her special sounds and, second, he'd know because he hadn't been asked to pay her. My father was in charge of the money. He never had a bank account but kept everything in his right-hand trouser pocket. That was he was never overdrawn and he didn't have any books to balance. Every night the bank was neatly hung over a bedside chair, and when cash was needed for groceries or for Clara my mother would tiptoe into the room, shake my father, and ask. He would reach out a pajamaed arm, take the money from the pocket, give it to her, and go back to sleep. Clara was my father's extravagance and my mother couldn't let her go without an argument that she was sure to lose anyway.

No matter what anybody says there must be such a thing as fate. There has to be, otherwise why did Clara leave? One Monday she told my mother that she wouldn't be coming back, she was getting married to a widower with three children and she was going to have enough laundry of her own to do without looking for more.

My mother should have been very happy but she wasn't. She knew my father too well, and if he found out that Clara wasn't coming back it wouldn't take him more than five minutes to hire another laundress, and then it would begin all over again. So what should she do? She thought. She thought of me. I wasn't running but I got elected—I was the only candidate in the house. I was about twelve and practically Clara's size. I liked playing games, and besides, whatever my mother said to do, I did. I became Clara.

The first Monday morning after Clara's departure we acted like it was every other Monday morning. The day started out with the doorbell and my mother saying, "Good morning, Clara. . . ." Since Clara hardly ever talked, my part wasn't hard. All I had to do was hum, so I hummed. I put on a bandanna, an old dress, my mother's slippers, and then, because my mother was, ahead of her time, a theatrical realist, I put burned cork on my hands and face and paraded up and down outside my father's door. Every time we heard him stir I ran so that I could be outside his door in case he happened to open his eyes. My mother wanted to be sure that the image of Clara registered. Between the two of us we did the laundry; and when we were finished my mother tiptoed into the bedroom, withdrew the money for Clara's wages, and then hid it away in a pitcher on a high shelf over the sink.

My father kept paying Clara for six months. It would have gone on longer but my father caught pinkeye from the son of a second cousin and he had to stay home. My mother and I were hoping that he would be cured by Monday, but medicine in those days wasn't what it is today so he wasn't. He was home awake, and irritable. When Monday came we all sat around the kitchen table waiting for Clara. My father kept looking at his watch and finally he decided she wasn't coming at all. My mother said she'd do the laundry, and my father wouldn't hear of it—he said he'd do it. My mother wouldn't hear of that, so we all did it. It was fun but it took twice as long as usual. It was a game for him but it was a torture for my mother who was torn between a bad conscience and saving for a rainy day.

The pinkeye lasted all week. It was terrible—not the disease, the patient. It was living with a caged lion. He was always finding something to do around the house. He made up his mind he was going to help, so he helped. He mopped the floors, he cooked the meals, and everywhere he went in the house there was chaos. The more he did, the more we had to do. He used every pot in the house for a single spaghetti supper, and when he set the table he used the best silver and the special glasses—also linen napkins, linen tablecloth, and candles! We couldn't wait for him to go back to work. Finally the pinkeye disappeared—he was cured.

But he got well on Monday and he wouldn't be going back to the restaurant until that night and that meant another session of waiting for Clara. Naturally she didn't come and as the time passed I could see that my mother was going to confess—better to get it over with than spend another day doing laundry with my father. Before she had a chance, my father said enough was enough. He left the house and an hour later came back with another laundress. Her name was Carrie and she'd be with us until Clara came back.

My mother and I looked at each other. Now what? It was going to start all over again; there was no way out. It looked like Carrie was going to be with us forever; we couldn't even hope that she'd get married—she already was.

My father was very pleased with himself, and my mother resigned herself. Somewhere in the Golden Book it was inscribed that Dinah Edelstein was entitled to one laundress every Monday morning. So who would argue? Like it or not my mother was going to have a modern convenience and nothing she could do was going to change that very simple fact of life. She learned to live with it.

8 *A Tailor He'll Never Be*

We lived a life that may have had hardships, but if we had them, nobody told me. All I know is that I was surrounded on all sides by love and affection and very little money. My father's attitude about money was that it wasn't meant to be hoarded. He worked for it so that we could have what we needed, what we wanted, and enough of it to have a good time. If he ran short, he never seemed to worry. He was young, strong, healthy. He could always find work of some sort because he was an optimist who was almost always right. Without thinking about it, I trusted him to take care of us, just as I trusted him to hoist me to our apartment in the dark dumbwaiter. Taking care of us was his job as much as it was Bubeshu's to cook Friday-night and Passover feasts. And he did it very well—in his own way. That meant that we never knew what was going to happen next.

After my father became a married man, the truth had to come out. That he wasn't a diamond setter his in-laws already knew. But that he didn't have any trade they didn't know, and as soon as they found out, they did what all good in-laws do; they tried to give him one.

My mother's father Harris was a manufacturer of men's suits in his own right by the time Jake married his daughter Dinah. In those days in that business there was always a job for a son-in-law, or for that matter, almost any other relative. So my father went to work for his father-in-law.

The day after Jake began working Harris came home to

report on him. Everybody had high hopes, and the report should have been glowing. It wasn't. Harris's diagnosis of Jake's talents as a men's tailor was less than hopeful. He shook his head sadly and said: "A tailor he'll never be." When he was asked why, Harris wouldn't say. It was as though the whole thing was too terrible for this gentle man even to hint at. But when my grandmother, Bubeshu, wanted to know something, she quietly found out. She kept after Harris until the whole story came out: Jake had put the fly in the back of the pants instead of in its traditional location, and that was something, according to Harris, that not even his most hopeless apprentice ever did. Jake had to go.

Jake was only too happy to go. He was only nineteen, and even if he didn't know exactly what he wanted to do, he was sure he didn't want to be a tailor.

The story of Jake's failure as a tailor ran through the family—both sides—from brothers to brothers-in-law, to aunts and uncles and even to first cousins. It became everybody's business to find Jake a job. Anybody who'd put the fly in the back shouldn't be let out in the street alone.

Offers began to come in by the dozens. He could be a butcher, a baker, a candy-store owner, but he didn't want any of them. The only job that interested him was one Sam Blechman, his brother-in-law, offered him. Sam had a restaurant. Why that interested Jake above anything else nobody ever knew. But he went to work for Sam Blechman, and to everyone's surprise, except Jake's, he was a success.

Blechman's restaurant, "The Waverly," was on University Place near Washington Square. This must have been about 1910 and the neighborhood was a mixture of brownstones and shops. Fourteenth Street was the amusement center of the town and Greenwich Village wasn't yet thinking of itself as the art center of the nation. The restaurant catered to everyone; manufacturers and businessmen and the more sedate and finicky diners who came for their evening meals.

I wanted to go to the restaurant every day with my father but he didn't want to mix his family and business. It was admirable, I suppose, but at the time I thought it was mean. My father said a restaurant wasn't for children so the most I could ever do was to come down every once in a while for supper. I always thought that if my father was running a restaurant he could feed his family for nothing but every time I ate there he gave me money to pay the cashier and a little extra to leave for the waiter.

In spite of the fact that my father didn't seem to understand that a restaurant could be fun I was proud of him. He didn't own the place but I acted as if he did. It wasn't big. The dining room was long and narrow and the kitchen behind it was just deep enough to hold two iron stoves on the back wall. A serving table inside the swinging doors was the only barrier that kept rushing waiters from running into the stoves as they came through the doors shouting their orders.

The menu was everything to everybody because of the neighborhood, which was a mixture. My father's theory was that it didn't make any difference what you cooked, it was what you called it that mattered. Corned beef could be served with cabbage and that made it a traditional dish for the Irish. With gravy it was sauerbraten for the Germans. Without cabbage and between two pieces of rye bread it could be Jewish or a plain American sandwich. Consommé is just chicken soup, but with noodles, my father would say, it was a Jewish lunch. Without noodles it was fancy and for supper. But no matter what he called it, on the menu it was listed as "soup du jour." After a while the customers never asked what the special soup of the day was, they knew. Every day my father made sure there was a "special" (chicken, a roast, or stew) and thirty-five cents included everything but the tip. My father was proud of his specials and he hated to see them go to waste so he would write a few encouraging words on a menu that announced the day's "special." Next to the fish, always the special on Friday, he would write in parentheses, FILET OF SOLE (BRAIN FOOD). Sometimes the sign made a difference.

My father was good at this work. He could order supplies from the wholesalers right down to the last crumb and seldom be a pound off. He could handle anybody, chefs, customers, waiters, even the owners he worked for. It wasn't long before people came to him for advice about their restaurants and he began to think that since everyone thought he was good, then maybe he was. My mother could guess what was going to happen even before father knew it. She didn't object, she just had to know. And the only way to get an answer was to catch my father when he wasn't ready. The best time was just before work when he was rested and six hours away from aggravation.

"What kind of a restaurant is it going to be, Jake?"

"Who said something about a restaurant?" My father always played the innocent when my mother asked a direct question.

"Nobody."

There was a little pause while my father looked at his wife trying to figure out if he had said something yesterday. "You think it's not a good idea?"

"It's up to you."

"You're not giving advice today, Dinah?"

"You didn't ask for any."

"So now I'm asking...."

"About what?"

"A restaurant. What do you think?"

Just as long as the way ahead was established my mother

would agree to anything my father wanted to do, so she said, "Why not?"

"That's what I was thinking," my father told her and the only thing that stood between him and his own restaurant was time and money.

America, in those days, was the land of opportunity, and everybody who lived then seemed to sense it. The country was not only full of opportunities but of optimists who knew what the knock on the door meant. Today is not like yesterday—it never can be and maybe that's good too—but today the style is different. It's not what you can do, but what you shouldn't do. This is the age of the expert, while, just those few years ago, it was the age of the man who didn't mind trying. Yesterday, if you wanted to start a business the only experts who could tell you you were wrong were your own family. Everybody had a father, a mother, in-laws, friends, who knew better and predicted bankruptcy. Today you have to hire a firm to get the same advice.

The family of today, in this age of psycho-this and phycho-that, is not so much afraid of the mistakes you'll make as they are of what will happen if they tell you about them to your face. Who knows, you could end up with a complex, and that's worse than being in the hands of the receivers.

Jake paid no attention to relatives and friends who tried to tell him he didn't know anything about the restaurant business. He knew what he knew, and he knew what he didn't know. He didn't have to bother his head with corporate setups, little business taxes, big business taxes, amortization, loans, banks, withholding, social security, and surveys to tell him if there were enough hungry people in the neighborhood where he wanted to open his restaurant. All Jake knew was that he wanted to open a restaurant where plenty of people would eat. So he did. He dug up his own money, borrowing a little from relatives at no interest except a couple of dinners at the restaurant when and if it should ever open.

No matter what the family said to Jake at home, outside it was a different story. They might call him foolish to his face, but to their friends and neighbors they said he was a "very successful restaurant owner," "a big man," "a success," and, above all, "the owner." To fail, within the family circle, that was normal, natural, a part of living. To admit failure to outsiders was a sin. There was a pride in having a man of business in the family even if the business didn't work out. But when Jake started something he had a way with it. Even if some of his restaurants didn't do so well, they never actually failed. This was his self-chosen profession; he was proud of it, and he never gave up. Maybe he sold out once in a while to start up elsewhere, but he never threw up his hands.

9 *Of Men and Restaurants*

My father used to have streaks. Other people would have moods, he had streaks—and when he had one nobody knew what would happen, least of all himself. He might spend a day dreaming of his own restaurant or he might leave the house in the afternoon, go to work, and come home a day later. Where he went was something for him to know and for my mother to try to find out. Most of the time he stayed out to talk about this and that with friends and play a few hands of cards—not that he was a card player or a gambler or a man who ran around, he just had streaks.

My mother never suffered but she wondered. My father loved her, she loved him, they were happy together and they knew they were lucky. My mother's philosophy of marriage was to give my father enough rope as long as one end was always tied at home. We didn't have Tennessee Williams problems; it was more George Kaufman.

When my father came home from his late nights there were no questions asked and that annoyed him. He wanted my mother to ask, he wanted her to be jealous, and because she knew that's what he wanted, she didn't ask. She understood him better than he understood himself, and she was smart enough never to say that to him. If someone was going to say something about it, let it be him—and he always did. "You know where I was, Dinah?" he would ask. "Where, Jake?" my mother would say. She always made sure that she was doing something domestic so he couldn't see her smile.

It was always a good story—maybe even the truth—but embroidered a little because my father liked a good story.

Most of the stories had to do with his work. He was at this time the manager of the Murray Hill Lyceum on East 34th Street, and it was a big job, though he wasn't an owner yet. My father would get to work about three in the afternoon and finish about three or four in the morning. He was in charge of the staff, the food, the orchestra, the kitchen, the decorations, and he catered the parties.

The Lyceum was a huge place that could take care of fifteen hundred people at a time and that's not counting the four or five private dining rooms upstairs. The Lyceum was one of those places that don't exist any more. It was not only big, it was *gemütlich,* it was where people came to laugh, and it was before publicity men talked about atmosphere. The ceilings were high and absolutely guaranteed not sound-proofed. The whole idea was to have a good time and not to be quiet. In those days silence was for funeral parlors, not restaurants. There were chandeliers that were chandeliers—all cut glass with teardrops and draped strings of little glass balls, not straight pipes with blisters on the end or holes in the ceilings that drop light on you. I'm not saying that those were the good old days. It's just that there was something about a bigness then that was friendly. Today if it's big, it's a bank or Grand Central or a cafeteria where you go in fast and come out fast. There's no place to relax any more except at home—and with the foam rubber they put into everything today, who can relax?

My father's job was not only to keep the Lyceum going but to make it into a place where people wanted to come. The work was hard and the hours were long, and this could have been the best excuse in the world for one of his streaks—but it was too easy.

One explanation my father once gave my mother for a streak was his friend Damrosch, who was the headwaiter at the Lyceum. He was a little man with a fringe of white hair around a very bald head and he always wore pointed shoes. I don't know why I remember Damrosch's shoes better than I do his face, because he had a very nice face—but he also had very nice shoes.

My father came home about eight-thirty in the morning—he usually arrived at 5:00 A.M.—but this was eight-thirty and a day late. He came through the door and hung up his coat in the hall closet and walked through the house to the kitchen. As usual my mother didn't ask questions. My father sat down at the table—still not a word. My mother put a cup of coffee in front of him without questions, he stirred in the sugar, and then he sighed. That was the prelude.

"Dinah," he said, "how should I tell you? You know where I was last night?"

My mother didn't say a word. She just pushed the coffee closer to him.

"I don't feel like eating. I'm not hungry," he said.

"Then drink," my mother told him, "it's not food."

My father drank. "You know my friend Damrosch?"

"Certainly."

"He died last night!"

"Damrosch?"

"Damrosch!"

"Such a nice man," my mother said. "What was it?"

My father shrugged and the shrug meant that if it wasn't a disease then it was the will of God—whatever it was, Damrosch was gone. "I had to go, Dinah," my father told her. "I was called the first one. Damrosch wanted only me. Me, his friend Jake, nobody else. That's why I was gone for such a long time. He lives in Fort Lee so I had to take a ferry boat, and then I had to walk, and when I got there he hung on and on—and the things he told me! Poor man!"

My mother cried. She kept saying that he was so nice, such

a good man, such a fine man. And then she said she wanted to go to the funeral. My father told her that Damrosch was being cremated, that there wasn't going to be a funeral—it was his last wish. My mother said she understood and I think she was relieved that my father had stayed out to do a good deed instead of playing cards.

It was about a week later that she saw Damrosch in the street.

What can you say to a man who's just died? Nothing. You pass the time of day with him, you ask him how he feels, what's new, you say good-bye and tell him to give your regards to his family. After he's left you make a remark about how he never looked better in his life.

What you don't do is go home and tell your husband you just saw one of his dead friends walking around in the best of health—especially when your husband is just recovering from such a terrible shock. Why make him feel bad in the middle of his grief?

Sooner or later my mother and father were bound to meet Damrosch face to face together—not in the great hereafter but in the ordinary right there and then. When something like that happened my family had only two ways to settle an argument —either they laughed or they quarreled. This time they did a little of both but the one who was the maddest and didn't laugh even a little when he found out about it was Damrosch. For weeks he went around asking people if he looked all right and peering at his tongue in a mirror. It was almost a year before he stopped taking his own pulse. And my father, if he had to stay up with a dying friend, always made sure it was someone my mother didn't know.

Jake's most successful New York City restaurant was called "The Samovar." It was in the Spencer Arms Hotel on West Sixty-ninth Street and that part of town was considered one of the best, especially for eaters. The Samovar was not only a place where you could eat, it was also a place where you could look, and after a while it got to be a place where you went to be looked at.

The time was just after the First World War, and it wasn't enough for a restaurant to be just a place with tables. Like everything else, a restaurant in the nineteen twenties had to make believe; reality, especially after a big war, is nothing that anybody wants to face, even when they're eating. The decoration in The Samovar tried to make people forget they were on West Sixty-ninth Street. There was a large samovar in the center of each table. Along the walls were gypsy wagons and in each wagon a table big enough for eight people.

The food was exotic: flaming shashlik served from a sword, caviar in icicles, Russian fruit soups—everything from a world that no longer existed. It was Russian food, but food the tsars ate, not the peasants. Yet people like my father who ran restaurants like The Samovar, had they lived in Russia in the old days, would have been eating black bread and cabbage soup, and would have been running from a sword instead of eating flaming shashlik served from one. This was America, and it was free, even for a man to believe in what no longer existed.

My father, the son of a man who had to run from his homeland because of the tsars, was making believe he was running a restaurant resembling "A Night at Yars." The waiters, the cooks, the busboys, were all part of the make-believe, authentic, American version of Old Russia. Nearly everybody who worked at The Samovar was a White Russian, and there wasn't a waiter in my father's Samovar who hadn't been at least a count, and all the chefs were said to have once been generals.

Whatever they might have been, they were good at their jobs. The number-one chef, who said he was a Cossack commander of thousands of horsemen, made excellent blintchiki and chicken à la Kiev. Maybe he learned how from his old mess sergeant, who was now probably a commissar.

It was only a matter of time before all the White Russians began to dislike being waiters or cooks, so they decided to be something else. Some of the waiters became actors, one went to the Art Student's League to become an artist, and one wanted to open his own restaurant. This man, Michael Artzbasheff, told my father that what he wanted to start was a French restaurant. By his way of thinking, that was the only logical choice for a man who wanted to get ahead.

My father didn't care one way or the other. What interested him was why Michael had decided on a *French* restaurant.

"Because," Michael said, "customers know absolutely nothing."

"That's not a reason," my father said. "That's an opinion."

"I worked it all out," Michael said. "I did a survey. On the menu you have Bœuf à la Stroganoff and as soon as a customer asks me what it is, if I say it's beef but with a French sauce, they order it. Right away, as soon as they hear a French name, they feel dumb. They also feel if it's French, it must be cooked very well and even if it isn't they think they're wrong and not the cook. So how can I lose?"

"With that kind of an attitude you can lose, believe me," my father told him. My father respected his customers.

Michael said that my father didn't understand. "In an American restaurant fried chicken is judged by comparing it to other fried chicken. But if I call it *poulet frit* it's French fried chicken, and who ever ate that?"

"Frenchmen."

"Would a Frenchman come into a French restaurant in America?"

"Suppose he did?"

"So when he goes back to France he'll say French cooking in America isn't French."

The last I heard of Michael he was night manager of a cafeteria that stayed open twenty-four hours a day.

Most of the waiters and kitchen personnel were real White Russians. The others, no matter what they were dressed as, made my father say that The Samovar was a little melting pot. The gypsy violinists were Italians with bandannas; the ear-ringed dancers were booked from a theatrical agent who sent over nothing but Irish girls. So long as they could dance and looked well in their costumes, who cared? After all, the customers, for the time they were in The Samovar, were making believe they were Russian nobility enjoying themselves with gypsies. Why not?

The restaurant was successful, my father was proud of it, and it would probably still be running today if it wasn't for one thing: spring. As soon as the birds began to chirp and the trees get green, Jake couldn't keep himself in the city. It was too much to ask. For a few summers he closed the restaurant in the summer months and ran hotels in the mountains. Finally, he decided that he had run about everything there was to run in the way of New York restaurants so he sold The Samovar. It ended just as suddenly as it began. My mother woke up one day to find we owned a restaurant. Then another day, a few years later, she woke up to find out we didn't. What we were going to be next, we didn't know, and we would have to wait until Jake told us. In the meanwhile we didn't worry, we knew it would be something grand.

PART TWO

THE COUNTRY

1 *Our Own Hotel*

My father and a friend, Mr. Nathan Engleman, used to rent hotels for the summer season. They had been doing it for a few years when my father decided he wanted his own hotel. I don't know what Mr. Engleman wanted; he was a bachelor of many years who had just gotten engaged, and I suppose he was a little restless, too. So he listened to my father's reasons for looking for another place, and when my father thought of reasons, believe me, they were whoppers. The area around Woodburne in the Catskills where they had always rented was getting too crowded, he said. In the hotel business that should have been good, but to him, right then, in need of a reason for moving, it was bad. In a mood to buy a windmill, Mr. Engleman and Mr. Edelstein went on an exploring trip to the other side of the mountains.

I was about six, and getting used to my father leaving the house without a word. He said he'd be back. To me it was an unnecessary remark but it made my mother worry. He was up to something, but what?

My father and Mr. Engleman found the little town of Griffins Corners which was about forty miles west of Kingston. It was a very small place with maybe five hundred people including traveling salesmen, but it had two names. The main part of town was Griffins Corners; the other part, near the railroad station, was called Fleischmanns. It got its name from the Fleischmann family who had made their fortune from yeast and gin. They even built the railroad station for their own use. A few years later the whole town was called Fleischmanns for convenience and Griffins Corners was no longer listed on the schedule put out by the West Shore Division of the New York Central.

The Fleischmann family had an estate high up on a hill above the station. There were five houses, a large one and four smaller ones. The view was magnificent. You could look down into the valley to where the town was and you could see across to the mountains on the other side with their patches of dark green farms and white threads of roads. It looked like Switzerland and I suppose the similarity was so great that the Fleischmann family spent their summers in the Alps instead of in Fleischmanns because it reminded them of home. When my father first saw the estate the houses were all vacant. My father began to think, and the more he thought the more he wanted to buy the big house and make it into a hotel. He had had enough experience to know that it would be a good one. Mr. Engleman also had had enough experience in the hotel business, so he bought a farm on the other side of the valley.

The first thing my father had to find out was if the big house was for sale, and the simplest way to do that was to ask. He finally found the lawyer for the estate, a Mr. Hirsch.

Mr. Hirsch had an office in New York City and that meant coming home and dodging questions from my mother. All we could find out was that he had gone to the mountains. What he was up to was a surprise and we had to be happy with that.

Mr. Hirsch's office was on Wall Street and Mr. Hirsch, according to my father's report later on, was the picture of a Wall Street man. He parted his hair in the middle, wore high collars, a cutaway and pince-nez glasses, and he was also a man who didn't like to waste time fencing with words. When my father was ushered in to see him he asked exactly what it was that he wished to discuss.

My father was also not a time waster. He told Mr. Hirsch he wanted to buy the Fleischmann house and he had come to see if it was for sale. Mr. Hirsch said it was and it wasn't—it all depended on the offer.

My father nodded like a big businessman and told Mr. Hirsch that he was willing to put down the sum of five hundred dollars towards the purchase price.

Mr. Hirsch didn't say "no." He simply said that the furnishings in one room were worth at least three times that amount and that there were twenty rooms in the house.

My father told Mr. Hirsch that five hundred dollars was all he had in the world except for his experience and his good name.

Mr. Hirsch said that he admired my father's forthrightness and honesty but, unfortunately, those virtues weren't bankable. He also said that he had confidence in my father's ability, and my father told him if he had confidence he should arrange for the sale. He assured Mr. Hirsch that the balance would be paid. Mr. Hirsch said he would think it over.

A few days passed but without a word to us about the surprise. The first my mother heard about a hotel of our own was when Mr. Hirsch came to visit. It was in the late afternoon; my father had gone to work, and when Mr. Hirsch knocked on our door, we thought he was a very high-class bill collector. My mother was shocked when he explained and she almost fainted when she heard what my father was offering for the main house of a big estate. Mr. Hirsch said that the offer was, of course, ridiculous, but being a businessman he recognized nerve when he saw it. He was impressed, and, foolish as it sounded, he said he was inclined to approve the sale. All he wanted was to see what sort of a family Mr. Edelstein had. He wanted to make sure the house was going to

the right people. We must have made a good impression because a few days later the papers were signed, and we owned
a hotel.

The first time I saw the house at Fleischmanns I didn't
know what to say. I had never seen anything like it. It was
beautiful, it was luxurious, it was unbelievable, it was out of
a storybook. There were stairs that led up to a veranda that
surrounded the house, and there were twenty white pillars and
seats that ran the length of the veranda. Inside there was a
large reception hall and a long staircase leading to the second
floor. To the left of the reception hall was a library; to the
right was a parlor, all done in white satin damask. Upstairs
were the bedrooms and a nursery. Each room was done in a
different color: one was blue, one was pink, one was yellow,
and one was all in chintz. The attic was filled with bolts and
bolts of material so that the furniture and the drapes could be
redone and rematched exactly. The whole house was decorated
in Biedermeier—handsome stuff, heavy and stately. Each of
the twenty rooms was more ornate than the other, as though
there were a contest going on. There was flatware in the side-
boards, dishes in the cupboards, enough for a hundred people,
and the kitchen was large enough to cook for at least twice
that many.

I looked at the house and I couldn't believe that this was
all ours. I turned to my father and asked him how he had done
it, and he said that he always wanted to be a businessman—
and he added, "for your sake, so that when people ask you
what your father does, you can say he's a Hotelman, that he
owns a hotel."

That was in the fall. The hotel opened the following spring,
and not only was my father in business for himself, we were
all in business with him. For better or worse, we had a hotel.

2 *Fleischmanns*

When somebody mentions the country, I'm sure he's talking about a place I know and I have to catch myself before I ask him, "Do you remember when——?" I suppose everybody has one place that's The Country, and Fleischmanns happens to be mine.

Fleischmanns is a small town. There's a sign on the road just before you get to it that says POPULATED AREA. Fleischmanns is populated with five hundred people, no more, no less. To a stranger it looks like any other little village in the Catskill Mountains. To a native it's a special place and every town he doesn't live in is a nice place to visit but he wouldn't want to live there—he wants to live in Fleischmanns.

So what has Fleischmanns got? It has weather. In the summer it's hot, in the winter it's cold. But it's not only weather; there's the village, and the village would be nothing, or almost nothing, if I couldn't close my eyes and remember the names of all the people who owned stores on both sides of the main street. The town begins at the bottom of a mountain with Todd's garage. Then the road makes a little turn and there's the fish store. And then comes Miller's drugstore that used to have wire-backed chairs and metal glass holders for sodas that nobody makes any more. After Miller's there's the Post Office, one story high, government style with wooden steps. Then comes Halpern's hardware store and Milt's candy shop, set back a little from the street. In the good old days you could buy penny candy, fireworks, and *The Police Gazette* from Milt. Across the street is the bowling alley, the Onteora movie house (matinee

81

Saturdays only)—then comes Babitzki's Photographic Studio which was the only house on the whole street with a bay window, but nobody could see in or out of that window because Mr. Babitzki pasted pictures all over the glass. Then there's the shoe shop with a big wooden man's shoe hanging out over the sidewalk. After that is Ritter's Hotel with a sign taller than the whole building. Across from Ritter's is Meltzer the Butcher, with the shop downstairs and an apartment upstairs.

The town should stop right there, but it doesn't. A sidewalk stretches out for another mile, where the village road turns left and goes over a bridge. To me that bridge is always summer. From the bridge I could look down into the stream and see catfish on the bottom or a few trout swimming upstream out of town. I spent hours throwing pebbles off the bridge at the fish. Just across the bridge is a restaurant-tavern called "The Cat's Meow." To this day I think of it as a place that's not for ladies, because it has a sign over the door that says LADIES INVITED.

The street that runs from the bridge goes up to the railroad station. This is the residential section with big houses and big trees. I always remember it as being quiet here, and in my mind all the houses seemed to be painted green, and they always looked empty. The only way you could be sure there were people in the world of that quiet street was to catch a glimpse of washing hanging on the lines in a back yard.

At the end of the street the road divides. One part goes up to the station, the other goes under a railroad bridge and up the hill to where we had the hotel.

The station was New York Central Gothic, every spare piece of wood carved with so many curlicues and little twists and turns that I thought the carpenter must have been daydreaming when he built it. In front of the stationmaster's office was a semaphore signal that was worked by hand. Fleischmanns wasn't a regular stop, and that annoyed the stationmaster. I think he had ambitions to be the stationmaster in a busier place. How he would have made out I don't know because he was very short-tempered. Everything bothered him, including the trains. He was a slow-moving little man with steel-rimmed eyeglasses and a green celluloid eyeshade that he wore night and day. He spent his time in an office that was a combination ticket booth, telegrapher's desk, and baggage room. He had a roll-top desk that he never unrolled, and everytime somebody wanted to buy a ticket he acted as though he was going to push the train himself. If you asked him what time a train was due to arrive he would say, "When it gets here," and then he'd stomp out to look up and down the tracks. Hardly any train was ever on time, and when a train did finally puff into the station he'd stand outside and yell at the engineer, " 'Bout time!" Then he'd hand mail and baggage up to the men in the baggage car, grumbling that he was doing the work of two and getting paid for the work of one, a midget at that. As soon as the train left he'd go back to his office, slam shut the window of the ticket booth and sit at the telegraph key waiting for a message. Very few messages came over the wire for him, and he'd sit there talking back to the key as it clicked orders for other stations on the line. "Number 18 take the siding at Highmount. What's the matter with this place? I got a siding here, ain't I?"

I think the only time the stationmaster was happy was when there was a passenger or two for a train that didn't make Fleischmanns a regular stop. He would make quite a production of the whole thing. He'd leave his office, pick up a pair of thick leather gloves from a window sill and then stride out to the tracks, look up and down the line, and pull the semaphore lever. The arm would swing up and out and when the train came to a noisy and begrudging stop, he acted as though he had finally got even with the whole New York Central system.

He was what, when I was young, we used to call a character. Of course he was rude, but his rudeness had style. Not like the ordinary, thoughtless sort you meet today. Our stationmaster worked at it.

In back of the station was a coalyard where kids picked up odd pieces of coal to throw at the engines as they came puffing through. That was fun, but first you had to make sure it was a through train, because who wanted to make the local engineer mad? I always thought putting pennies on the track was more fun. I remember waiting for what seemed like hours for a train to come along and flatten out my penny. Believe me, that was a trophy to have! A smashed penny with a long-faced Lincoln was a treasure!

After the trains had come and gone it always seemed time to go home. Home was at the top of the hill. In Fleischmanns anything from a bump to a mountain is called a hill, and this wasn't a hill, it was a mountain. The road, all dirt and rock, went up to 2,500 feet, and was maybe two miles long, but for a happy child what's two miles, even straight up? The road was bordered by daisies, sunflowers, and milkweed, and the higher I climbed the more I could see below. The town was in a valley and little pieces of roofs or a church steeple would stick out from the tops of the trees. It always looked peaceful and it reminded me of what the little boy in the flagpole must have seen before he fell, shot, living long enough to say to Napoleon, "I'm killed, sire"—and smiling, fell dead. I often played "Incident of the French Camp" going up the hill; sometimes I was Napoleon, and sometimes I was the little boy, and sometimes I was the terrible Englishman who shot him.

Around one of the many turns in the road there was a patch of blackberry bushes, and if I was hungry from marching with Napoleon, and had the time, I could always have dessert before I got home for supper.

At the top the road divided again. To the left was one guest house and in front of it a tree we called the "umbrella tree." What a naturalist would call it I never found out; to me it was handy in a summer rain. It didn't keep out the rain, but if I could make believe, who wanted to be dry? To the right of the tree was a small hump of ground with the top flattened to make a croquet field, and in back of that was another guest house. To the right, at the end of the road, was the main house with a big, heart-shaped stone wall in front of it. Inside the stone wall was a landscaped garden that grew, it seems, only pansies. To the left of the main house were two more guest houses, and in back of them a line of small cottages for the help; that is, all the help but the musicians. They were put way back in the woods where they wouldn't disturb the guests with their practicing, their late hours, and their whatever.

In front of the two houses near the main house was a terraced field that was a playground for the children, and beyond that, to one side, was a big apple tree, and then, behind the apple tree, was a large meadow surrounded by pines. The meadow had a gigantic rock right in its middle, a rock that for us was always a boat. It was the *Santa Maria,* the *Monitor,* the *Merrimac,* a submarine, a whaler, a steamship, anything the children wanted to make it. That poor rock went around the world at least a hundred times a season.

The hotel was surrounded by scenery. Mountains in front with their green sides scratched by a giant fingernail to make brown roads run up and down. There were woods in back of the hotel, a sky full of big clouds, and if the apple trees weren't in bloom, the lilacs were.

If there happened to be nothing in blossom, all you had to do was turn slowly, forget nature, and watch the guests. They were as much a part of the summer's tapestry as the grass. They were part of nature, only they had two feet, and they had their seasons just like the trees and the flowers. They came with the first blooms, and they left with the leaves.

The hill is still there, Fleischmanns hasn't changed too much. Babitzki's Photographic Studio has boards over the bay window, Ritter's Hotel still has its sign, but the management has changed. There is still water running down the hill for the horses, but there are no horses. The railroad station is empty because trains don't stop there any more except to drop a few pieces of freight. The weather is still clear and bright, and the scenery is still green, and it's still the only place to call country.

3 *Credit*

That first season in the hotel was something new for my mother and myself. What the both of us know about the business was what we were told by my father. And, as his apprentices, we started doubling not only in brass but in boiled chicken and paper work.

I was seven when the hotel started. My chin just about came up to the top of the reception desk counter. Obviously if I was going to be of any help I had to be taller. I asked for high heels and I was turned down. My hair, which was worn long or sometimes braided, I wanted to have cut so that I could look older, and that idea was also vetoed. I wanted to wear "older" dresses instead of middies and skirts and, naturally, that was refused. So I had to put up with myself as I was, a little scrawny, a little gangly in the legs, a little self-conscious, but eager to learn.

The first thing I ever learned at the hotel was about smiling. Everybody who works at making guests feel at home has to know how to smile. Guests are sensitive: they come in room sizes: doubles, singles, or suites. And they always check in with bag, baggage, and troubles. If the people around them don't look happy the conclusion they come to is that there must be something wrong. What a guest doesn't know is that there are two sides to every counter and if the boss doesn't smile good morning it doesn't mean measles has broken out. It could mean the groceryman wants to get paid or an unexpected rainstorm turned the June figures from black to red. I learned very soon that frowning was a luxury my family couldn't afford, so from

87

Memorial Day to Labor Day we all smiled. The whole staff looked like Pagliacci and his friends.

The second thing I learned was not to try figuring out what guests will do because it is like calling heads or tails. It must be one or the other, never both, and half the time you're wrong anyway. It was just like gambling, only with people, and the odds were always against the house. Over and over again I learned that almost anything will make a guest leave. It was our job to figure out how to keep them happy and registered.

The third lesson was not to be afraid of work. In those early days it would have been easy to be a coward, especially when we looked around to see what there was to work with. There was a house that we had to turn into a hotel—and empty rooms that we had to fill with people. Theoretically, these people were to come from the lists of former customers gathered together during the years of renting. With what little money there was my father printed circulars, mailed them, and waited. Meanwhile we had to have hope and help—and credit. Without that one commodity it is impossible to run a hotel.

With credit you can order in April and pay in September— if you're lucky. The storekeepers in Fleischmanns wanted to give credit; they wanted hotels because that meant business, and if the hotels had a good year, they had a good year. Everyone was willing to work on the cuff, and people figured that if they couldn't collect one way, they'd collect another. The whole hotel business was built on credit right down the line. The shopkeepers got credit from the wholesalers, the wholesalers got credit from the manufacturers, and the manufacturers got credit from the banks. Where the banks got their credit from I could never figure out; they must have made it up. You can believe me when I say that there were years when not a penny passed from one hand to another; renewed notes were the coin of that realm.

Everyone from the president of the bank to my father hoped that each season would be a good one. And what was a good season? No rain. If it rained in August, if four or five families went home because of it, everyone's credit would have to be extended into the next year. And then everyone would congratulate everyone else because it could have been worse.

I learned about credit from experience. I was the bookkeeper for the first year, and what I didn't know about keeping books, I made up. One side of the page was for the guests' names and the rooms they took and the price they paid. The other side of the page was for when they paid. In another book I kept an account of what we took in and what we paid out. It was very simple. The black ink on one side meant things were good and red ink on the other side meant we were going to have a bad winter. It got so that my mother would look at the books to see how much red there was. If there was more black than red she would take me out to buy clothes; if there was more red than black she'd go through my clothes looking for hems to let out.

A hotelkeeper has a lot to worry about. Even if he's doing well there's always some crying need that liquidates the profits —new rooms, new decorations, advertising, maybe a pool to keep up with the competitors. Money was something we never had in the hotel business. The only ones who left after a season with money in their pockets were the help, and if we kept on their right side for the season, maybe we could borrow enough to last through the winter. Most of the time we were very lucky; the red and the black balanced each other, and that meant we could pay our bills and have enough left over to buy our tickets back to New York.

But you never knew. How could you? There were always things happening that we never could have predicted. Like the horse we bought to go with the buggy. We used to hire a man to drive our guests up the hill from the station, and when we got a little ahead we bought a buggy, waited for another good spell and then bought a horse to go with it. We had her for two weeks and then she dropped dead coming up the hill. I don't blame her, it was some hill. So we went back to hiring transportation; it was better not to know the horse personally.

Little things like that make the hotel business a gamble, that and rainy days, sick or temperamental help, weather that's too cold for some of the guests and too warm for others, not enough to do, too much to do, too much quiet, too much noise. We needed a mathematician with a crystal ball to figure the odds. We became experts in expecting the unexpected, so much so that when something happened that couldn't possibly have happened, we had already been expecting it for a week and were wondering where it was.

4 Country Confessions

When I was in the country I was very glad that my father ran a hotel, but in the city I used to tell all my friends that my father owned a summer estate—it sounded better than a hotel—with fifty rooms and thirty in help. That wasn't entirely a lie; at least the figures were accurate.

I felt free to say whatever I wanted to say while I was in the city because I was sure that none of my friends would ever come up to the country to see. I was so sure that I even added a swimming pool. I was going to put in a stable and horses, but even I thought that would be going too far. I settled for a Duesenberg instead, and if anyone wanted to know why my father wasn't driving it in the city I could always say it was too long to park on Lexington Avenue.

Claire was my favorite confidante to whom I spoke about the country estate. Her father was a well-to-do doctor and she understood all about percale sheets, silver service, and how to speak to chambermaids. If the sort of estate I dreamed of existed today, the taxes would be so impossibly high that my father would have to donate it to the state for a public park—the government would be the only organization capable of keeping it.

One day, one summer, naturally, my sins came home to roost. I was in the village, when I saw Claire, her grandmother, and an aunt riding down the main street on horseback. They just happened to be staying up in the hills somewhere on a farm, and because I'm the kind of person whose sins always come full circle to smite me, they just happened to be riding through the village when I was there.

Claire was overjoyed to see me. I would have been happy to see her except for memories of what I had told her about the estate. I was in too deep to invite Claire and her grandmother to the hotel—and because Claire was my dearest friend, how could I not invite her? At first I tried to avoid all questions that I could see were going to lead to the "estate." The first thing I just mentioned, in passing, was that the house, all fifty rooms, were being painted and that the immediate family, my mother, my father, and myself, were occupying the guest cottage, a small shack with only three rooms. As soon as the house was all painted, they simply *must* come up for a visit, and as soon as I made the invitation I knew it would take all summer to finish the painting I had just started.

Claire's grandmother was one of those district-attorney ladies who, if you said it was a nice day, cross-examined you on exactly what you meant by that highly controversial statement. She wanted to know, room by room, what color everything was going to be. By the time I got to the second floor I ran out of colors.

Actually Claire helped me out by reminding me of all the things I had told her about the "estate" during the winter, little imaginary details I was forgetting under the glare of her grandmother. It occurred to me in a flash of insight—and I should have known it months ago—that Claire knew there was no such thing as an estate. After all, I had written her English compositions at school and she was familiar with my style of living. But Claire was that kind of friend. She understood being caught in a lie and having to live with it. She knew, in those early days, what it took me years to find out: the difference between the real world and the world you make up in the mood of the minute. You can, if you want to, be an orphan when you're talking to your mother and father, the Queen of England on the Staten Island ferry, or, if you have a good friend, you can live on an estate instead of a hotel.

Imagination plays games that have no rules, and mine always makes trouble for me. I can feel sorry for myself in a second or I can feel just wonderful in the same amount of time. Also I can relive embarrassing moments as though they were happening in front of me. I have total recall for terrible things and the worst thing about it is that I can't tell myself to stop. It goes right on and I can't walk away. Even a book in the window of a store can remind me of the time when I was a nine-year-old criminal.

Fleischmanns had a library, a small, white house donated to the town by the Skenes, a wealthy family that had an estate in the hills above the village. From the outside the library looked like any other private house, but inside it was the real thing, complete with the special smell that comes from bookbindings, a little dust, and library paste. The librarian was a lady who looked like a librarian, tall, thin, with eyeglasses and a bun on the back of her head. She was the only person in town who could move across the wooden floor without squeaking a board. Whenever I came in to borrow a book she was ready with suggestions and advice. So my crime was not only against society, but also against that very nice lady.

I happened to borrow *The Deerslayer,* a very long book, believe me, and even at that age I felt I had to finish any book I started, if not for myself, then out of respect for the author. I kept the book for a long time, so long that it became overdue. At first the fine was two cents, then four, then eight. It was approaching fifty cents when I became panicky. I was reluctant to tell my mother and disappoint her, and I didn't dare to face my father. Every time I walked through the village I crossed the street to avoid the library. I walked up back streets and through alleys until I was sure that I had passed it. I was positive that everyone in the town knew of my terrible crime, and at home, when the doorbell rang, I shuddered: it might be the sheriff or the librarian or the mayor coming to take me and the book away.

A child can be desperate. I know now that if I had told my parents I would have got a little lecture and the fifty cents to pay the fine, but that was then, and who knew?

I felt that there really wasn't anyone I could turn to, not even my closest friend, Kenneth Avery, who, at the age of eight, was a financier. There are some children who cast shadows of themselves as adults and Kenneth's shadow was rich. He grew sweet peas in his father's back yard and sold them at The New Switzerland Hotel. (The New Switzerland was Kenneth's territory, he explained, since it was the closest hotel to his house.) His price, depending on the size of the bouquet and the attitude of the customers, was five or ten cents a bunch. During the sweet-pea season Kenneth might average three to four hundred dollars. But that wasn't the end of it: he would lend the money to his father at six per cent interest. He was the wealthiest self-made eight-year-old I ever met.

I didn't want to ask Kenneth for the money because I was too ashamed to tell him, but his mother was a different story. Finey Avery was a comfortable woman, a lady who understood children and always had cookies in the oven and a ready ear for children's problems. I don't know why I felt that Mrs. Avery would be more understanding than my own parents except that she looked the part, and besides, she was familiar with high finance through her son. I decided to confess to her.

Committing a terrible deed is simple compared to confessing it. I approached Mrs. Avery's house four times before I had the nerve to go in. Of course she welcomed me as though I were an innocent child. She didn't know yet. How she would feel about me in another minute was something I didn't want to think about. Maybe she'd never let me see Kenny again; after all, a self-confessed criminal wasn't a good companion for a young tycoon. I built up my nerve by eating the cookies she placed on the table. When I finished the last one I went into a long explanation about what I was going to tell her. First, I wanted her to promise not to say a word to my mother or my father, and, second, I wanted it understood that what I was suggesting was a purely business proposition. As the mother of my wealthiest friend she could understand that. I finally told her about the overdue book. Mrs. Avery looked very serious. I thought she was going to say no, so I reassured her that I would pay her back at the rate of one cent a week for fifty weeks, plus six per cent interest. She nodded and said that she would extend the credit. She handed me two quarters—and suddenly the world seemed to be a brighter place; it began to look as though I really had a future. My heart stopped pounding and my hands stopped shaking. I tried to thank her but the words didn't seem to come out right.

I ran home. I got the book and marched up the main street to the library. I went inside like an honest woman, paid the fine, and walked out—free!

I paid Mrs. Avery one cent a week every week, secure in the knowledge that no one knew about my debt except the two of us. I should have known better, but I didn't until many years had passed. Of course Mrs. Avery told my mother, and they had a good laugh. Can you imagine? They laughed at my suffering, and years later my agony became one of my mother's favorite stories. Even when I was married and the mother of two children I still felt the hot flush of shame whenever my mother started to tell the story. In some ways a person is always a child and whenever I think about the library and the book I'm nine years old again and I have no place to turn.

The other sufferer in this affair was Mr. James Fenimore Cooper. I never could read him again.

5 *The Bellboy*

The first person a guest meets at a hotel is the ambassador of the entire staff. The ambassador at Fleischmanns was Whitey.

Some people you have to know for a while before they really become characters. Whitey was a character at first glance. As soon as you looked at him you knew it, and as soon as he looked at you, he knew too much.

Whitey was sixteen and not so sweet when he began working at the hotel. Ten minutes after he started he was acting indispensable. Whitey was a wise guy, nicely wise—he could even have been called charmingly fresh. He was small, a little stubby, bowlegged; he had blue eyes and a head of very light blond hair. He also had ambitions but they didn't run him, he ran them.

The guests loved Whitey. He was the bellboy and almost the first contact a guest had with the hotel. He set the mood. Whitey could look at a guest and tell you what he was going to order for breakfast—which ones were the pot-cheese eaters and which ones were the dieters. He knew people, he knew what they were inside, what they wanted, and exactly how to treat them. The men thought he was a funny kid, the women loved him like a naughty son, and the young girls ran after him. He had something. I don't know what it was. Ask a woman what there is about certain men and they won't be able to tell you anything except that it is there. Whatever it was, Whitey had it.

Whitey knew everything that went on in the hotel. I thought I knew quite a bit, but he knew scandals and gossip, who was going with whom, where, when, and even how. And if there is anything that bothers me, it's not knowing. I was that way when I was born and I haven't recovered. When I would ask Whitey to tell me a few of his juicier secrets, our conversation would be like a list of unanswered questions. If there was a rumor that interested me, such as a married lady guest taking long walks with an unmarried male guest on week days and avoiding him on the weekends when her husband came up from the city, I would try to get the real story from Whitey.

"Whitey," I would ask, "when is Mrs. Lehrer's husband coming up?"

"Isn't he going to be here for the weekend?"

"Mr. Korn is going to be disappointed."

"Is he?"

"Isn't he?"

"Well, if I was Mr. Korn . . ."

"Yeah?"

Whitey would look at me with his innocent eyes and make believe that I knew the story and he didn't. There was nothing I could do but tell him what I suspected and he would act shocked and then tell me that he didn't think I could be right. Why, Mrs. Lehrer was a fine lady, he'd say, and Mr. Korn was a perfect gentleman. Whitey always left me with the impression that I had made up an impossible story without a word of truth in it. He knew that I knew and I knew that he knew but there was no satisfaction in that for me. Once I complained to him that it wasn't much fun talking to him if he wasn't going to say anything. He told me that being in the hotel business meant that seeing should never be believing and the whole trick was to act as though nothing ever happened. The guests were always right and always perfect.

Every once in a while Whitey would get on my father's nerves. My father thought Whitey talked too much, that he had too many jokes and not enough respect. I think it was mostly the jokes. Whitey would walk up to my father looking as though he had some very confidential information to impart and he'd say, "What has one head, four legs, a tail, and eats hay?" The first few times my father bit and would say, "It sounds like a horse," and Whitey would step back and look at him with amazement. "Boss!", he'd say, "that's right! Thanks! Who would have thought of that!" Later on when Whitey would start another "riddle" like "What has two legs, feathers, sings, and . . ." my father would say, "I don't want to know," or, "There's a dictionary in the office. Look it up after you cut the grass."

At the end of every season my father would swear that Whitey would never be hired back, and the beginning of every season would see Whitey right there. He kept coming back for fifteen years. Their relationship was in itself a kind of joke because my father liked Whitey and Whitey liked my father, but it was my father's opinion that he was being blackmailed into keeping him on.

My father blamed it all on electricity. The hotel made its own and at least once a week the generator would stop and the hotel would be pitch dark. My father would yell for Whitey. The machines must have loved him because he was the only one they would work for. After the yell for help, "Whitey, the lights!", Whitey would go off to the generator house which was way back in the woods, and do who knows what to the machine—and there would be light.

That was a pretty strong hold Whitey had on my father, but in spite of that he would be fired at least once a week. But he never left. He would go to my mother—he was her favorite—and tell her that the boss had fired him again. My mother would rehire him immediately. Whitey had a saying: "The boss fires, the missus hires." And there wasn't a truer statement in the world. My father was resigned to it.

When the hotel got prosperous enough we bought a bus to pick up the guests from the railroad station. The bus was very modern for those days but today it would look like something you see in a French movie about Mexico. It was long and high and it loaded from the back, up a little step and in a door with a shiny handle. The seats—they used leather then—were placed longways on each side of the bus so that the passengers faced one another. It was green with gold letters on the sides. *The Fleischmanns Mansion* it said, and it looked elegant!

With great pride, Whitey would drive the bus to the station to meet every train. He never missed. He started for the station late and got there early. And the reason he got there early wasn't fast driving, it was because the train was always late. At the station there were always buses from the other hotels and I'm sure if it had been called for, Whitey would have fought with the other drivers for their passengers. He didn't for two reasons: first, everyone who came to the mountains had a reservation at one hotel or another, and, secondly, anybody who wouldn't choose The Mansion in the first place wasn't the sort of guest Whitey wanted.

I remember standing with Whitey on the porch of the hotel and watching guests drive up in their cars. Whitey would shake his head at me and say, very seriously, that someday he was going to have his own Cadillac and a chauffeur. It wasn't a bitter thing, it wasn't an envious remark. People, according to Whitey, were entitled to the comforts they could afford. It was just that someday he wanted them, too, and the car and a chauffeur were the symbols of his ambition.

Whitey liked people and he respected them. Some a little more than others. He seemed to know the good ones from the bad ones but everybody got the benefit of the doubt. Guests would give Whitey tips on the stock market. He took the tips from the people he liked most and forgot the tips from the people he liked just a little. He would buy what he could afford and little by little he began to be able to afford more and more. When at last Whitey left the hotel, he went to Texas with, as he said, "A few bucks in my pocket." If this were fiction I suppose the ending would be that Whitey took his few bucks, invested here and there and became a rich man with a Cadillac and a chauffeur.

But this happens to be a true story. Whitey has two Cadillacs but only one chauffeur. He lives in Texas with his family and several oil wells. He writes that he's getting bald but he still signs the letters "Whitey."

6 *One Headwaiter + One Cook = Trouble*

If vanity is the name for women, what should a man be called? In this case it should be Emil, because a vainer, more self-loving person never lived, and he had nothing to be vain about and nothing to love himself for. Emil was tall, even for a headwaiter. His face looked as if it was being held up by his nose, as if he was following it and it was getting away. Emil was getting bald on top. He combed his hair to cover the bare spots so that when he was standing it looked all right but when he sat down, the masquerade was over.

Emil came to America from Austria when he was five, but he kept his father's accent because it sounded Continental. He probably could speak as well as Noel Coward but since an accent got him the jobs he wanted, he cultivated it until he sounded like a headwaiter in a movie.

According to the people who worked with him, Emil looked like a human being but that's as far as it went. The guests felt the same way but wouldn't dare say it; they were afraid of him. They would say things about him when he went from the dining room to the kitchen but when he came back they changed the subject.

Emil was a very good headwaiter but he felt that guests should eat and not ask for favors. Once in a while a guest would put his courage on the table and complain to Emil that, maybe, the soup wasn't hot enough.

Emil, always the gentleman, would say, "Hot soup, my dear sir, is very bad for the liver."

101

Sometimes the guest was a brave man and would continue. "Make the soup hotter, please."

"I don't think I should take the responsibility."

"*That* hot you don't have to make it!"

"Sir, I give service. If you want hot soup I'll have it made hot. However, its present temperature is healthfully pleasant, believe me."

"You're a doctor?"

"That happens to be the latest medical information. I'll have the waitress take the soup back and have it heated."

"Never mind. I'll eat it lukewarm."

"Very wise of you, sir." And then Emil would turn and, like a rooster, look around to see if there were any other problems he could solve.

Emil had no use for people; he acted as though they existed only to annoy him, that God was mad at him and invented people as a punishment. The only thing Emil really loved besides Emil was horses, so everyone was surprised when they heard that he was almost engaged to Schoene Helene.

Schoene Helene was our first cook. She was called Schoene —pretty—because that's exactly what she wasn't. She was short, dumpy, and very ugly. Her face was a mixture of all the features of her ancestors carelessly assembled. She had her father's nose, her grandfather's mouth, and one eye might have come from her mother, the other came from who knows where. Her face was lumpy like oatmeal bread. Nature gave her a heart of gold and hard work gave her a bank account.

Emil became her one and only admirer. Instead of bringing her candy and flowers he brought her compliments from the dining room. He reported everything the guests said about her cooking. For Schoene Helene these were more than diamonds —and if sometimes she slipped a little and put too much salt in the soup, Emil would make up compliments. Helene bloomed for him. She was never a laugher but she could always manage a giggle for Emil. And she rose to new heights after so many years of neglect; she cooked stuffed cabbage and strudel that are remembered even to this day. She gave Emil everything he wanted, and since all he wanted was money, Helene gave it to him in the same way she threw raisins into a pudding. He told her he needed it for his sick mother (in the third race) or his brother (who was running down in Florida). She gave him the money without question. They were engaged, after all, so it was all in the family.

Emil lost more than he won. My father tried to tell Helene, without being insulting or putting her in a mood so that she wouldn't cook, that Emil was only after her money. Helene wouldn't listen. Emil couldn't help it if he had such a sick family; she loved him and it was her duty to help. My father had to leave it at that. He didn't want to lose the best cook he ever had.

Naturally the summer passed and just as naturally Emil never set the date. He made excuses and Schoene Helene started to get depressed, and a depressed chef is the worst curse a hotel can have—better a guest with a contagious disease than a sad cook.

My father began to worry; the guests were complaining that there were lumps in the gravy, too much salt in the fish, the stuffed peppers weren't stuffed enough and the strudel dough tasted like thick celluloid. Even the help began to grumble about the food. In a way, that wasn't serious because the help always complained. If they could have got away with it they would have said there wasn't enough heat in the sunshine. But they added to my father's worries. He had to do something. He even asked me to talk to Helene, distract her if it was possible, tell her love stories, buy her true-romance magazines, something, anything. I tried, but every time I said the word "love" she would start to cry. She spent more time wiping her eyes than she did cooking. Sometimes I would come into the kitchen and find her standing by a huge pot of soup stirring it with a ladle in one hand and a pepper shaker in the other. She would be staring at the back of the stove, stirring, shaking pepper into the pot. The rest of the kitchen help would be standing around looking at her and nodding their heads in sympathy in time with the pepper shaker.

It was a good thing the season was almost over. My father did the only thing he could do; he told Emil that he would not be welcome back next year. It didn't bother Emil, but when Helene heard, she was furious. She made it very clear that if Emil wasn't coming back, neither was she. The madder she got, the better the cooking became. Her anger somehow took her out of herself and she was able to concentrate. But it wasn't a cure for love, only a temporary remedy.

My father made up his mind that Emil or no Emil he had to do something about Schoene Helene. If he couldn't make her see that she was being fooled he would have to protect her in his own way. Schoene Helene's soft spot was her heart—she was the sort of lady who cried in the movies and my father was the sort of man who could invent things to cry about. He went to see her in the spring just before the hotel opened again. He put on his saddest face. He told Helene that he was in trouble: there were bills to be paid and if they weren't the hotel couldn't open for the next season. He asked her for a loan, just for that season, and he would pay her back at six per cent interest.

Schoene Helene was torn between my father's bills and Emil's family. She didn't know what to do until my father convinced her that Emil would approve. After all, her money would be earning interest and they would have more in the bank in case his family got sick again. Helene agreed.

When the hotel opened my father "rehired" Emil, who returned with new diseases for new relatives: his sister had a baby, an aunt in Chicago suddenly developed a heart, and an uncle in Danbury had a liver. Schoene Helene explained what she had done with her money—she had invested it, and it couldn't be touched. She told him she had done it for them, for their future, their happiness, their security. Emil saw the handwriting on the wall. He quit early in the season.

Schoene Helene's cooking was very bad for a few weeks. My father hired a new headwaiter but he made sure of three things: that he was good-looking enough to cheer up Schoene Helene, that he didn't play the horses, and that he was married. He wasn't taking any chances. It took a little while but the cooking got back to normal. And the six per cent interest that my father paid to Schoene Helene was chalked up to running expenses. It was worth it.

What happened to Emil? He found a woman with money that wasn't tied up in investments. He also found a horse he could depend on. He took his gambling earnings and bought a partnership in a hotel across the valley from us. And Schoene Helene never got over being saved from Emil. She couldn't stand being so close to him and finally she left us and went to work in Florida.

My father never got over her ingratitude.

7 *Conrad*

Conrad was a dishwasher. It was the first job he ever had when he came here from Poland, and it was the only job he had until he went back. He was a tall, strong man. He had light, almost blond hair that was getting a little thin on top, and his eyes were a cold blue. He spoke with a thick accent and he had a way of getting his words so mixed up that sometimes he would just stop speaking. And whenever he had something to say, he said it as though he was going to be wrong. Sometimes I would see him walking all alone. He would look so sad that I felt I'd have to say something to him even if it was only to ask him where he was going. He would stop and very carefully hold out one finger as though he was going to conduct himself. "I am," he would say, and then stop to see if he was saying it correctly so far. "I am to storeroom have to go. Boss say so. I said all right words?" I would tell him that he said everything very well. He looked too lonely to correct and he seemed to be a man with so many heavy things on his mind. Besides, I was a child and I didn't think it was right to correct a grownup even if he asked.

No one who worked at the hotel ever made fun of Conrad's speech. For one thing, most of the help spoke with accents themselves, and for another, Conrad had a terrible temper and the strength to go with it. If anyone wanted to laugh at him they had to wait until he went to bed.

Conrad worked hard. He washed the dishes, peeled the potatoes, lifted the fifty-pound bags of flour as if they were balloons, and cranked the ice-cream machine for hours without even changing hands. I used to sit with Conrad while he pumped the machine, and he let me put rock salt into the casing and then more ice as it was needed.

"Little girl," he would ask sometimes, "you like Conrad?"

I always said I liked him, and then he'd ask me who I liked better, ice cream or Conrad. I could see from the way he looked that there could only be one answer. He made the question sound like a joke—but it wasn't. He would laugh as though saying "thank you" when I said I liked Conrad the best and then he'd tell me, "You be nice girl." Then he'd let me test the ice cream as a reward and to make sure it was frozen just right.

Conrad was up at five and in bed at ten. It was a long day but he had a reason for working hard. Only two people knew—my mother and myself. Conrad liked me, but he loved my mother. Of all the people in the hotel she was his favorite. He called her "Missus" and confided everything to her. He would let me listen, but when he talked he never looked at me, only at my mother.

Conrad owned a small farm in Poland. His wife was still there trying, Conrad said, to make the farm earn a living. Every payday Conrad would take his money and send it to his wife. Each letter was sent with careful directions about what to do with the money: it was for a plow or a horse, or pigs, a wagon, a new stove. Every week that went by made the farm a little bigger and a little better.

Conrad wasn't a man who talked much but when he let go he could talk a week's worth in an hour. His favorite listener was my mother. Between chores he would light a cigarette that always had two wet spots from his thumb and forefinger, puff deep puffs, and say, "Missus, by God, Missus, I got damn fine farm now. I got damn fine wife and soon, by dammit, I go home and be farmer. I live like king over there now. Conrad no damn fool, work it hard to get it amimals and machimes for farm so be like in Unites States. You come visit Conrad, Missus? You and Boss and little girl? I treat it you damn fine, all right, Missus?"

My mother always said, "Yes." His plans for his farm became almost her own and she would ask farmers for their advice and even send Conrad off to see them and to talk about the best ways to grow corn or feed pigs. She took Conrad seriously and she became his very special friend.

Every once in a while my mother would tell Conrad that he really needed a new pair of shoes, or a new suit, or a hat, and Conrad would listen to her, keep out a little money and go to one of the stores in the village. He never wanted to, but if the Missus said, he would. One day Conrad cashed his check at the desk and went down to the village for new shoes. He came back to the hotel later in the evening drunk and without the shoes.

I was in the kitchen with my mother and Schoene Helene. I was supposed to be on my way to bed but I had delayed it a little bit by asking for a glass of milk. The kitchen at night after supper was like a factory slowing down. The huge wooden cutting tables and the serving table had been scrubbed white with a wire brush. The big stoves were banked and were being blacked with a wire brush and a pan of something that looked like thick ink. The floors were still damp from their mopping. The only real activity was in the bakery at one end of the kitchen where the baker and his assistant were getting ready for the morning, mixing dough in huge round-bottom copper pots that smelled of vanilla, sugar, butter, yeast, and always made me hungry.

I was drinking my milk when Conrad banged in through the screen door. He looked funny but I didn't know why. He seemed like a brick wall that was going to fall but didn't. He was singing and he seemed happy for once. He smiled at everybody and I remember feeling glad that Conrad was in such a good mood. He slapped the men on their backs and he kissed every woman he could reach. He yelled that everyone should feel good, "Like Conrad, like me!" Then he danced around the room, clapping his hands for music.

My father must have heard the noise. He came running in from the empty dining room. He saw what was happening and started to walk towards Conrad. I was getting scared. The happiness I felt for Conrad was gone because there seemed to be such violence in his dancing and laughing. I felt safer when I saw my father, and my mother must have felt the same way, because she was holding on to me and saying, "It's all right, Jake's here." Conrad looked at my father. "Hello, Boss," he said, and then he danced up to me, held out his hands and said, "Little Girl, you dance with Conrad?" I didn't know what to say and I looked to my father who was next to Conrad. Conrad turned to him and said, "Boss, Conrad don't hurt little girl. What kind man you think I be, hah? Conrad just drunk not crazy. O.K., Boss?" I didn't know what my father was going to say but I didn't want to see Conrad sad again, so I held out my hands. Conrad laughed and picked me up and then he danced me around the room singing in Polish. Finally he put me down on a table, leaned against it for a moment, and then sat down in a chair.

Someone brought him a pot of coffee but he pushed it away. He told everyone that he had stopped for a drink. "And by dammit is good fellows in dat place. Conrad buy drinks, fellows buy drinks, then more drinks—go to shoe store, is closed. Good joke on Conrad. Wear old shoes. Missus don't mind, feet don't mind, only shoe man mind but he closed so who care? Not Conrad!"

One minute he was laughing, the next he was silent, and then he began to cry. He must have realized that he had spent his money on drinks and hadn't sent anything back to his wife in Poland. "Dumb Polack," he yelled at himself. "Stupid Conrad!" he said. He wasn't fit to live with people, he yelled, and he begged someone to hit him, to punish him. He asked God to strike him dead, and then, still crying and banging his head with his fists, he staggered to bed, my father helping him.

The next morning I made sure I said an especially nice hello to Conrad. He smiled down at me and said that I was a very good dancer and then he stooped down to peer into my face and asked, "Conrad hurted you maybe?" When I said that he hadn't he nodded and told me, "Must never hurted childrens. Is not nice." When I told Conrad that I didn't think he would ever hurt a child he stood up and said, "By goddammit is right! Excuse it language."

Conrad never took another drink. The next time he needed something from the village he asked my mother to get it for him. He worked for us about ten years before he went back to Poland and to his wife and his farm. When he got there he found that his wife had been living with another man ever since Conrad had left and that she had a child by him. The money for the farm? It was gone, spent, wasted. Conrad had worked hard for another man's pleasure.

We got the news in a letter he wrote to my mother and after that we never heard another word from him. We always wondered but never knew what had happened to him. I used the story for a radio show many years later. My story had a happy ending.

8 *Music Hath Charms—But*
Food Is Better

In the city spring comes, not with budding trees but with the opening of windows. In the country it's the robins. In the hotel business it's musicians, because when they arrive, summer can't be far behind. They were easy to recognize, these harbingers of summer. They didn't need to carry their instruments to be spotted as musicians; they were always five pale young men, and no matter how many bands came to the hotel over the years, they were never anything but five pale young men.

Watching the musicians was sometimes more fascinating than listening to them, and the more I watched, the more I was sure that there was such a thing as magic. There was no other way to account for the change. From thin and pale, they became fat and tanned. They always said it was the mountain air. It wasn't. It was the food, the girls, and the sun, probably in that order.

There was a special quality that set the musicians apart from all the others who ever worked at the hotel. In those days— I don't know how it is today—a musician had to be more than just a boy who could play a saxophone. The first requirement was that he had to be unmarried; the second that he had to be a student—and not any sort of a student, but a student of medicine, law, dentistry, or, a new fad, business administration. Liberal arts were out—no self-respecting mother wanted to have her daughter in the possible position of being engaged

111

to a young man whose lifework was to be English, or Music, or, God forbid, Philosophy. So, for the good of the hotel, every musician was an embryonic professional man in the best sense. In all the years that we had a band, none of the musicians ever married a daughter of a guest, proving, I suppose, that they might have been studying for a profession, but deep down they were musicians.

And they were a race apart. They can't help it, it's something they learn along with reading music. They're not like people. First of all, nobody hires a musician. A musician works out of the goodness of his heart. Secondly, if a musician decides he'll do you a favor and be on your payroll, you have to remember to treat him very gently. By nature he's a mingler, and he thinks that the guests at the hotel have been invited to keep him happy.

One of the first things a hotelkeeper has to learn about musicians is that they should not be allowed, under any circumstances, to have living quarters near the guests or the help. There are good reasons, believe me. For one thing, musicians practice; they practice any time they think they want to practice, and if you tell them to stop, you're nothing but a music-hater, and an obstacle in the road of cultural progress. The second fact to bear in mind is that musicians make friends very easily—but only with women. That's something they can't be blamed for, but that doesn't mean they should be encouraged, either.

After a few tries, my father found the best place for the band. It was an old corrugated tin garage, way back in the woods, maybe a quarter of a mile away from the hotel. He converted the garage into living space, and, on the pretense of privacy, lured the musicians into their new home. There they could practice any time they wanted—and there they could invite any lady foolish enough to go. Unless you are a lady yourself, you will never actually realize just how foolish one of us can be.

The first item on the band's agenda—after scouting out and setting aside the prettiest waitresses—was the friendship of the chef. If the chef was Hungarian, the band would rehearse night and day one of those wild gypsy airs; if he was a Viennese, there would be waltzes; if he was Bavarian, German *Landlers* would make their appearance. If, and this would be too much to hope for, the chef happened to be a woman, then the band would be in seventh heaven. Because then they wouldn't have to play at all.

One of the ways to butter up the chef was to ask for an opinion. After a rehearsal the chef would be approached and his criticisms of each number would very deferentially be asked for. I have yet to meet the chef who could resist the chance to criticize.

The critiques would take place in the kitchen over coffee and cake, naturally. And the chef would hold forth—that none of *them* ever went into show business is a miracle. While the chef talked, the band would nod, sip coffee and eat cake. The length of the conference was always determined by the size of the cake. At a really successful critique, the chef would insist that the "boys" taste the goulash or the roast—while the chef delivered still another musical opinion.

Nobody at the hotel seemed to be musician-proof. I don't know why five young men who played the drums, the double bass, piano, saxophone, and trumpet should have had such an air of glamor about them. Maybe it was their look of collective irresponsibility. Or maybe it was just that they were a bunch of boys on a paid vacation. Whatever it was, it drew admirers.

I particularly remember one saxophone player, a twenty-year-old not-so-good-looking redhead called Sonny who made it a practice or a hobby to walk around looking like a lost little boy. Everybody fell for him. His pose worked wonders especially among the young females at the hotel for their two-week vacations. Every time a new crop arrived Sonny would look them over like a shark and then, when he had found what he was looking for, he began his attack. The attack was simple —it took advantage of the softer, trusting, feminine natures of the young girls looking for husbands. For one girl Sonny made believe he had consumption and was going to Switzerland either to recover or perish—and the way he told it, most likely the latter. When she left after two weeks they had an "understanding." Of course Sonny couldn't ask a girl to marry a man in his condition. The next victim succumbed to a long story about artistic integrity. (That can be a disease too.) For that particular two weeks Sonny was a composer who was demeaning himself by playing jazz saxophone in order to make enough money so he could finish his symphony. When this patroness of the arts had to leave for home, Sonny's new approach on a new girl was almost the truth, only backwards. He told his new love that he was a medical student. That much was the truth. The rest of his story was that he really wanted to be a musician but he had a very cruel father who had forced him into medical school so that he could carry on the family name in surgery. He, Sonny, was going into brain surgery—but his heart wasn't in it.

My father told me the real story because he knew Sonny's terrible Philistine father. As a matter of fact, that's how Sonny got the job at the hotel. It was a favor to a friend. Sonny's father played violin in a German restaurant and there was nothing he would have liked better than to have his son to be a musician. In the first place it was cheaper. The poor man had been supporting Sonny for twenty years and he was looking forward to the time when he could stop. But could he? No! Sonny wanted to be a doctor and that meant four more years of medical school, two years as an intern, and on top of all that he'd have to set Sonny up in an office. My father's attitude was, "God forbid, that that poor man should hear what his son is saying!"

My mother also fell for Sonny and her greatest concern that summer was that Sonny should get a decent night's rest. She kept telling him that girls wouldn't disappear off the face of the earth if he got to bed early one night. And Sonny kept telling her he didn't want to take the chance.

My mother had a soft heart, especially where the band was concerned. But once, early in the season, in one of the first years of the hotel, she told my father that she was afraid the band was going to eat them right into the red. My father knew very little about music, but a whole lot about musicians. He hadn't run restaurants in the city without learning something. He told her to wait, to watch and to be patient. This was, after all, only the first week of the summer season.

My mother waited, watched, and was patient. At the end of another week she told my father that maybe there was something wrong with the food: the musicians weren't eating so well. My father looked like Sherlock Holmes, shrugging "Elementary" to his dear Watson, and pointed out that the pale thin young men were now sunburned and putting on a little weight. They had eaten themselves into a normal state after a long winter of half-rations. In short, they were full.

At the end of the season my mother began to worry about how the boys would manage through another hard winter. My father shrugged. It was hard to kill a musician. There was nothing to worry about. Musicians practiced magic on the side. They had to, otherwise they would never last a week the way they lived.

But in spite of magic, my mother always packed a picnic lunch for "the boys" when they left at the end of the season for the city and the hard, cruel world.

9 *Guests Are Named, Not Born*

Does a child ever grow up to deserve the name his mother gave him? I don't think so. Mostly a child grows up, takes a vacation, and gets a nickname that should have been given to him right in the maternity ward. Mothers of the world! Wait! When your child becomes a guest in a hotel he'll get the name he deserves. Anything else is wishful thinking.

The staff of any hotel has a way of naming people in such a way that each name is better than the original and fits like a glove. Having a name is like having a dog—you get the one you deserve. Men who own bulldogs look like bulldogs, ladies with Pekineses look like Pekineses. Have you ever seen a fat man with a greyhound or a tall man with a Chihuahua? Probably it's the people in the pet shops who arrange for these right combinations, or maybe it's nature. In the hotel business it's the help who make the necessary name changes—it's a tradition.

The minute a guest checks into a hotel he becomes public property. And when he checks out, the second scullery man probably knows as much about him as his own family.

The first person a guest meets is the bellboy, whose first job is to find out which side of the fence the guest is on, theirs or the other side. Is he a friend or an enemy? By the time the bellboy puts the bags in the guest's room, he knows. A guest who is a friend is a person who laughs, even a little, about a joke and doesn't think the bellboy is just hired help: which he is, but doesn't want anybody to know. Every bellboy likes to think of himself as the owner's son just learning the hotel business —and he wants to be treated that way. He likes it to be understood that America is a democracy and he's the President. Any guest who doesn't understand that is an enemy.

The second person to look over the guest is the chambermaid. Listening to them talk when they were having their coffee break on the back steps of the kitchen I could have been a cynic and the only reason I escaped was that the chambermaids were humanitarians. They took human nature as they found it in the rooms they had to clean. I seldom heard them say a word against a guest. What was, was, and they only made comments, not judgments. If you want to know how solvent a guest is, don't ask Dun and Bradstreet, ask a chambermaid. She won't be far off. The chambermaids would sit quietly drinking their coffee and then, all of a sudden, one of them would say, "That Mr. Leeds! He must be pretty rich." The other maids would nod their heads and agree. Once I asked how they knew. I helped in the office and all I knew was that Mr. Leeds booked a room for two weeks. They let me in on their secret.

"Look, honey," one of the younger chambermaids told me. "Leeds checks in. He goes to his room. Then what's he do?"

"He unpacks."

All the other chambermaids nodded in agreement. "He puts away his clothes but you can't tell from that. He could of borrowed them from a rich brother. You know what counts? The medicine bottles!"

I didn't understand. I couldn't see what medicine had to do with it. I was too young.

"Honey," the maid said very patiently, "a poor man don't buy every pill in the store. He gets a prescription and he uses it until it's empty. Then he gets another one. A rich guy, he can afford lots of pills. So, the more pills and bottles a guy unpacks, the more he's got in the bank. And I don't mean aspirins, I mean that prescription stuff with the doctor's name on the label."

Well, it was a new way to look at the world. I always thought that people with just a few bottles of medicine were healthy; now, all of a sudden I had found out it meant they were poor.

The third test for a guest is the dining room, and here is where he finally gets his new name. No matter how nice a person seems in the lobby, when it comes to the dining room he gives himself away.

For instance, take Mr. Goldstein. Mr. Goldstein was a very friendly man; he laughed at the bellboy's jokes and he filled his bathroom cabinet with pill bottles. He could have been in the staff's Hall of Fame except for a couple of little things. First, he came at the very beginning of each season and he left at the end, and he didn't tip until he checked out on the last day. Because he was one of the first to arrive, he would try to get special treatment from my father. He knew that at the beginning of the summer business could go one way or the other; it might be a good year, or it might be bad. Mr. Goldstein would take three rooms for himself and his family for the whole season, and three rooms booked for the summer is nothing to sneeze about—especially since he always paid cash in advance and cash in advance in a hotel is like an oil well on the front lawn. My father always agreed to Mr. Goldstein's request for a discount. He didn't have any choice and Mr. Goldstein knew it.

The second mark against Mr. Goldstein was that he liked prunes. He liked them for breakfast, for lunch, and for supper. He insisted. I would listen as he argued with the headwaiter who told him he had insulted the chef's chopped liver by always asking for prunes. After one week in the hotel Mr. Goldstein became—inevitably—Mr. Prunes, and for the twelve or fifteen years that he came to the hotel I never heard him called anything else. To his friends and his family he was a busy, important man of the world, but to the hotel, all he was was a dish of cooked fruit.

Then there was Mr. Lefcourt and his family. Mr. Lefcourt

also passed the first tests. He didn't have too many pills but he had a heating pad, and that counted for a little something. Mr. Lefcourt was a very protective man. He wanted only the best for his family and he was always worried that some guest in the dining room was eating something that his family wasn't getting. He was always looking around to see what was being served to the other tables, and the waiters were afraid he was going to wear out his eyes. They began to call him Cockeye. The waiters would run in and out of the kitchen getting orders and giving orders and every once in a while they would yell, "Cockeye wants a meat ball," or "Cockeye wants a roll with seeds." I thought it was funny but my father felt a man should deserve better for being so concerned about his family.

We once had a guest who came down to breakfast in her peignoir. She was called Madam Queen because it didn't bother her that people stared, and also because she spoke with a very thick English accent.

Madam Queen wasn't any bother to anyone. She ate what was put in front of her and never fussed if things were hot or cold; she just wore the peignoir to breakfast. Everyone excused her because she was so nice, and because she probably didn't know any better. She came from South Africa and everyone thought maybe that's the way people acted in the hotels over there. Not even the headwaiter, who was supposed to know everything, wanted to admit that he didn't know what ladies wore to breakfast in African hotels. He acted as though he had seen it all before and so it was accepted. The only thing we were afraid of was that bathrobes at breakfast might catch on, become a style for the other guests. It didn't, but we worried all summer.

I remember another guest, a bachelor, but he didn't stay with us very long. He was a bald lawyer by the name of Hiller. The waiters called him Eggs and when he walked into the dining room, they just shivered with fear. He always ordered eggs for breakfast but that's not why he got his name. He got the name because he always sent the eggs back—there was always something wrong with them: the fried eggs were too runny, the boiled eggs were three and a half instead of three and three quarters, the poached eggs weren't round enough, and the scrambled eggs were too mixed up. You couldn't please him and if you argued with him about the eggs he'd talk back like a district attorney. On his last day at the hotel—he didn't know it was going to be his last—he sent back seven orders. The chef was going to quit and the waiter ready to collapse from the exercise. My father got mad. He knew that the help could stand just so much and no more. He could see that the camel was getting a sore back.

I knew something was going to happen because when he got mad my father would walk in a straight line to whatever and whoever was making the problem. I saw him start from the kitchen, go through the swinging doors, then across the dining room, and stop in front of Mr. Hiller's table. The waiters knew the walk and they stopped right where they were; even the headwaiter stopped. My father was calm but firm. "Mr. Hiller," he said, "There's a farmer right across the mountain from here. He's a friend of mine and he has chickens—very fine chickens. My friend, the farmer, sells his chicken eggs to a grocer—also a friend of mine. I buy the eggs. I bring them to the hotel— and the chef, also a good friend, cooks them exactly to your order. The point, Mr. Hiller, is you've insulted all my friends. So, please, pack your bags, go to another hotel, and don't come back. Good-bye, Mr. Hiller." My father turned and went back to the kitchen, but not in a straight line. He stopped to talk to a few guests on the way. I relaxed and the waiters began to move and the headwaiter began again to snap his fingers at the busboy.

Mr. Hiller left. Where he spent the rest of his vacation I don't know, but wherever it was I felt sorry for them.

Once a guest got a name it stuck. No matter how many years a guest came to the hotel—and no matter how many times the staff changed—the name remained. It was like a legacy. There are people whose faces I can see, whose clothes I can remember, but whose names I can't recall except for those given them in the privacy of the kitchen. I remember a Mrs. What's-the-Matter-No-Butter?, Mr. More-Bread, Mr. No-Noodles-in-the-Soup junior and senior, and a widow, Mrs. I'm-Not-Hungry-To-day, who always asked for doubles.

I feel like Mrs. Good-bye-Mr.-Chips calling the roll. Some guests were always trouble, some guests were never trouble, and some of each kind left their mark. It's hard for me to eat a quiet meal at the Plaza without naming the people around me. I know the waiters must have names for everyone in the room, maybe a little more upper crust than what I remember, but the meaning is the same. Maybe the lady in the Hattie Carnegie dress is called "What-Is-the-Matter-Have-We-No-Paté-Maison?" It's a name and it probably fits. The only thing that bothers me is what am I being called. Not that I mind, I'm just curious and I'd like to know—and then again, maybe it's better if I don't.

10 *The Triple Standard*

Mrs. Marcus lived a life that would have made a movie
—but it would have been banned in Boston. Her life was exactly opposite the way our guests lived and that's what made
her fascinating to them. She was doing exactly what they
thought she was doing. There are some people who dream, some
people who wouldn't dare—and there are the Mrs. Marcuses
that do. Maybe she didn't have any imagination or maybe she
had too much, but whatever it was, she was different.

Mrs. Marcus knew she was by no means above suspicion; she
only acted as though she was. And when she asked me to read
her palm, something I pretended I knew how to do, I knew
I was going to have to say no or make up a story that didn't
fit the facts.

When Mrs. Marcus held out her hand to me there were only
two ladies on the porch watching. By the time I had sat down
next to her every lady guest in the hotel was gathered around,
watching and waiting. I looked at her hand and the ladies looked
at one another with winks and significant raising of eyebrows.
If Mrs. Marcus was nothing else she was an earful and the
ladies wanted to hear everything. I saw three life lines in her
hand and three long lines for wealth, but that was only because
I knew about Mrs. Marcus. And what I knew I couldn't tell.
What I told her was that she was going to take a trip and I
knew I couldn't be wrong because when she didn't go to
Europe during the winter, she went to Palm Beach. Mrs. Marcus
spent her life recuperating.

After I finished with Mrs. Marcus I had the ladies to contend with. Every place I went during the day I was stopped by little groups who seemed to be waiting around corners for me.

"Let me ask you a question," was the password. "So what was in her hand besides a trip? You saw men? Us you can tell." I had to say that I wasn't even sure about the trip. I couldn't persuade them that I didn't know anything. They knew better and they were right. I would never have found out about Mrs. Marcus, even from her palm, if I hadn't heard my mother say to my father late at night, "Shh, you'll wake the child." "Shh" meant there was something going on that "the child" shouldn't know about and so I sat on my bed with my ear to the wall until I found out all about Mrs. Marcus.

The only difference between Mrs. Marcus and the other guests was that she was a little bigger than life. She had a flair. You knew she was somebody when she walked into a room. Saints have halos—people like Mrs. Marcus look as if they have spotlights on them. And if you think she was beautiful, you're wrong. She wasn't even pretty. Handsome maybe, striking. She was tall, with a nice figure, well-groomed, and she had the most beautiful clothes. If anybody was à la mode at Fleischmanns, it was Mrs. Marcus. And it's not true that you can't tell by looking. Maybe you can't tell everything, but if you have eyes you can tell there's something.

Mrs. Marcus had all the normal ambitions. She wanted the ease and the comfort that other people wanted; she wanted a vacation in the country like everybody else and she wanted the best for her children. So what's so different about her? The big difference is that she knew how to get it—and that's a big difference.

She wasn't rich, or to put it another way, her husband was poor. Mr. Marcus worked in a dress factory in New York. When he came to the hotel, which wasn't often, he looked, acted, and was treated like a poor uncle who had to be invited for the weekend. He was a small man with great big eyes and he looked like he was always asking, "What happened to me?" Nobody could give him an answer because nobody knew. He was like a character actor in a movie—the kind that as soon as you see him on the screen you know he's the one who is going to get the pie in the face, have an accident, or just drop dead. That was Mr. Marcus. One look and you knew that here was a man who had tempted the fates and was being punished. What was his crime? Nothing. He did nothing, that was his crime.

Mrs. Marcus didn't fit into his life. She was a piece of a jigsaw puzzle from another set. She came to the hotel each year at the same time—for the Fourth of July—and she took the best rooms for herself and her three daughters. Mrs. Marcus always arrived on the Rip Van Winkle Flyer which was the fastest and fanciest train on the West Shore Division, and she came with seven trunks. She was the hotel's showpiece. For years she was as much of an attraction as the fireworks or the Masquerade Ball, not only because of the sort of person she happened to be, but because of what she brought in the trunks.

Normally a guest, female, would come to the hotel with a few new dresses that she could show off at dances and at supper. During the day an old dress would do—why get a new dress dirty playing croquet? But Mrs. Marcus had a new dress for every activity. She had one for gossiping on the porch, one for lunch, one for tea, one for watching tennis, and even a dress for "checking out." Every time she went back to her room to change the guests would gather on the porch and wait.

It was like a movie. Mrs. Marcus would leave the Main House—her rooms were a suite in one of the smaller houses— she would walk like a stately lady to her rooms, disappear for a few minutes, and then she would reappear, a changed woman. Each dress was fancier than the last, and each dress, even if she had made them herself—and she didn't—must have cost a fortune.

How could Mr. Marcus, a cutter in a dress factory, afford such luxury? He couldn't. Maybe Mrs. Marcus was an heiress? She wasn't. So how could she be so fancy? Very simple. She had two rich lovers. One was a dress contractor who always had good seasons, and the other was a stock broker who clipped coupons. And between the three men Mrs. Marcus lived very, very well.

It's possible that Mr. Marcus objected to his wife's arrangements, but I don't think so. She wasn't the kind of woman to pay attention to the kind of man he happened to be. Not that she didn't like him—she did. But he was a worrier. Sometimes I would hear Mrs. Marcus telling him to stop worrying or he'd get an ulcer. She was right, because he was just the kind of man who worried about what he didn't have just in case someday he'd get it. His health was very important to him, almost a hobby. After all, some people are vegetarians, some people walk five miles before breakfast and some people like to be healthy.

Of course, Mr. Marcus could have been a freethinker, but he didn't look like one—they wear sweaters. Mr. Marcus always wore a vest.

It's not unheard of for a woman to have two lovers and one husband—maybe it's what could be called a triple standard. Among people anything is possible, and the interesting thing is not what people do but why they do it. Mrs. Marcus wanted to be loved. There are different kinds of love and Mrs. Marcus wanted them all. She wanted people to like her, and if a bellboy smiled at her she tipped him—to her that meant for twenty-five cents the bellboy was her friend. She gave private parties in her room for some of the guests, and to her that meant, because they drank her champagne and ate her hors d'œuvres, they liked her. But instead of love she was getting attention. People talked *about* her, not *to* her. She was a freak, not a friend. And she was envied because how many nice, well-brought-up, middle-class ladies had three men and seven trunks of clothes?

If Mrs. Marcus was different, her three men were even more different. They were very liberal. Mr. Marcus and the dress contractor lived in the same apartment with Mrs. Marcus and her three daughters. They even played pinochle together. The stock broker was a visitor. The children called him "Uncle." They were all respectable men whose favorite writer must have been Colette. They were also happy. They didn't bother people, they didn't drink, and they didn't have wild parties. What they must have had was a schedule, like the New York Central, otherwise can you imagine the traffic jam?

The three daughters, Laura, the youngest, Yvonne, the middle, and Arlene the oldest, should have grown up to be delinquents, but they didn't. Mrs. Marcus was very strict. She was a moralist in spite of herself. She knew right from wrong, and if she couldn't help herself she could help her children. She kept an eagle eye on them all the time, waiting, I suppose, for some sign that they were taking after her. If she saw Arlene sitting alone with a boy on a bench, she would send Laura out to keep them company. Better than anyone else, she knew that three's a crowd.

Her girls didn't look like sisters. Laura looked like the stock broker, Yvonne looked like the dress contractor, and Arlene looked the image of Mr. Marcus. A wise mother who has three different daughters tries to find a common denominator for them, and by Mrs. Marcus's figuring that meant three rich men. An ordinary mother trying to find somebody rich for one daughter has a big job, but for three the mother needs a miracle. Mrs. Marcus never gave up. She looked and looked—and when a woman like that looks, she finds. Mrs. Marcus found three rich men, and as each girl reached twenty-one, she got married. It was automatic, it was almost electronic, and also it was unfair. At least that's what a lot of the guests thought. Here they had been leading blameless, faultless, harmless lives, and what was their reward? Their daughters had to marry for love, and that means, always, boys without a cent.

They say that crime doesn't pay and the wages of sin are supposed to be death. And when someone dies what happens? They leave annuities, insurance policies, a business, and other little odds and ends. And who does it all go to? The beneficiary. That was Mrs. Marcus after her three men passed away. She became a very rich woman without a worry in the world. She had three happy daughters who had married for money and found love. And each one respected her mother. So is virtue its own reward? Ask Mrs. Marcus.

11 *The Philosopher's Store*

There was a spring that started flowing from the ground somewhere high up in the hills and ended in a wooden wellhouse where the water was always cold and clear and fresh. I remember that a cup was always kept in the wellhouse—it was hung on a hook or stood on a ledge just where the water emptied itself into the well. The cup was an old-fashioned measuring cup—blue enamel on the outside and white on the inside, and where enamel had been chipped off you could see the black of the metal underneath. The cup was as much a part of the well as the water. In the summer the cup stood on the ledge, mouth up, in the winter it stood mouth down waiting for the summer. The water was to me the best-tasting water in the world.

When I was young I thought I had discovered the well, that I was the only one who knew how fresh the water tasted and how cold it always was. I kept the secret to myself until one day I found out that everyone who lived around Fleischmanns also knew about the well. It was a disappointment to discover that my secret was the whole world's. The only person in town who seemed to understand my feeling about the well was Alfred Alpert, and the only way I knew that he knew was one day when he handed me a new tin cup and said, "It won't make it taste any better will it? But it'll look nicer." The next time I went to the well I put the cup on the ledge. It stayed there until Alfred Alpert died.

When I first met Alfred Alpert he was already an old man, a born father who never had a child. I was seven and he was

128

fifty. And to a child of seven anyone with gray hair is old and probably a grandfather. He was always a favorite of mine because he always seemed to have time for me. There was never a minute that he was too busy to pick me up, give me a kiss, or tell me a little joke, like: "What happened to the man who swallowed a feather?" I never answered that the man in the joke was tickled to death because it was too much fun to hear Mr. Alpert tell it and I didn't want to spoil any of the others that might follow, like "I see said the blind man as he picked up a hammer and saw." In the years I knew him the jokes never changed and there was a comfort in that.

His department store was just like Mr. Alpert. It was big and it was friendly and it looked like the kind of a place only a man would run. There were long lines of counters filled with everything in the world and arranged with absolutely no order at all. There were rolls of oilcloth right next to the kerosene lamps. The scissors and knives were on the same counter as the candles and work shoes. The calico and ticking separated the nails, tacks, and screws from the hammers and saws. And in spite of that he knew exactly where everything was.

Sometimes he would play games with me. He would say that if I was going to grow up and be his assistant I would have to know the store in the same way he did. While he was waiting on my father he would send me off to find something that was needed, like six cakes of brown soap. I knew where that was. It was next to the work shirts just behind the gloves and the ready-made bow ties. When I would bring the soap to him he would ask my father how much he wanted for me, and the two of them would dicker a little. Mr. Alpert would say that girls were going at seventeen cents a pound that year. My father would think it over and say he'd keep me until the price went up to twenty-one and then Mr. Alpert would tell him he was being foolish because he heard girls were going out of style next year. I would listen to them and laugh and never worry. My father wouldn't sell, and the matter would end when Mr. Alpert would say, "I tell you, Jake, even if I bought her I wouldn't know where to put her. All the counters are filled right now anyway."

I'm quite sure he could have found a spot for me because there was a place for everything in his shop. His own place was behind the counter, at the rear of the store. He was as much a part of that back counter as the hanging scale with its two metal scoops, the brass markers on one of the counter edges where he measured the lengths of material, and the huge roll of brown paper and spool of string that he used to wrap things in. No matter how many people were in the store, if Mr. Alpert wasn't there it was empty, and no matter how empty it was, if he was there the dark, quiet place was full of life.

Mr. Alpert had a wife, and she seemed to be in charge of the outside of the store. Her name was Tessie and she had a habit of sitting in a rocker on the front porch of the store with her legs crossed and a red rose in her black hair. Somebody once told her she looked Spanish and she believed it. From across the street there was the suggestion. She was a pretty woman, but I always wondered why she wasn't prettier. I think there was nothing behind her eyes, nothing to make the pretty woman into a pretty person. She seemed empty inside, and my father used to say that she needed a little salt.

Mr. Alpert and his wife hardly ever talked to each other during business hours. They were like separate people, not husband and wife, held together by dry goods instead of love.

People didn't mind Tessie. She could be charming and pleasant if she wanted to be but what charm she had came out only when customers went into the store. If someone was a well-known browser she couldn't be bothered. The real reason people were polite to Tessie was because she was Alfred's wife;

their affection for him carried over to her. As a child I could never understand why my father would say to my mother about Alfred, "Poor man," and my mother would answer, "Maybe he loves her." "That's a big maybe," my father would tell her, and then she'd hold a finger in front of her lips meaning that he should be quiet and not talk about such things in front of me.

Tessie Alpert was a very religious woman. In her time she went to every church of every denomination in Fleischmanns. When she first was married and moved to Fleischmanns the population was Protestant and so Tessie went to the Protestant churches. A little later a Catholic church was built and Tessie went to the Catholic church. Later still when the synagogue was built, Tessie went there, too. It wasn't out of any One World, Brotherhood of Man, conviction. It was for business, and if the town had become Arabian overnight Tessie would have been the first to face east. She practiced absolutely nothing that the religions in the town preached. It was a commercial duty and had nothing to do with her soul.

Alfred, on the other hand, paid no attention to religion. He was an intellectual, and he believed that if a man needed a religion he should have one, and if he didn't he shouldn't. But no matter what a man finally decided he was going to believe in it was Alfred's idea that it was nobody's business but his own. He called this his Categorical Imperative and it applied to everyone except Meltzer the Butcher. Meltzer was also an intellectual and a very religious man who acted as the rabbi for Fleischmanns. The two men liked to argue with each other about religion. They made it each other's business and they kept trying to convert each other. Alfred had philosophers on his side to back up his arguments. Meltzer also had philosophers, different ones, and their discussions sounded like a faculty tea in a graduate school. Meltzer would quote something and Alfred would quote right back. "True happiness is the union of in-

tellect with divine intelligence," Meltzer would say. And Alfred
would ask Meltzer where he got that piece of misinformation.
Meltzer, very proudly, would say, "Judah Abravanel," and Alfred would get annoyed because he didn't think it was very fair
to quote such an obscure philosopher.

"You know what Kant said," Alfred would ask as he leaned
across the counter, pointing himself at Meltzer. " 'True knowledge cannot transcend or go beyond experience' . . . that's what
he said. He didn't mix himself with divine intelligence."

Meltzer would look at Alfred very sadly and shake a finger
in his face. "Alfred, why do you read only what you want to
see? You know what he also said? You won't like it! 'Two
things fill the soul with wonder and reverence—the starry
heavens' "—and Meltzer would point to the ceiling—" 'and the
moral law within' "—and he would point to his heart. "He's
your friend, not mine."

"That doesn't mean what you think it means, Meltzer. If
you don't mind my saying, you should read more Voltaire.
That's where you'll find out about the moral law. You know
what Voltaire said? 'Man can shape the future with the results
of science,' science, Meltzer, not superstition! And also by 're-
sisting arbitrary power and intolerance.' That's Voltaire, a man
who knew what he was talking about!"

Meltzer would smile gently. "Alfred, you know Spinoza?"

"Of course. Who doesn't know Spinoza?"

"You mean what he said? 'He who knows nature knows God.'
What does that mean?"

Of course they never convinced each other about anything.
They argued this way for twenty-five years and the only thing
they proved was that each side of the argument was right.

Tessie Alpert had no use for senseless discussions. She was
all business. When she thought the talking had gone on long
enough she would cough discreetly from her place on the porch.

Alfred knew what that meant and he would say to Meltzer, "You came for nails or an education?"

Meltzer understood. "From you, nails," he would say. Then Alfred would walk him to the front of the store slowly so that their discussion would last a little longer. When they got to the porch the talking would stop because they were now both in Tessie's territory. Meltzer would nod good-bye to her and Alfred would turn and go back to his place behind the counter.

I always thought that Alfred and Tessie should have been a very romantic couple. They had the background. Alfred was one of three brothers, Tessie was one of three sisters, and they were all in-laws. The three brothers married the three sisters and none of them lived happily ever after.

The three sisters were born and raised in Margaretville, about six miles west of Fleischmanns. Their parents were the first Jewish settlers in that part of the mountains and the three girls grew up to be as native as the natives, complete with nasal twang.

Alfred and his brothers, Lew and Harry, were immigrants from Russia. Lew was the oldest, Alfred was in the middle, and Harry was the youngest. The mountains attracted them and they arrived at Margaretville as peddlers selling pots and pans, cutlery and clothes. Their wagon became a store and the three brothers settled. The one thing they had in common was reading. It was an obsession. Anything printed on paper they read. They educated themselves in everything except how to get along with one another, and when it was decided that they should open a branch in Fleischmanns, Alfred jumped at the chance. The six-mile separation would allow the brothers to remain friends.

Both stores did very well and Alfred liked being a businessman. He invested in everything and anything, and he made his business judgments according to whether he liked the person, not the proposition. It usually turned out well for him because either he liked the right people or there were only a few wrong people in the town. Alfred wanted to invest in my father's hotel and advance enough money to build a larger place. It was a very tempting offer. My father would have done it if it hadn't been for my mother, who had a fear of being in debt to anyone —even Alfred Alpert.

In spite of his being well liked there were a few people who were very careful about Alfred. They had my mother's opinion of him: that he was too sharp or a little too good to be true. One of the people who was afraid of Alfred was his own brother, Lew. I don't know how and I don't know why but the two stores, the one in Margaretville and the one in Fleischmanns that had been set up as a partnership, were dissolved, separated from each other. Everything was all very friendly, except when it came to Harry, the youngest brother. Alfred, who was a good deal older than Harry, had treated him like a son, and when Harry decided to stay in business with Lew instead of going with Alfred, Alfred looked on the decision as a betrayal. From that day on he never spoke to Harry or to Lew, or to Lew's two boys, Mort and Jimmy. The six miles between the towns became an ocean and the Alperts became a family of strangers.

Time went on and everybody got older. I became fifteen, sixteen, then twenty, and still Tessie Alpert sat on the porch with a rose in her hair, and Alfred got richer and sicker with diabetes. It was in the spring of the year when he took to his bed and Tessie and Alfred found out that they didn't know each other. They were like two strangers. The store was their marriage, and when Alfred had to leave it there was nothing to hold them together. Tessie, everybody thought, was a strong woman, but she was only strong because she had Alfred to lean on. And when Alfred was forced into his bed, Tessie left the front porch of the store and sat at home, rocking in her rocker in the living room, staring out the window—the rose still in her hair. Tessie could do nothing for Alfred. She couldn't cook or clean or make him comfortable. Instead she waited for Alfred to get better and take care of her.

Spring was life—and Alfred Alpert in his sickroom was death. Alfred knew that, too. I remember him pointing out of the window and saying that he wished he could live to see another spring but that he wouldn't.

Alfred began to put his affairs in order, and he went about it like a man putting his things into storage. My father, who liked Alfred very much, was a constant visitor. One day Alfred told him that he had decided to leave everything to me. My father, a wise man, asked him not to. He knew Alfred liked me; if he wanted to leave me something let it be a trinket, nothing else. By leaving me everything he wouldn't be doing me a favor, my father told him, and he didn't want to see his daughter involved in a lawsuit. He didn't want Alfred to leave me trouble because that's all it would be, and Alfred understood.

Alfred was getting too sick to stay in his own home. The doctor wanted him in a hospital; the nearest one was forty miles away in Kingston. The day Alfred left his home and Fleischmanns he gave up the convictions of a lifetime. He sent me for Meltzer the Butcher, whom he wanted not as a friend but as a rabbi.

Meltzer knew why I had come for him. Solemnly he walked me back to Alfred's house without a word passing between us. He entered the house in silence, walked into Alfred's room, and closed the door behind him. I sat down to wait, and I watched Tessie Alpert, who hadn't moved or said a word but kept staring out of the window.

For a few minutes there was nothing to hear. Then Meltzer's voice, quiet, calm, strong, started the Kaddish, the prayer for the dead. I could hear Alfred's voice a few words behind

Meltzer's like a counterpoint, punctuated by sobs of sorrow and resignation. There was a finality in the rhythm of the prayer—it was the end of a life, the end of hope, and the wondering if there would ever be another beginning.

Meltzer stayed with Alfred, and when the door opened they both came out. Alfred was dressed for his trip to the hospital. The car was waiting for him. Alfred, leaning on Meltzer, stopped for a minute to look at Tessie. She didn't turn away from the window. Alfred nodded a little nod and went out through the door.

Outside, his brother Harry was waiting for him—he had come to say good-bye. Alfred walked past him without a word and got into the car. Harry ran to the side of the car where Alfred was sitting and looked at him, begging him to speak. Alfred looked straight ahead. The car began to move and Harry ran after it crying, "Alfred! Alfred! Speak to me." But the car moved off and Alfred just looked straight ahead. Harry followed the car until it reached the main road and turned towards Kingston. He stood there watching until it had gone from his sight.

I went to visit Alfred in the Kingston Hospital a few times. The first time I went there he asked me to bring him water from Flagler's well—water that reminded him of his first days in the mountains—and before I came the next time I filled a five-gallon jug for him and brought it to the hospital. I don't think he ever got to drink any of it.

The jug stayed at the hospital and the water—what can happen to water?—it evaporated, disappeared, and came back to the earth as rain—maybe for another well or another stream or another Alfred Alpert.

12   "Where Is It Written?"

Mr. Banks was always called Banks the Butcher until he left town and the shop passed over to Meltzer the Scholar who then became automatically Meltzer the Butcher. Meltzer was a boarder with the Banks family. He came to Fleischmanns directly from the boat that brought him to America from Russia. He was a learned man and a very gentle soul. He was filled with knowledge of the Bible and the Talmud. He knew the whyfores and the wherefores but he was weak, very weak, on the therefores. Banks the Butcher took Meltzer the Scholar as an apprentice and he made it very clear that a man of learning must be able to do more than just quote the Commentaries of the Talmud in order to live. So Meltzer learned a new trade from Banks, who supplied the town and the hotels with meat.

Banks had a family—a wife, a daughter, and a son. The daughter, Lilly, was a very good friend of mine and I always had hopes that someday she and Meltzer would find each other. They lived in the same house and it didn't seem to be such a hard thing to do, but the sad realities of Lilly's life and the fact that Meltzer didn't love her never satisfied my wishful thinking.

Banks the Butcher was a hard master and a hard father, a man who didn't seem to know the difference between the living flesh of his family and the hanging carcasses of his stock in trade. He treated both with equal indifference and with equal contempt; perhaps he was a little more sympathetic to the sides of beef that hung silently from his hooks.

Lilly Banks and I became friends. She was the opposite of everything she should have been—a positive pole in a negative

137

home, a living reaction of warmth and kindness to the harsh reality of her father. And Lilly's whole family seemed to be an apology for Mr. Banks. Her brother Karl was a very gentle soul, her mother was a quiet woman who said little but who had hard, probing eyes. For every rude word of Mr. Banks's the family had five in apology.

Every chance I got I left the hotel to visit Lilly. I was free but she was bound to her duties that not even the coming of Meltzer lightened. She had to clean the glass on the display cases in the butcher shop, help her brother scrub the cutting tables with wire brushes, mop the floors, put down new sawdust on the floors and help check the outgoing orders. When these chores were finished, only then, was she allowed whatever freedom she could find.

I helped Lilly in the store. To me it was a game, to her it was the deadly seriousness of life. I wanted to help so that we could find time to play. And Lilly allowed me to help so that she could have her few little hours of escape.

When the work was finished, we would walk. The road past the butcher shop took us along the side of a stream. It ran north, away from the town and the people, through woods and past the nothingness of a graveyard.

Lilly preferred the loneliness of that walk. I would have liked the town and the busyness of its people but I always followed Lilly into the peace of the silent and unstaring road.

It wasn't hard to understand. To me Lilly was a fine and lovely girl. To people who didn't know her she was a gawky, badly dressed kid whose arms were too long, whose legs were a little too bony. She had the hips of a boy and a loose-jointed walk that reminded me of a string of beads strolling down the street. And she had the kind of crossed eyes that shocked. It was unexpected, unexpected because Lilly walked with her head bent down, down, and her mark of friendship was to look into your face. I accepted her crossed eyes as she accepted my childishness; childishness compared to her grown-up understanding that life was a punishment for as yet undisclosed sins. We were almost the same age, she was fifteen, I was twelve, and where I felt there was a life to look forward to Lilly felt she had had as much of it as was necessary.

When we went for our walks Lilly's brother would come along every once in a while. Karl was an almost exact copy of his father physically and it was strange to see the expected become the unexpected. This huge hulk played the guitar and he would take it along on our walks and play for us as we sat alone in the woods or by the stream. Karl played well and his favorite song was a Schubert lullaby. He spoke no German but he could sing it and the words of the song were the only ones he knew in a foreign language. The song, he said, was called "The Stream's Lullaby," and when he sang, "Gute ruh, Gute ruh, Mach't die augen zu" there was such longing and such simple sadness that it frightened me. Later, when I was older, I found the song was part of Schubert's *Die Schöne Müllerin*. And even hearing it in a concert hall surrounded by hundreds of people the words and the melody would make me a little colder and I would reach out for my husband's hand.

The brother and sister seemed to be a sort of mutual-aid society, a little fortress of kindness for each other in a hard world. I felt very flattered to be included in the protection of their company even though I had nothing to be protected from. But friendship being what it is, their enemies were my enemies, and mine, if I had any, would have been theirs.

Lilly's mother was someone I could never get to know. I had a feeling about her, a feeling that was almost fear, not for myself or for Lilly or for her brother, but rather for Mr. Banks. She had such an air of an avenging Greek mother about her that sometimes I half expected to see Mr. Banks lying cold in the midst of his meat. What I didn't know at the time was that there are more ways of revenge than the simple, obvious ones.

Mrs. Banks's job was to take care of the cash register and the household accounts. I have often tried to figure out how many years it took to save two thousand dollars by ringing up ninety-eight cents instead of a dollar. Mrs. Banks must have begun her revenge years before I met them, but however long it took, when the time came Mrs. Banks was ready.

I never gave up thinking that Lilly and Meltzer would finally find each other, and every time the summer came to an end and I had to go back to the city and school, I expected that during the winter to come I would hear news about them. I always made Lilly promise to write me about everything and anything that happened to her. I told her I would see her next spring— and why not? We had been going through this ritual of good-bye for the five years we had known each other.

That was the last time I ever saw Lilly Banks.

When the hotel opened the next summer, I ran down to Lilly's house. The sign over the store that had said BANKS THE BUTCHER now read MELTZER THE BUTCHER. I asked Meltzer what had happened. I asked where Lilly was, hoping to hear that she was in the back cooking his lunch.

Meltzer shrugged. "Gone," he said, "all gone, the mother, the brother, the father, gone."

I asked him where they had gone.

"I don't know," he answered. "Ask God. Last month they were in Kingston, not the other one, the New York one. This month, only God knows."

I had to know what had happened. I kept after Meltzer until I found out that Banks had suddenly decided to sell him the business. Meltzer said that if I knew Banks I also knew that when he decided something, it was done. He acted as though he had no choice in the matter. "Where is it written," he asked, "that a scholar should be a butcher?" He shrugged again and said, "But where is it written that a scholar shouldn't be a butcher?"

Meltzer clucked sadly at me. Mrs. Banks, he said, had taken money from Mr. Banks, and he quoted from the depths of memory about a wife, a husband, trust and devotion. He added, as an afterthought, that Lilly had been in a hospital.

I begged Meltzer to tell what had happened to Lilly. Did Mr. Banks finally become violent? He shook his head, "no." Had Lilly hurt herself? I hinted at self-destruction and romantic suicide. Meltzer looked at me as though I were the most foolish person he had ever seen. He slowly pointed to his eye. "Operation," he said. "The eyes," he said, "and Banks didn't even know. They went away to Kingston, New York, to the hospital. Can you imagine," he pleaded, "that a man should support a family, a wife, for twenty years and she should do such a thing to him?"

"What thing?" I asked. "What was so terrible?"

Meltzer took a deep breath. Mrs. Banks, he said, took Lilly, without even asking permission from the head of the house, to Kingston—he underlined New York—with all that money. She made Lilly have an operation. "If God hadn't meant Lilly to have crossed eyes, would He have made her that way? Tell me, where is it written that man should tamper with the will of God?"

I was about to get mad at Meltzer. He seemed to be the focal point for everything that had happened. "But," he interrupted my anger, "where is it written that God didn't make doctors so they should fix a person's eyes?"

It was a problem, and he pondered the ways of God and finally said that the operation had been a success, and Lilly was going to college.

College? I was beginning to wonder about God. What college? Meltzer said he didn't know, all he knew was that when Mr. Banks heard about it, he decided to sell the store. Did that make sense? he asked.

To me it did. What better revenge against a tyrant who thinks people are helpless than for him to find out that they are not, and that they don't need him but, rather, he needs them.

Lilly wrote to me a few times. She did go to college, she became a secretary, and then, for some reason, she stopped writing. The news I had of Lilly from then on was the secondhand news that came from people who never knew her. "You remember that cockeyed girl?" the news started. I don't remember any cockeyed girl. I remember Lilly Banks, the sweet girl with the mean father and the avenging mother, and Meltzer the Scholar who became Meltzer the Butcher and who should have married Lilly Banks.

The people who remember Lilly always talk about her as though somehow she was doomed to a terrible life. I once talked to Meltzer about that and he looked at me, sadly, and asked, "Tell me, where is it written?"

It's not, thank God.

13 Portrait of the Actress as a Young Palm Reader

Everybody talks about the weather but the only people who do anything about it are hotelkeepers. They pray.

In a summer hotel the worst thing that can happen is rain. Even on the sunniest day, the hotelkeeper looks around the horizon for clouds. Worry is as much a part of the hotel business as clean sheets, and the biggest worry is always the weather. If the bills are paid (a miracle) and the guests are happy (another miracle) there's always a big black cloud that may arrive just in time for the weekend. Maybe the farmers like rain, but in a hotel you're not raising corn—from rain you don't get crops, you get bank loans.

The whole trouble is the guests—guests don't like rain. They don't mind if it sprinkles a little after supper, but if it starts in the morning and goes on all day and into the next day and the next, they begin to look a little grim. It is hard to get a sun tan rocking on the porch and listening to the water dripping off the roof. Guests get restless, and who gets the blame? The hotel proprietor. If the place was being run right, it wouldn't rain, and they can tell you about other resorts they went to for years and never saw a drop. The whole problem is how to keep them from packing up and going back there.

A hotelkeeper quickly learns bad-weather symptoms. The first sign is rocking. When the ladies gather on the porch in a line and rock in the wicker rockers, that's bad. When they sit there tight-lipped and don't even talk to one another, that's terrible—especially when they stare at the puddles in the driveway. And

143

if one lady heaves a deep sigh, it becomes contagious and travels from one end of the porch to the other.

The summer, in a hotel, is made up of fifty per cent women, forty per cent children, and ten per cent husbands who commute to commune with nature on weekends only. All that guests want out of life is sunlight in the summertime. So rain, when it comes, is an insult and they all consider it to be nature's way of telling them to check out.

The only cure for that is to make the guests forget it is raining, a difficult feat when everyone is walking around in raincoats and rubbers. Though it takes a lot of doing, anything is worth the effort as long as it makes them stop sighing and it keeps Mrs. Leicht from telling Mrs. Rubin how nice the weather is in Woodstock.

A hotelman has to be prepared in advance to stop the trend. As soon as the first drop hits the ground and the guests run inside for protection, he has to be ready. He knows that his guests should never be allowed to think, "What am I going to do next?" Even before rain starts, the bridge tables have to be ready for the guests who like cards, and for those who don't there has to be dancing or bingo or supervised gossip. They have to be entertained.

That became my department. I was put in charge of keeping the ladies' minds off the weather. I learned that as long as they could be kept talking they would be happy. I worked hard because I liked the job and I think I was the only person in the hotel who looked forward to the rain.

As a matter of fact, this is how I started to become an actress. In bad weather I became a fortuneteller. I read palms and I told all. And the reason I could tell all was because I heard all—and in a hotel that's a lot. The first time I listened was a mistake. I loved to read and my favorite reading place was the window seat in the main lobby. In the warm weather the windows would be opened wide, and one day I heard the ladies gossip on the porch. I heard plenty. I didn't understand half of what I heard because I was a young and innocent child of fourteen but old enough to like gossip. So the second time I sat in the window seat was on purpose. I would peep over the top of the seat and look through the window to see who had just said what. I got to know everybody—their families, their friends, and their medical histories.

I found out, for instance, that Mrs. Engle had a son who was running around with a girl that worked in Mr. Engle's office, and that Mrs. Engle was afraid it was going to get serious. "Listen, they've been going together for three years already and who knows what could happen?"

Mrs. Landau had a story to match: her daughter had a crush on a married teacher. I heard that Mrs. Mayer was going to have a (whisper, whisper) operation and the doctor said (mumble, mumble) but she didn't care because it was the least of her troubles. The most of her troubles was Mr. Mayer. Well, it wasn't really him, it was his partner. They had nothing but trouble with that man; the partner wanted to relocate the store uptown and Mr. Mayer wanted to stay where he was. The partner's wife and the partner were on one side of the fence; Mr. and Mrs. Mayer were on the other, and if anybody wanted Mrs. Mayer's advice it would be "dissolve the partnership!" But nobody was asking and she wasn't going to say—at least, not again until the next time.

I peeped over the window seat and got a glimpse of Mrs. Mayer, an arm folder, arms across her bosom, glaring with raised eyebrows at Mrs. Engle, who nodded back at her.

I stored up everything I heard just like a squirrel. At first I didn't know what to do with all the information. But whoever said that necessity was the mother of invention was probably in the hotel business. I remember when the idea of fortunetelling came to me out of the blue and I couldn't wait for the rain. I had always liked to dress up and play parts and it was going to be a game for me even though I knew how important keeping the guests happy was for my father and mother.

As soon as the weather began to sprinkle I ran to the kitchen. I went in one swinging door myself and I came out the other a gypsy. I wore a linen napkin around my head; slippers on my feet borrowed from Helene; I stuffed towels inside my dress; I took a coat from one of the waitresses; I bent myself over like an old lady and I hobbled out to the porch.

I didn't have to ask for volunteers. The guests acted like it was their guaranteed right under the Constitution to be amused, so I started at one end of the porch and worked myself to the other end. Everybody wanted their fortunes told, everybody wanted to be fooled, and at the same time everybody winked at everybody else to show they knew they were being taken in. I must have been the only person on the porch who was being serious.

Mrs. Engle was the first lady. I walked to her very slowly and very bent over. I looked into her face with its sunburned wrinkles and gray eyes. She smiled at me but I didn't smile back —gypsies who see the future can't afford to smile. I picked up one of her hands and looked at the back of it for a second or two; it was for effect that I did it but the hand said things to me. The blue veins told of an age, the wedding ring looked like it was born with the hand, the fingernails were covered with red that tried to paint over the cracks that came from hard work. And the way the nail polish was put on only showed that the hands were on vacation, too. I turned the hand over to look at the palm and the hand shook just a little. I began to feel sorry for Mrs. Engle and I made up my mind that what I was going to tell her would be the truth, with a little hope thrown in for good measure.

"I see," I said, "a boy. You have a son?"

"A son," she answered. "Stanley." It wasn't a name, it was a statement.

"I see an office . . ."

"What kind?"

I was only a fortuneteller, not an architect, so I didn't go into it. "The boy is in the office; there's an older man—he seems very nice . . ."

"He's all right."

"Your husband?"

"Who else?"

"There's a girl, I see a girl, she's young."

"Sure there's a girl—she'll put me in an early grave." By this time some of the other ladies who couldn't stand something happening that they didn't know about gathered around Mrs. Engle's rocker. "So go on. What's gonna be with her?"

I hadn't heard enough to know whether or not Stanley was going to marry the girl but I knew what Mrs. Engle wanted to hear. But suppose Stanley finally decided to marry the girl? A nice boy like Stanley would have to get married sooner or later, so I said, "I see a wedding . . ."

"I'll die! Who?"

"Stanley . . ."

"Who's the girl?"

"It's not clear . . ."

"So use the other hand. I'm going to call my husband in the city! Listen," she said to her friends, "a boy has to get married but God forbid it should be that girl!" Mrs. Engle shook her hand away and like a steam engine in a corset she crossed the porch, went into the lobby, and straight to the phone.

I watched her go, afraid that maybe I had done the wrong thing. All she had to hear on that phone was that Stanley had finally made up his mind and the hotel would have lost a guest.

I was hoping that Stanley, who had waited three years, could hold out to the end of the week before he made any decisions. I turned back to the waiting ladies. The nearest hand belonged to Mrs. Mayer—the one with partner troubles.

Her hand was nothing like Mrs. Engle's. This one was a nervous hand with long fingers and bitten fingernails. Even when I held it, it was always moving, like its owner. I thought I knew exactly what Mrs. Mayer wanted to hear so I said, "I see trouble ahead!"

"I can't stand it!"

"I see two men . . ."

"They're talking?"

"They seem to be . . ."

"So! They're still partners!"

"One man wants to move . . ."

"Sure he does! A fool, the man's a fool, that's why he wants to move! So go on, what's he saying?"

"I see two stores . . ."

"I'll pass out! Two stores?"

I nodded.

"You heard?" she said to the women who were listening. "I have to tell my Joe so he shouldn't worry; there'll be two stores. It's all settled." She gave my hand a squeeze. "The phone is in the lobby? I have to call the city. You're a smart girl," Mrs. Mayer said as she got up and started across the porch. She walked with fast, little steps—like a typewriter, click, click, clickclickclick—to the double doors and in she went.

Rain or no rain, I thought, I might have done enough damage for one day; two ladies calling home could mean two ladies going home to solve their problems in person. I wanted to stop right then and there but I was surrounded by a fence of hands. The show had to go on. I picked another hand. This time I wasn't going to be so smart. I was going to try to keep my next "client" away from the phone.

I picked Mrs. Landau, a lady with a daughter problem. Suddenly I was a social worker instead of a fortuneteller. What should she do about her girl and a married teacher? I was only supposed to see the future, I wasn't supposed to give treatments. However, I saw something—not in her hand but in my head. Mrs. Landau's daughter and Mrs. Engle's son—a change of air couldn't hurt them.

"I see a young man," I said.

"Yeah? Where?"

"Shhh!"

"Beg pardon . . ."

"I see them . . . in the country. . . ."

"He's married?"

"Not yet," I said.

"He's got a name?"

"I can't see that but he works in an office. . . ."

"A lawyer?"

"Shhh!"

"I wouldn't say a word. A doctor?"

"I heard someone calling him . . . Stanley."

"Stanley? Mrs. Engle's Stanley! Where's the phone?"

Mrs. Landau's walk was like a chicken's. She couldn't move two feet without pecking—stopping to talk with someone and then moving on a few yards only to stop to talk to someone else. But this time she jumped up from the rocker and went across the porch to the telephone like an arrow.

So far three ladies had gone into the lobby. Between the rain and my fortunetelling I was sure the hotel was going to be empty. I tried to give up being a gypsy but I wasn't allowed. I was inside a ring of ladies who all wanted their hands read. I looked at hands but I was very careful about my predictions; I didn't even tell Mrs. Varsen that her daughter Charlene was going around with Sonny, the sax player—that's all I'd have to say and there'd be two more checkouts. I told Mrs. M. not to worry. She was our star worrier and I figured it wouldn't hurt to tell her to stop even if I knew she wouldn't; she was already worrying about why I told her not to. I told Mrs. Strauss that her health was going to improve. She was a pill taker; why she was taking them I didn't know, but I had faith in the medical profession and I figured if she took enough pills they would cure anything that was wrong.

Mrs. Landau and Mrs. Engle finally came out to the porch, talking to each other so hard they didn't notice the rain. Was that a good sign or a bad one? They pulled two rockers together and kept right on talking. Well, they weren't packing, anyway.

By the time I got through reading palms the rain was beginning to stop and it even looked like the sun might come out. I started back to take off my gypsy uniform and when I passed Mrs. Landau and Mrs. Engle they stopped me and thanked me. They told me that Mrs. Engle's son and Mrs. Landau's daughter were coming up for the weekend. And they had booked two more rooms and they were hoping that since I had seen a wedding maybe it meant their children—anyway it couldn't hurt to try.

When I got into the lobby, Mrs. Mayer stopped me. "See?" she said. "You were wrong!"

"Trouble!" I thought. And it crossed my mind that being a gypsy wasn't easy.

"There's not going to be two stores," she announced. "Nobody's mad on nobody any more. My husband and his partner and that wife of his are coming up for a conference. See how wrong you were?"

I told her I was delighted and I told her that lots of times things weren't always clear and even a gypsy can make a mistake.

Mrs. Mayer was a friendly woman, even a forgiving one. She looked at me for a moment, then she gave me a shove and laughed. "Some gypsy!" she said.

So I wasn't a gypsy, but whatever I was, I was lucky. Five new guests and not one checkout. And the sun was even peeping through. There might even be a wedding between Mrs. Landau's daughter and Mrs. Engle's Stanley. I was feeling very proud of myself and the feeling lasted until Miss Landau and young Mr. Engle met on the following weekend. They didn't like each other, not even a little, not even enough to be platonic. The two mothers realized that there was just so much leading they could do and they both told each other sadly and over and over that there was "no chemistry"—and for that they couldn't blame the fortunetelling or the hotel.

14 *The Gentleman Caller*

When I was a very advanced thirteen I met a man with an English accent and I paid hardly any attention to him at all except I loved to listen to him speak. He fascinated me because he had really been born in London and he spoke like a Waverly novel. He said "whilst" and "hence" and "shed-yule." Of course, since I paid so little attention to him, out of the corner of my eye I saw that he was good-looking, that he dressed quietly and simply and wore a straw hat. If I had had the nerve I would have told him he looked smashing. I also found out, by calculated ignoring, that he was twenty-three and a graduate chemical engineer on a two-week vacation. I had a feeling for engineers. They were romantic, they wore puttees and tropical helmets and spent their time building railroads and canals. What a chemical engineer would be doing in such a setting I never bothered to figure out.

We said very little to each other, I was never shy with boys, but I had to divide my time between all the boys and unattached men at the hotel, so I had to ration myself. Also I was very impressionable. If I met a boy who was going to be a lawyer I saw myself as a lawyer's wife, or a doctor's wife, or a businessman's wife, even an engineer's wife. I daydreamed so much I didn't have time to make up my mind what sort of man I really wanted to marry. Besides, I was too young. Thirteen was not an age to make any commitments. And, anyway, my engineer didn't ask.

By the time I reached my teens, I looked older than I really was and so I had overheard or had been given every line in the book of Man. Some men were going to teach me about life— that was a remark that came from short men with little mustaches and from them I didn't want to learn. Some men knew how to make me into a woman—that was from big men who talked to me while their wives were dressing the children. I was going to be one anyway and without their help. The young boys had their lines: devotion, undying love, and Dante Gabriel Rossetti. I didn't knew what a Pre-Raphaelite was at that age, but I knew I didn't care for them anyway. But there was one line I always fell for and that was being ignored. I couldn't stand it, and the only man who saw through me was the engineer. I paid no attention to him, hoping that he would make an effort, and he paid as little to me. All I could do was to hope he was playing my game, too.

Lewis Berg was the engineer's name so the plot is no longer thick. The outcome is obvious, but at thirteen it wasn't. When Lew left the hotel after his two-week vacation was up I didn't see him again for four years. In the meantime I went with other men and other boys. I was growing up and I must have fallen in love at least once a week. In the city, during the winters, I fell in love with a shop teacher at school, not because he was handsome, but because he was going to Teacher's College at night and he looked romantically tired. I stayed in love with him for three days until I fell in love with one of my father's waiters, a man with lovely black hair that was maybe a little too long. I had to worship him from afar because my father didn't like me around the restaurant. That love lasted almost a week. The boys I went out with (as distinct from the men I didn't) and held hands with for real were never objects of my love. They were nice, some were even charming, but they were only boys.

My father was very concerned that I should know about men and women but I assured him I knew. After all, I had spent years at the hotel, the chambermaids were my friends, and

Whitey the bellboy was what you might call a Catskill Kinsey. "All right," he said, "if you know so you know, but one piece of advice let me give you?" He shook his head before I could interrupt and said, "If you love a boy, a man, and you go out with him and you go to a restaurant, order the omelet. If you don't care about him, order a lobster." That bit of advice I passed on to my daughter, and as for my son, I told him early to make sure he had enough money in his pocket because I knew sometimes a girl can love a man but she can also feel like lobster. As a matter of fact my son married a girl whose favorite dish is lobster, Newburgh and otherwise.

When I was seventeen my engineer came back to the hotel. As soon as I saw him I started asking questions. Not of him, but of people I had seen him talking to. I wanted to know why four years had gone by. I was pretty, I had a good figure. I was five feet two inches, my waist was twenty-six, my skin was smooth and I could even play the piano. I thought I was quite the catch and I wanted to make sure I wasn't fooling myself.

I found out that Lew had been working hard and steadily as a sugar technician in a plant in Brooklyn. He had also been taking courses at Columbia School of Engineering, Brooklyn Polytech and Cooper Union. So it wasn't me, or even another woman, it was knowledge that had kept us apart. I didn't like it but I felt better.

The first words Lew said to me on his second vacation at the hotel were: "I came back to see what sort of a person you grew up to be—and I'm disappointed."

I was shocked. Men didn't talk that way to me. That was no way to make a pass. But as I thought about it more, it occurred to me that it was exactly the right way, at least for me. Lew had an air about him. When he looked around things seemed to fall into place, cause had an effect, two and two made four, and there were more things than love that made the world go round. I wanted to fit into his word of Newton's three laws and if he said I had disappointed him I wanted to know why.

"You're a very pretty girl," he told me when I had gotten up the nerve to ask him exactly what he meant and where he thought he got off saying such a terrible thing. "But you've done nothing with your mind, and it's a good mind."

This was a new angle if I ever heard one! My mind! But beneath my hurt vanity, I understood what he was saying. In his way he was telling me he was interested, more than interested.

He looked at me for a minute. I was never the sort of girl to turn my eyes away from anyone but this time I did. "It's not that serious," he said, and I told him it was, he was right, I was wrong and what should I do? Lew smiled a little at me and I decided right then and there I'd get to know that smile very well. It meant he had won a point. "Give me a little time," he told me, "and I'll help you be the woman you want to be."

Was there ever a more arrogant and infuriating approach?

Was there ever a better approach?

All my life I had been waiting to fall in love and when I did I knew it, felt it, accepted it, wanted it, and yet it all came without warning. I thought there would be, at least, music and clouds and floating through the air. There wasn't. It was better than any romantic love fantasy I had ever read. I felt like myself, and I knew that I was one thing and not a collection of meaningless little sexperiences and half-developed thoughts. I was me.

Lew and I spent his vacation going on walks, sitting under trees, playing croquet, talking, holding hands. He hadn't asked me to marry him but we both knew he didn't have to. Between us he had asked and I had said "yes." He was my protector even against my father—and that's something nobody had ever done before. One afternoon Lew wanted me to go on a ride with him. He had rented a horse and buggy but my father put his foot down. "No riding alone in the country!"

I was spectator for once. I wanted to go but I had someone to argue for me.

"Why not?" Lew asked.

"Because I said so," my father told him.

"Don't you trust your own daughter?" Lew asked quietly, with his polite English accent.

"I didn't say. . . ."

"That's precisely what you've indicated."

"Listen, professor, I trust my daughter, all right?"

"Then let her go for a ride. Have enough faith in her."

"If I have faith in her, what should I have for you?"

"Have enough regard for my respect for your daughter."

"So if I have regard for your respect, how do I know you can drive a horse and buggy? In my experience city men don't know about horses."

"Then you haven't had enough experience. I am acquainted with the methods of driving a carriage."

"So go! But come back before sunset. I mean it!"

"You have my word, Mr. Edelstein."

Lew took me over to the horse and buggy and handed me in as a gentleman should. He went around to the driver's side and climbed up, picked up the reins, and without turning his head asked me quietly, "How do you make the horse start?"

I looked at him and started to laugh and he told me kindly to wait until we were out of sight. I told him to say "Giddyap!" and slap the reins on the horse's rump. We started off and from a distance it must have looked all right because my father turned and went into the hotel.

Lew told me that he had decided we were going for a ride and nothing was going to stop him. He admitted that he wasn't given to telling "fibs" except in extremely good causes. I told him I liked "fibs," especially in a London accent. It wasn't a thing he wanted to make a habit out of, he said, but he felt my father really had it coming. I agreed, and he added, "I must hasten to assure you that I meant everything I said about my respect for you."

I was about to open my mouth and tell him not to have so much respect when he said, "And, of course, a great deal of love."

During that two-week summer vacation Lew became so much a part of me that I wondered if there was ever a time when I didn't know him even though he liked to talk about ideas and all I wanted to talk about was him. It took me a long time to find out the who, what, when, and where of Lewis Berg.

Lew was born in the Cheapside section of London. He went to school at St. Jude's, which later became a London County Council School, something like an American public school. When he was fourteen Lew had to go to work as a clerk. He called it "clark." At the same time he went to high school—secondary school in English—during the evenings. It was during his high-school days that he got into trouble with his father. Lew's father was a very religious man, very orthodox, and a strict patriarch. He demanded that his family of six girls and two boys follow in his footsteps exactly. Lew said that he probably would have done exactly that if he hadn't started to read George Bernard Shaw and René Descartes. At fifteen, he said, he became what he called a Shavian Cartesian. Reading changed his mind, turned his world around, and he had no choice but to become a doubter. He felt it was his intellectual duty to refuse to go to Hebrew school or to temple. Lew's father didn't speak to him for almost a year. It took that long for him to realize that his son was a rational human being entitled to his opinion, whether or not he, the father, liked those opinions. The reconciliation came when Lew's father turned Descartes inside out. He told Lew, "You think so therefore you are? So if that's the way you think, what are you?"

From then on the question of religion was never mentioned. Neither of them had an answer that seemed rational to the other.

In the early nineteen hundreds things were very bad in England and Lew's family decided to come to the United States. Lew's father took one of his daughters over first and then was going to send for the rest of his family. But he found things were difficult here, also, and he had to delay bringing over his whole family. Lew, at sixteen, gave up a scholarship offered to him by Oxford, borrowed money to pay for the fares of five children, his mother and himself, from the Jewish Board of Guardians where he "clarked" and started off for America.

Lew worked during the day, went to Brooklyn Polytechnic Institute at night and paid back his loan in one year. Lew is one of those people who thinks that doing what he did was like going around the corner to buy a paper. Anybody could have done it. When I tell him not me, I couldn't have done it, he gets bored and changes the subject.

When I returned to the city Lew was a constant caller. He and my father had gotten over their first squabble and Lew was put through my father's testing ground, a pinochle game. If you want to know about a man, my father always said, play cards with him. Lew passed with flying colors because it became obvious that he liked to play for the fun and not only to win. He didn't have much of a poker face but he didn't need it because his mind could remember every card that had been played and as a consequence knew almost exactly where each card remaining must be. Lew and my father were evenly matched and before the first night was done, they were calling each other Jake and Lew.

Lew always got on especially well with my mother, and after

I was married she told me why. She was sitting on the porch, she said, when Lew and a friend walked by. She overheard their conversation and, since it was about me, she listened twice as hard as she ordinarily would. My mother said I happened to be passing by on the road below the porch when Lew pointed me out to his friend. "That's the girl I'm going to marry," he said, "but there's one thing that worries me about her. She looks like the kind of girl that likes to have her own way."

I asked my mother why she didn't object and come to my defense. She said why should she? Lew was right. Maybe he was right—then. But I've found out over the years that the only time I get my own way is when he decides it's all right for me to have it.

Every time Lew came to see me, and we arranged that it would be almost every evening, he would bring a new book. Some evenings we would spend reading them out loud together. We read H. G. Wells' *The World Set Free* and finished feeling like idealists; we read Romain Rolland's *Jean Christophe* and felt like romantics. We read Kipling, but not much, because we both thought he was a little too predictable and just a little superior. Chesterton's *A Short History of England* opened my eyes to the idea that history could be a wonderful mixture of fact and paradox instead of the flat facts and dates of a school-book. We read Beatrice and Sidney Webb's *The Manor and the Borough* and from everything Lew had told me about them, I was sure the book was very important. I felt very ashamed of myself for not being enthusiastic, but it was written in such a styleless style that I found I was taking deep breaths at every comma. We had planned to read *The Prevention of Destitution* next, but not even the romantic idea of a husband-and-wife team could make me look forward to it. I asked Lew if there wasn't some other book we could read without being lectured at. He said he was very relieved, and even though we owed the Webbs quite a debt, he agreed that enough was quite enough—and so we started *Candide,* which I found a wonderful relief from the constant guilt feelings I had been getting from the Webbs. Lew told me that probably the only person who had ever been bored by *Candide* was William Wordsworth and I told him I was sure that the compliment would have been returned. I was beginning to feel quite educated.

On the evenings that we didn't stay home and read we went out for supper (omelet) and then perhaps to a play—especially if it was a G. B. Shaw play. I think Lew would have walked to Chicago if Shaw was playing there. We went to operas, museums, and the Cooper Union lectures every Monday and Friday night. Lew opened up a new planet for me that included the new theories of Dr. Freud—theories that were being laughed at almost every place. I heard lectures about why women should run for mayor and lectures about the new music in France by Stravinsky, Ravel, and the "Terrible Six." I began to find out, with Lew's help, that there was more than one way to look at things and that the imagination of creative people is one of the most exciting parts of living. I even stopped laughing at Coué because I was no longer so sure he mightn't be right. I began to have an open mind and I started filling it as fast as I could. I was being directed from one idea to another instead of skipping here and there and finding things that interested me only because they were easy to understand. I learned how to learn and that was something no teacher had ever been able to make me see. I was doing what I should have done years ago because now I had someone I loved and who loved me. And, believe me, if love can do that, it can do anything.

When I was nineteen Lew and I were married. I was prepared for all sorts of problems as far as the ceremony was concerned. I knew how Lew felt about the formal aspects of religion and I also know how his father felt. I wanted to be a dutiful wife and

I also wanted to be a loving daughter-in-law so I was prepared for a civil ceremony.

I prepared wrong. Lew said he thought we should be married in my father's house by a rabbi but he made very sure that I understood it would be a Reformed rabbi. He said he hoped I didn't mind. Perhaps I looked at him in a way that made him think I thought he was giving in and not sticking to his principles. He explained that he wanted a religious ceremony and not a civil one only for his father's sake, as a mark of respect. I told Lew I would be honored.

The two of us started a new life with just us to lean on, depend on, and to love. We had gone "steady" for two years and knew each other well, but it wasn't until our first wedding anniversary that I got up enough nerve to ask for something I had never asked for before. We were in a restaurant in New Orleans when I asked. "Lew," I said, "I love you . . ."

"And I love you but I know that look. What do you want?"

"You do believe I love you?"

"Of course. . . ."

"Then could I have a lobster?"

Lew gave me that look of his that said, "Euclid and Eddington make sense but my wife is insoluble." He held my hand. I could see him give up. "Have ten if it'll make you happy." Then he leaned forward as though he had found the solution and asked me if I was pregnant. I told him I wasn't and his face fell. It would have been such a good solution.

PART THREE

THE STUDIO

1 Down on the Levee

Lew and I live in Manhattan, on Park Avenue, in a duplex, and it's a long, long way from our first home in Louisiana. When we first went down there we had nothing to bring but our clothes. We hadn't been married long enough to accumulate all the paraphernalia that comes with the years and it was easy for us to put what we owned into two suitcases and go. Sometimes I think that today we need moving vans just to go to the country for the weekend.

When Lew and I pack for a trip we sometimes talk about that first one we made together. And as we pack we look around us and there on the dressers are pictures of our daughter, our son, our son-in-law, our daughter-in-law, and five grandchildren. I don't know how many times I've said to my husband, "What did we start here? Just look at what two people did all by themselves." And each time I say it Lew tells me that when people get married you can never tell what's going to happen. I ask him where time went. One minute ago our daughter, Harriet, was sitting in a play pen shaking a rattle and one of us was chasing after our son, Cherney, to make sure he hadn't swallowed a marble. Now our daughter is a mother and our son is a father. Lew says it's all in the nature of things.

"Look at you," I say to him, "you're a grandfather."

"Did you see my wash-and-wear shirts?"

"Don't change the subject," I tell him, because Lew is a subject-changer. He thinks ahead. He can see sentiment coming before it's even started.

"I like being a grandfather."

165

"And I like being a grandmother."

"Good. Where are my socks?"

"But doesn't it make you feel a little funny?"

"No."

"The time's gone so quickly. We were just married and look at the family we have."

"Tillie, dear, the time hasn't gone quickly, there are still twelve months in every year and twenty-four hours in every day and maybe our family will get even bigger. And while you're looking for my shirts and socks see if you can find my handkerchief and blow your nose."

That's what happens when you live with a scientist but it's a good thing because of the perspective. By the time I found the shirts and the handkerchief Lew had me feeling that, grandmother or not grandmother, I hadn't changed much over the years, that the two of us were the same two we had always been, and that it was the world that changed and not us. Lew says that grandchildren are nature's way of getting even, not with us, but with our children. Our son and daughter can now have a little taste of the medicine we had when they were kids. And when I ask him if what we had was so terrible he says it wasn't and that a family is the best thing he could wish on his children. It's just that he's waiting to see history repeat itself in terms of raised allowances, two-wheel bikes, a dog, and arguments about piano lessons. He hopes one of his grandchildren will want to play the oboe. And when he says that I have to laugh because that's what happened to us. It was Cherney who wanted to play an oboe, and I suppose I can be happy for little favors. At least it wasn't the cymbals.

Our son was thirteen when he decided the oboe was what he wanted to play. Where that idea came from I'll never know. I asked Cherney why he wanted to play the oboe and his answer was, logically, to be an oboist. I asked him if that was an ambition for a boy; didn't he, at least, want to be the conductor of the orchestra? No! He wanted to be an oboe player. If you've never heard an oboe being practiced by a beginner you haven't heard anything. It's a Chinese torture the Chinese didn't even think of. We had oboe playing in our house for seven years combined with the scratching of the viola that my daughter decided she wanted to play. The only reason I was happy to see them both go off to college was because of the silence. But after a while I began to miss the noise and when I mentioned that to Lew he said I ought to take up the trumpet if I missed music so much.

In my time I had to get used to change. Lew and I went through plenty of things together and one of the biggest was not having the children at home. The apartment was emptier than it had even been before.

When we were first married I thought being a wife was going to be the greatest change of all and at that time it seemed to be exactly that. But, in a way, it wasn't as sharp a change as I had expected. After all, I had been living with married people all my life and I knew a little. I knew, as an instance, that married people never spoke to each other in the morning before they had coffee. I also knew that the lady of the house got her shopping money on Monday morning and it had just better last the week. What I didn't know was Lew. He didn't need coffee first thing in the morning to be pleasant and, as for money, as soon as we were married he opened a joint checking account and whatever I needed I took. From the first minute of our marriage there were no secrets except for where I happened to have hidden his handkerchiefs.

Two weeks after we were married Lew became chief technologist at a sugar plantation in Reserve, Louisiana. And his contract said that it would be for three years. I was excited. We were going South! I had visions of what it was going to be like—and all my visions came from books and were wrapped in crinoline and Spanish moss. I could see the river, the paddle-wheel steamers, the levees. Everybody was going to look like Mark Twain, the women would carry parasols and the men would be as polite as Lord Chesterfield.

The trip was lovely until we got past Chicago. The further south we went, the hotter it got. Air conditioning was a rumor in those days—something like weekend trips to the moon are today. If you opened the windows on the train you couldn't live with the smoke from the engine; if you kept the windows closed you couldn't live with the heat. By the time we got off the train at New Orleans I was ready to turn around and go home. I didn't because I wanted to see the city.

Well, I saw it. There were hot, wide streets, charming Old World houses—all hot—wonderful hot restaurants, and lovely, well-decorated, hot hotels. In the evening, when the sun goes down, the heat goes down also but the humidity goes up. It's no wonder that Tennessee Williams and William Faulkner write such good tragedies. With air conditioning maybe there'll be a change in our Southern literature.

The day finally came when we had to report to the sugar plantation. And the word "plantation" was enough to make me forget that I was hot. If there was nothing else there would be mint juleps on the porch.

We rode for many flat, dusty, hot and humid miles until we came to the plantation. And the plantation was nothing. Miles of sugar cane, a group of small frame houses, and a huge re-finery throwing smoke into the air. It wasn't exactly romantic. The only thing that was nice was the house we were given. It was like the other houses, a cottage with a peaked roof and no basement—two bedrooms, a living room and a kitchen. And it was ours for the three years we were supposed to stay. We made it into a home. It became a refuge from everything outside, and when I looked around at the "scenery," at the Mississippi flowing by, the levees I had dreamed about which were nothing more than mud banks, the paddle-wheel steamers that pushed barges, and the miles of sugar cane stretching shadeless across the muddy fields, I always felt better when I ran into my home and closed the door. I could hardly wait for my husband to come home every night, and when he arrived we had our own world together.

Sometimes we would have to go visiting the foreman or the general manager or one of Lew's assistants. Each evening, though in a different home, was exactly like the evening before in the previous home. When we went to visit the foreman his guests were Lew and myself, the general manager and his wife —and then maybe one of Lew's assistants and his wife. Then when we went to the general manager's home the guest list was exactly the same. The conversations were also the same. They practiced segregation; the men talked in one section of the living room and the women talked in another. The men talked about the quality of the cane, the yield in the crushing plant, and the words, "levulose, dextrose, sucrose" would float across the room and mix themselves up with the words of the ladies, "gingham; I can't stand the heat; you never tasted catfish, honey?" It never changed. It went on and on and after a few months we let it go on and on without us.

The nights we stayed at home were the best. There was nothing like radio or television, and sugar plantations don't have Radio City Music Halls around the corner. We made our own amusements and that was mainly reading out loud to each other. We went through H. G. Wells' *Outline of History*, Eugène Sue's *Mysteries of Paris,* Tolstoi's *War and Peace,* Van Loon's *Geography,* and anything else that was good and thick.

Intellectually, the years on the plantation were my formative ones. I really learned what a book was and what a book meant.

I went into reading without any preconceived notions. Authors' names were just names, some I had heard of, some I didn't know. I read whatever I found or Lew sent my way. Some I liked and some I didn't. I had the advantage of being an unintellectual reader who read for pleasure and when I found a book I liked, I kept it; when I didn't like it I gave it away. Lew never insisted on my liking anything.

I never thought that I would write, it never even occurred to me. What little writing I had done at the hotel I did for the amusement of the guests, little acts not unlike my fortune-telling routine. The other writing was purely personal. I found that if I was feeling bad, sad, lonesome, a little depressed, I could get out of a mood by putting it on paper. And when it was all written out, I wouldn't even reread it. I would throw it out. It was my business and not for other people to read. I was what you might call a lonely sufferer. I wouldn't even show my little stories to Lew. I would tell him how I felt but I wouldn't read it to him.

Sometimes I would sit and think about how it would be if I were, say, Gogol. He was one of my favorites and I liked his idea that he was a writer whose business was "to speak with living images, not with arguments." I liked his humor and his sudden descents into black fits and then the way he had of rising back out of the darkness and into a laughing look at what had just depressed him. I could never get over the fact that Gogol wrote *The Inspector General* and *Dead Souls*. How could one man have that much fun in him and that much sadness? I would tell myself that I had a nerve wanting to write like that. I tried writing like Shaw, but I could never be that clever; I didn't know enough to be like H. G. Wells. The only writer I could be was myself and I didn't like that at all. But I kept on writing and I kept on tearing up what I had written.

There was one story, something that happened down on the

levee, that I always tried to write and rewrite but it never quite got down on paper. It was about a young girl I had met on the plantation. Her name was Marie LeDoux and she was a very pretty girl—tall, a little thin but with one of the wonderful lithe figures that some of those long, stately women have the luck to be born with. She was a dressmaker. She made dresses, but only for herself. She lived with her mother and father. Their house was way at the end of the living area on the plantation. I met her one day when I saw her sitting on her porch shortening a hem. I introduced myself, we talked for a little, and then I asked her if she would shorten a few hems for me. In those days dresses went up and down from year to year just as they do now. She said she would be happy to, so the next day I brought over a few dresses. While I was there her father came out of the house. I could see where she got her good looks because Mr. LeDoux was also tall, very straight, and absolutely blond, but with sharp, bright, black eyes. He was in charge of the cane fields, the friendliest man on the whole plantation. But a joke had to be explained to him word for word—and the point of the whole joke had to be told and retold—still, he wouldn't understand it. But even if he didn't have humor he had something else. He had the understanding that made him able to take things as they came. He made no excuses for people, for himself, or for things that happened. And it wasn't that he saw a preordained pattern that made him so able to live in his world. It was just that things were a certain way, and to live a person had to live with them and not let them get in the way.

I was on the porch with Mr. LeDoux and Marie for a little while when the front door opened shyly and a lady looked out. My first thought was that she was the maid. My second thought, seeing Mr. LeDoux's face and the look of sad understanding that went across it, was that the lady was one of those women I had always read about—the white boss's black mistress. It wasn't, it was his wife.

Mr. LeDoux introduced me. I tried to do my best not to show that I was confused. Mr. LeDoux, his wife and his daughter, must have been expecting some reaction from me and I had none to give. I made it a habit to go and see them almost every day. If I stayed away it would only be because of the sort of marriage it was, and that wouldn't be fair. It's a good thing they were nice people because if they weren't I would still have had to visit them, and that would have been awful for all of us. That would be tolerance, and that's the last thing that should happen between friends. Tolerance is for speeches, not for living.

We would see the LeDoux about once a week and it was always a very pleasant evening because there was no pretense. Mr. LeDoux was incapable of it, his daughter was exactly the same, and Mrs. LeDoux followed her husband in everything. The only thing that did happen when we went to see the LeDoux was that soon Lew and I stopped getting invitations from the other people on the plantation.

I was so naive I didn't know why. I asked my husband and he explained it to me. There's a difference between knowing something and living something. I asked Lew what we should do, and he asked me what I wanted to do. What I wanted to do was to go out and give lectures and fight the good fight, but Lew said it would be wasting time. All he asked me was, did I like the LeDoux. I said I did. He asked me if I wanted to see them again and I said I did. Then he said we'd see them anytime they wanted to see us and to forget about anything else. They were friends, he said, and if the others didn't like it they didn't have to. That also was their business. Fools would always be foolish.

I tried talking to Mr. LeDoux about race, man, history, and

Darwin's conclusions but he would have none of it. He refused to believe that man descended from apes. It was, he said, an insult to us all. And he didn't need proof that one person was as good as the next because he held that they weren't. Science had nothing to do with it, Darwin was wrong, and he could show that limey scientist some people even the apes wouldn't have. Mr. LeDoux held that God made us all. The Bible said we came from Adam and Eve. But nowhere did it say that everyone was equal to everyone else. Some people were just plain no good and that's all there was to it.

The LeDoux were our friends for three years and in all that time I could never explain to Mr. LeDoux what I was trying to say, and I suppose it was foolish of me to try. He knew better than I, maybe even better than Darwin, that we're all variations on a theme and that Darwin was right even if he didn't like the whole idea.

Life on the plantation was an endless row of days for me. For Lew it was a different story. He had his work and it was work that he loved. The three years went quickly for him because he enjoyed the technicalities of making sugar. The three years went a little slower for me but I had the good luck to be able to go back to the hotel for the summers. We would try to arrange Lew's vacation so that we could go together and then he would return to the plantation alone. But the hotel season wasn't too long and there was only about a month that we were apart.

2 *The Goldbergs Are Born*

The summers I spent at the hotel during the first few years as a married woman were only different from the others in that I was anxious to get back to Louisiana and Lew. Another difference was that I wore a wedding ring and the men and boys didn't seem as friendly as they had in previous years. I worked a little harder because I had more time and it wasn't necessary for me to be in love once a week any longer.

Besides keeping the books, my work was trying to entertain the guests. Between the two jobs, I don't know which was funnier. My bookkeeping was homemade; it was adding up receipts and subtracting them from expenses. If I came out on the plus side of my ledger everything was fine; if I came out on the minus side I would work all day to try to change the inevitable. Sometimes I would even put a dollar or two of my own into the bookkeeping account to try to even up the score. I felt responsible if things added up in the red.

The entertainment was a different story. Originally I had started writing in order to keep the children of the guests happy. I wrote little playlets for them to put on and it amused them and their mothers. The plays I wrote depended on the number of children registered for the week. The ones who I knew were going to be around all summer I gave the speaking parts to; the others had to be satisfied with walk-ons.

One day my father, who took to calling me Maxine Reinhardt, told me that my timing was all wrong. "Don't put on the plays in the middle of the week," he said. "Put them on Saturdays, late." And he pointed out the reason: "If I was a

father in the city with a wife and child in the country and I
got a telephone call—long distance—and my wife said, 'Jake,
your dear child is the wicked witch in Hansel and Gretel on
Saturday night,' what would I do? I'm a father, so I would
say 'I'm coming up. Don't let them push her in the oven.'
What kind of a father would stay away? So twenty children in
a play—Saturday late—means twenty fathers on the train Friday night and that means a full house for the weekend. And
another thing, every child in the play has to have a part,
words, they have to say words—and don't talk to me about
art. They have to say words."

I changed the production schedule to Saturday late. I wrote
new characters into my playlets and I drowned the whole thing
in dialogue. I remember my favorites were *Snow White and
the Twenty-eight Dwarfs, Twenty-two Who Pass While the
Lentils Boil,* and, for the younger children, *Thirty-three Blind
Mice.*

As I got older I began to entertain the adult guests with
skits I both wrote and acted. Many of them were about a
woman called Maltke Talnitzky. Maltke was a figment, an
illusion, and a combination of all the Maltkes I had ever met.
She was a woman in her fifties and if anything bad happened
anywhere in the world it was because of her, or if there was
a tragedy in the making she was an essential ingredient. She
was a woman with an inferiority complex and she had a husband who was a no-good. He wasn't bad by intention, just by
circumstance, and could he help it if strange women happened
to fall in love with him? He couldn't. So, the sketches involved
a dialogue between Maltke and the other woman, Maltke and
her husband, Maltke and the lawyer, Maltke and the judge,
and Maltke and a marriage counselor. I thought the sketches,
the monologues, were very funny. At least the guests laughed
and stopped watching the water dripping off the eaves.

I think I was fourteen when I invented Maltke. During the first summer she was part of my routine, we had an invasion of lawyers and judges as guests and I wanted to do something especially for them. They spent their days talking about cases and decisions and appeals and it may have entertained them but nobody else. So I decided to stage a mock trial using the lawyers and judges as lawyers and judges in the skit.

Another one of the guests was a singer, Lillian Shaw, who was a headliner at the Palace at that time, and she agreed to go on with me. We decided to ad lib a skit after working up the material. I blocked out a case between Maltke and The Other Woman based on alienation of affection and a comparison of Maltke and her rival. Maltke's case was essentially that she also was a woman, she had a face—"And maybe, Your Honor, sir, Judge, if it maybe'll please the court, Your Highness, my face is not on top of such a long neck but it's a face, no?" Maltke had a figure, too—"So the legs are a little short, the knees maybe knock a little but who listens? There's a few lumps here and there and the waist isn't so ay, ay, ay, and the dishwater eats off the nail polish, but whose fault is that? And if I'm not stylish can I help it if skinny dresses don't fit me? Did I ask for what I look like? I'm a woman, a plain everyday woman, and you think my husband is such a Beau Brummel he needs something better? He doesn't. Believe me. For the kind of man he is, I'm good enough."

We must have ad-libbed for an hour in front of the judges and lawyers and the final decision was in Maltke's favor. It was in mine, too, for the hotel rang with legal laughter.

Lillian Shaw asked me, afterwards, if I was a professional. I told her that I had never thought about it before, but I started to think right then and the more I thought, the nicer the idea became.

I did a lot of thinking about writing and during the winters when Lew and I finally returned to New York I played around the edges. By 1928 I found myself a housewife and the mother of two children, but still possessed by a compulsion to do something with all the words I had written. The refinery in Louisiana had burned down and theoretically we were waiting for it to be rebuilt. I was hoping it would never happen and I think my husband had the same hope. We never admitted it to each other but we took a New York apartment on the Grand Concourse and started to live as though Louisiana just wasn't there.

I knew I wanted to do something in the way of writing or acting. Lew encouraged me, and whenever I wrote something, he always told me it was wonderful. My father told me to be satisfied with my lovely family, that I was looking for bubbles and rainbows and trouble. And I told myself I was being foolish. But I simply had to find out if there was something there or if there wasn't. So I went looking.

I kept on writing. I tore up more paper than I kept but gradually Maltke began to turn into a woman from an extreme caricature. She began to become human when I gave her a new husband, one who wasn't such trouble and who was a little more helpful. I made her younger, about thirty-five or forty, and I gave her two children, a boy and girl more than a little bit like my own two. Her name changed, too. Maltke became Molly. And Talnitzky was no longer suitable. It was too much, it was trying too hard, and I couldn't take my character seriously. I changed the name to Goldberg because it sounded right and that was the only reason. After a while Molly Goldberg began to sound euphonious and so I kept it.

The first presentable script was five hundred words long. I had absolutely no idea what to do with it, but it was script number one and it went like this:

MOLLY (*calls*): Rosie! What's de matter Sammy ain't back from the *cheder?* It's nearly time for your papa to come home.
ROSIE (*at the piano practicing*): What time is it, mama?

MOLLY: Looking at de clock already? Practice, practice, go ahead. (*Sings.*) La, la, la. Is costing me enough money. Where is Sammy already, maybe he got himself runned over by a cabsitac. Dey run around so fast like cackroachers.

The script was written in dialect. I was trying to be authentic. I made the children Americans and the parents immigrants; the dialect, I thought, gave me the effect. I also had clashes between the two worlds. When Sammy finally came home, he walked into the kitchen, lifted a cover from a pot and smelled the soup.

SAMMY: Hello, mum.

MOLLY: Vat's de matter so late, Sammy? Let me look on your hands. Playing marbles, ha? For vat is your fadder slaving for vat I'm asking you? A marble shooter you'll gonna be? A beautiful business for a Jewish boy!

SAMMY: What's the matter with the marble business? Didn't Uncle Morantz pay five thousand dollars just to get his name on a piece of marble?

MOLLY: Don't answer back! Go vash yourself and take de violin. No wonder is a saying in America de parends obey de children!

When Jake finally came home I established the fact that he was a cutter in a dress factory, a very good one, and that he had ambitions: "Yes, Molly," he says, "embitions meant vat you're never satisfied with vat is." And the whole plot is that Jake needs a little money to go into business with his partner-to-be, Mendel, who worked next to him at the factory. Jake and Molly run through the people they might be able to borrow from:

JAKE: Maybe your brodder?

MOLLY: Gott forbit! I should batter die before I esk him.

JAKE: So dot means I'll die a piker.

MOLLY: Don't pike so much and think some more. Stend yourself on a chair and bring me down de blue peetcher on de shelf.

JAKE (*little does he know*): Vat's de peetcher all from a sudden?

It develops that Molly, too, wants things to be better for her children.

MOLLY: So I safed a liddle here, a liddle dere—and liddle by liddle I safed dis. Take it, Jake.

JAKE (*choked with emotion*): Molly, you'll see in fife years vot'll be. Big signs all over—"De Molly Cloik and Soot Company."

MOLLY: Ull right! Be careful. Don't be a splonger.

Finally the family sits down to supper. The world never looked brighter to Jake.

JAKE: Molly, your soup is feet for a kink.

MOLLY: You mean a president. Ve're in Amerike, not in Europe.

JAKE: Oy, Molly, Molly, soon ve'll be eating from gold plates.

MOLLY: Jake, d'you tink it'll taste better?

JAKE: Soch a question?

And they all laugh.

So now I had a script but what was I going to do with it? I called everybody I knew. But it turned out I didn't know anybody who knew anybody who knew somebody who was even vaguely connected with show business. I had a glimmering of an idea that my show would do for radio. I didn't have to convince Lew and I didn't have to persuade my father. They both agreed that if I thought radio was the place, then radio was the place. My problem was how to get there.

Lew knew Herman Bernie, the brother of Ben Bernie, and Lew kept telling me to call Herman.

I've never been very good on the phone; face to face has always been my forte, and I debated with myself for almost a week about calling him and asking what to do. Finally I got up enough nerve and when Herman answered I stuttered out who I was and I told him what I wanted. He said he would call a friend and let me know. It was just an outside chance, he said, but if that didn't work he insisted that I call him and then he'd try someone else.

When I put down the phone I plunged into a glorious daydream. I was already on radio and I could hear an announcer say, "... And now, The Rise of the Goldbergs!" I lived with my daydream for three days. There were no calls and the announcer was getting fainter and fainter. I was about to call Herman Bernie again when a call came for me. I said, "Hello," and a voice barked at me.

"Boig?"

"Yes?"

"Listen, kid, Herman Bernie gayme a buzz so come on down here and maybe I can wrastle sompin' up. O.K.?"

"That's very kind of you...."

"Na! Tomorrow, O.K.?"

I said tomorrow was just fine and he gave me his name and address.

Willie Kamen was a one-man operation. He had incorporated himself three flights up on West 42nd Street. When I went to see him I thought he was a character actor who had gone out of date. He was over six feet tall, bald, fat, smoked a cigar and had a voice like a foghorn.

"You Boig?" he said as I walked in. "I got no time to be sociable. Tell you what I want ..."

I was going to tell him what I wanted but he ran me over. I couldn't say a word.

"Look, Boig, I put on lots a shows, see? I got one now for the road and I need a writer. Got it?"

I nodded that I got it.

"The name a the show is *Boomalay*. A African bit. Mostly it's dancin' but I need woids between the dances. You gotta explain what's comin' next or you ain't got a audience, get it?"

I got it.

"So the job you're gonna do is writin' the woids. Simple? So here's the breakdown of the acts, the names of the numbers and go write."

I asked Mr. Kamen about the authenticity of the dances and he shook his head at me, sadly.

"What's with you? You think anybody in Hohokus is gonna know real from what I'm givin' em? What are they, cannibals, they should know? Listen, I got dancers. They're dark but they're a hundred per cent from New York. And the dances— it's the Lindy Hop with feathers. Don't worry, just write."

So I went home. I was happy, nervous, and a little afraid. I sharpened pencils, put paper on a card table and sat down to write. And, surprisingly, everything went easily, without a hitch. I wrote the lead-ins and the lead-outs and the whole revue seemed to hold together. I sent the script to Mr. Kamen and after a few days he called.

"Boig? I got the script. It's O.K. I like it. You done good and I'm sendin' the check. I think I got another one of these here revues goin' out so I'll call you."

And Mr. Kamen hung up before I could get a chance to thank him. When I put down the phone I was already telling myself I was a professional writer. I had a credit and a check to prove it. I was also out of a job.

Because of Lew's friendship with the Bernies I persuaded him to show my first Goldberg script to Herman, who, if he liked it, could show it to his famous brother. Ben read the script and sent word for me to call a Mr. Schwartz, program director of radio station WMCA. When I walked into Mr. Schwartz's office in the Empire State Building with my script under my arm, I learned the first lesson about executives: they are always on the phone.

Mr. Schwartz waved me to a chair. I sat, he talked on the phone. He finished one call and told me to go ahead, read my script. While I was reading, he was on the phone again. We both finished at the same time.

"I like it," Mr. Schwartz said. I wasn't sure whether he meant the script or the phone call.

"You have a very good voice for radio," he added after a pause. "Ever do commercials?" When I said I hadn't, he asked if I would like to try. I told him I would be happy to. He poked around in his desk drawers for a while, pulled out a typewritten page and handed it to me. It was headed, "Christmas Cookies #1," and was a recipe for pinwheel cookies. I read it aloud to him, and he said I was pretty good. Then he told me it was a commercial for Consolidated Edison and that it had to be read in Yiddish. A Christmas cookie in Yiddish for a public utility in America seemed a little odd, but it gave me my second lesson in radio: Be surprised at nothing.

On my way home I got nervous. I suddenly remembered I couldn't read or write Yiddish, I could only speak it. Lew came to my rescue once more. He could read and write both Yiddish and Hebrew, and he wrote out the commercial phonetically for me.

I practiced for hours and by the time I got to the studio I had it memorized. For those few minutes that I was there I don't think any words but the Yiddish commercial went through my head. I got my cue and the words from "Our sponsor" issued forth from my lips like a news bulletin from the Tower of Babel with its combinations of Yiddish and English.

"Eire freindliche gas and electrische company brengen alle menschen fun New York eine speciele reciepe far cookies far dem Yontevdiken seison. . . ."

For that job I got $6, and I felt I had arrived. My ambition nourished by this great success, I sat down and wrote and wrote. My next story was about two worldly young women who worked in the Five and Ten, and I called it "Effie and Laura."

It was a sophisticated slice of life full of stark realism, economic problems, and the endless search for the meaning behind life. Effie and Laura worked behind the same counter at the dime store and they talked more than they searched.

EFFIE: Say, Laura . . .

LAURA: Yeah?

EFFIE: I was thinkin' . . .

LAURA: Yeah . . .

EFFIE: It'd be great if a millionaire walked in here right now, wouldn't it? What would you do?

LAURA: I'd sell him somethin' . . .

EFFIE: I don't mean that. I mean, how'd you act . . . know what I mean?

LAURA: Like I always act. Just because a guy's got money don't mean——

EFFIE: Hey! Here comes that floor walker. Start lookin' busy or he's gonna ask for another date . . .

LAURA: That heel! He can't even afford to take me to the Automat on what he makes.

When I wrote *Effie and Laura* it seemed quite up to date and very modern. Being a writer I'm not going to say my early plots and characters sound old-fashioned. It's not my fault that times change.

After I finished the script, I walked in cold—trembling, in fact—to the offices of the Columbia Broadcasting System. I told myself that I should feel confident. I had two credits, didn't I, an "African" review and a cookie commercial?

In those days radio was a new medium. Nobody knew what

to do with it and the people in charge listened to ideas. They needed something to fill up the time. I read *Effie and Laura* for a Mr. Seaman, who, like Mr. Schwartz, didn't seem to be listening. He loved it, he said, and asked me to do an audition. Fine—why not? I got hold of an actress and we read the script in a studio over a real microphone with a real engineer to a real executive and I got a real reaction. Mr. Seaman repeated that everything was wonderful only—only is a word you have to watch out for in radio and television because it can mean NO very politely and it can mean "We don't want the show and do we really have to make up our minds?" In this case it meant that the two voices were too much alike. So I went to Equity and found another actress, a Gertrude Mudge, with a voice twice as deep as mine. We auditioned again and one Wednesday night at six-thirty I found myself on the air and walked out of the studio a woman with her own show.

Next morning two things happened: Ben Gross reviewed me in the New York *Daily News*. He liked the show. Soon after I read praise that morning and enjoyed it, the telephone rang. It was C.B.S. They canceled the show. Someone "upstairs" didn't like it. I was heartbroken and ready to give up. Lew also was depressed for me. Only the two children playing happily on the floor were blissfully ignorant of the nature of the hard, cruel, outside world.

It was 1929 and Lew was feeling depressed for reasons of his own. The refinery in Louisiana had not yet been rebuilt, and he was awaiting word from Arbuckle Brothers, sugar refiners in Brooklyn, about a job there. My father, too, was worrying about how to keep busy in the winter and was toying with the idea of a hotel in Florida. He said he needed an assistant to look over prospects with him, so I took a week off, and we drove down to Florida in September, 1929. We didn't know it when we set out, but dark financial clouds were gathering to add to our other troubles.

For one of the first times in his life Jake had empty pockets, but he also had his usual high hopes and big ideas. We soon discovered that the days of $500 down and the rest on time to buy a hotel were over. My father remained unreasonably optimistic. I had always admired his cheerful lack of fear, but right then I was in no mind to keep smiling through.

We started back to New York with me in a black mood, and my father exuding brightness. He kept saying he would make another trip to Florida in a few months and see whether he couldn't pick up a hotel. I suggested he forget Florida and concentrate on Fleischmanns. He guaranteed me that within six months he would be the proprietor of a hotel in Florida. He accused me of dreaming, with my radio ambitions, and I accused him of the same, with his winter castle on the sands. But I realized that he was saying to me all the things I had been saying to myself, though I wouldn't admit it.

We kept up our quarrel, punctuated by silences while he was driving and I was looking glumly out of the window. Then suddenly we discovered we were lost. Somewhere during the argument Jake had taken a wrong turn. He pulled into a gas station and asked where we were. After he had listened to the man telling him to turn right, then left at a white farmhouse, go over a bridge to a dirt road and then come out on the highway, Jake decided the native didn't know as much as he did and he started to argue with him. This was too much. Not only was he telling me I didn't know what I was doing, but he was doubting the directions of a man who had lived in the neighborhood all his life.

I was so mad I got out of the car and started to walk to New York. My father followed me in the car, trying to get me to get back in. But, as usual with me, I had to wait until I had gone through my mood and out the other end. Sometimes that process took a few minutes, sometimes days. This time I was mad enough to walk if it took a year.

While walking I had plenty of time to think, and I made up my mind to one final thing: I would never go back to the hotel business. I would follow what Jake called my "bubbles and rainbows," until the one burst or I found out what was at the end of the other. Having made that decision, I stopped being mad and got back into the car. Then it was Jake's turn to be mad. He wanted to know what it was so awful he had done, and we were almost in New York before we could talk to each other without starting the same old fight. We were on the 42nd Street ferry before we both had our problems aired and the steam out of our systems. I told my father I was sure he would find a Florida hotel sooner or later, and he told me great radio success was just around the corner.

The day after we got back to New York the stock market crashed, and, having decided on the ferry not to worry about tomorrow, we now had all our tomorrows to worry about real hard. It wasn't any comfort to have plenty of company in such problems. We didn't have any stocks, so we didn't lose anything in the stock market. But the side effects caught up with us quickly. In October my father was getting cancellations for Fleischmanns in June; people were giving up their summer vacations before winter had begun. Then Lew got the news that the Louisiana sugar plant wouldn't be rebuilt under the circumstances. But there was one piece of good luck: he was offered the old job with Arbuckle Brothers in Brooklyn at a healthy salary, at a time when most people were losing their jobs.

I, too, went to work with renewed energy. I decided that there is no giving up in this entertainment business; you have to take encouragement from little things, such as someone liking your script, even if he didn't use it. If you give up, you're in the wrong line. Almost everyone I have ever known in entertainment has gone through this long apprenticeship in disappointment.

In those days there weren't many radio stations to try, but there were plenty of executives to telephone for appointments. I went from one to another and finally ended up at the National Broadcasting Company, where I left a script that I called *The Rise of the Goldbergs*. They seemed really interested and I was told I would get a decision in two weeks. I was determined to be good and not fret. I might just as well have saved my breath. Before I was home an hour I began to worry. I kept asking whether there was a call for me. Only at five o'clock did I stop worrying because I was naive enough to think that in radio people went home. If I knew then what I know now, I would have worried through the night.

How my husband put up with me, I'll never understand; I guess it must have been love. Being of a scientific turn of mind as well as a man with a heart, he tried to make me see the slim mathematical possibilities of a series of scripts from an unknown being accepted. But I was never good at figures. All I could see was, N.B.C. liked the script or they didn't, and if they didn't what did they know, and they should tell me quickly, thank you, and I'll take my business elsewhere.

I tried to protect the children—Harriet two, and Cherney, five—from my worries and moods. I did it by playing Indians with them under a card table, with a sheet for a wigwam. The children would have been content to stay under the table all day, but how long can a worried adult sit still under a table? Also, the game had to stop every time the phone rang. The kids trained themselves to be quiet the moment I grabbed the receiver. They knew I was waiting for something, and the two of them would stand around the little table that held the telephone and look like nervous script writers, junior size.

By the time the fourteenth day crept up on me, and nothing had happened, I decided to go out. I went shopping, I took a subway ride downtown, I walked. Then I went home, looked at a pad near the telephone—no calls. Well, I figured, that was that: The man said two weeks, two weeks was fourteen days, and I might as well try to forget about the project. Then the children came home, and their nurse, a Miss Schmidt, came home. She looked at me and remembered something. There had been a call, an important call, so important, she had written out the message and put it in a cereal bowl in the dish closet where all important messages went. I went for the cereal bowl and read the message. It said I was to be at N.B.C. next morning to discuss a contract.

I couldn't quite believe it. I told myself the nurse must have got it wrong, or the call was for someone else. But I finally gave up and let out a yell of joy. The children stared at me as if they had seen their first crazy woman. I began to cry, hugged and kissed them, and danced around the floor with them. My husband was on his way home from Brooklyn in the subway, where I couldn't telephone to him, so I went to the subway station to meet him. I told him right at the subway entrance and we both stopped in the middle of the street and laughed like children.

Waiting for that next morning was even harder than waiting for the fourteenth day had been. Sleep was something that never came. I read, I drank warm milk. Finally, I gave up, went to the kitchen, closed the door and washed, ironed, folded clothes while watching the clock to see how fast it was moving. By the time everyone was up in the morning I must have done a week's wash. Then after making breakfast, dressing the children, washing the dishes, I was ready by the time Miss Schmidt arrived for my big appointment.

N.B.C.'s offices were at 711 Fifth Avenue and the man I went to see was Bill Rainey, head of the program department. He asked me to sit down and told me he liked the script and wanted more. He asked me to read the script for him, and when I finished, he said he was giving me a four-week contract at $75 a week. I said, "Fine." If at the end of four weeks, N.B.C. renewed, I would get $100 a week for the next four weeks. I said, "Fine." Then he asked if I would like to play the part of the mother, Molly. I said, "Fine." Then he told me to write a few more scripts and be ready to go on the air on November 20, 1929, which was one week from that day. When I found myself out on the street I came to and realized I would have to have three more fifteen-minute scripts with a beginning, a middle, and end, all in one week. It seemed impossible.

When *The Goldbergs* went on the air we went on sustaining. I didn't know the difference between sustaining and commercial and even if I had, I wouldn't have cared. All I knew was that I was on the air, that somebody out there must be listening, and that there wasn't a happier person in the world than me. The problem of what to write about solved itself easily when I decided that what I had was two families—a real one and a radio one. I translated my life with my grandmother, my mother and father, my friends, the people I had heard about, into the Goldbergs and began to relive it on the air.

Molly, when I first began to work with her, was an amalgam of my mother and my grandmother, Czerny. Into that combination I put in a few characteristics of some of the guests at the hotel that I felt Molly should have. Some of the people who stayed at Fleischmanns experimented with the English language and from them Molly developed a manner of speaking that put the horse in the cart and threw an eye into the soup. From my grandfather Mordecai, Molly picked up her formal English. This manner of speech I used only when Molly was in a situation where she thought a little educated talk was needed. In some scripts she spoke to her son Sammy's violin teacher, an educated man, in a self-conscious manner to make up for her own simple beginnings. "Professor," she might say, "Maestro, kind sir, how is the progressing of my offspring with the three B's, Bach, Beethoven, and Berlin?" or, just asking a policeman directions, Molly finds herself torn between what she knows the police to be in America and what she knew them to be in Europe. With respect tinged with an almost forgotten fear, she says to them, "Mr. Policeman, Officer of the law, Your Honor, could you be so kindly if you would to inform me of the location of where is Fourteenth Street?" And when the cop, a word she would never use, tells her she is on Fourteenth Street, Molly's reaction is the relief of many immigrants at not only having found their way but also of not being arrested for asking a simple question. "You are most kind, dear Mr. Officer," she would say, and "very pleased to have made your acquaintance."

Molly's respect for learning came from all the immigrant families I knew in New York City. America, for them, was a land of opportunity and the greatest opportunity they found was the chance to give their children an education. America was full of good and wonderful things and the schools were the best. Everyone I knew wanted his boys and girls to go to college and the parents worked hard to accomplish it. In return, the greatest pleasure they could have was to see their child handed a diploma. Of course there were other pleasures like hearing their boy saying educated words or playing the piano or watching him read a book.

Molly became a person who lived in the world of today but kept many of the values of yesterday. She could change with the times, as did my grandmother and my mother, but she had some basic ideas that she learned long ago and wanted to pass on to her children. Next to the Constitution of the United States, the Ten Commandments came first. Not only were all men created equal, they also had to honor their mother and their father. Abraham, Isaac, and Jacob interchanged easily with Washington, Lincoln, and Jefferson, and the Philistines had nothing on a person who didn't vote.

Molly's husband, Jake, too, was a combination of people and their ideas. He was more like my grandfather Harris, I think, than anyone else. But he had touches of my father Jake's stubbornness and ability to go from one mood to another without reason or explanation. He also had a bit of Lew in him. He was a stickler for being correct in his dealings with everyone and he was too kind to be a good businessman. Not only could Molly and the children take advantage of him, but so could anyone else—if he liked them. If he didn't, it would take a little longer before they could get the better of him.

The children, Sammy and Rosie, were myself, my cousins, my own children, and some parts of all the friends I had grown up with. They also expressed a point of view: that of the first-generation Americans who were trying to make sense out of growing up in one world, America, but coming from another, the European world of their parents. They were being pulled by the new and held back by the old. It was a difficult position even for two nice children. For instance, they felt they had to correct their parents' pronunciation. But European immigrants of that generation did not take kindly to correction from below. Also, authority didn't mean to them what it meant to their elders. They weren't afraid of it. (This was an American tradition that they learned very easily.) Sammy and Rosie were important to *The Goldbergs* because they helped to teach their immigrant parents how to become Americans. At the same time, the parents tried to teach them some of the rich traditions of the Old World, thus combining the best elements of two dissimilar worlds. Or such was my intention anyway.

The first script in what I called *The Rise of the Goldbergs* was taken from a real-life situation. It was the one about Jake working in the dress business and wanting to go into business for himself. He needed some money to rent a loft and some machines. There was some money in his own home that he didn't know about—hidden away in a teapot in the dish closet. Molly had been saving it for a rainy day and when Jake told her what he wanted, she considered that the rainy day had arrived. Down came the teapot and the hundred dollars, which just made the difference. The saved money idea came from my grandmother, who was always putting away a penny here and a penny there for when something would be needed. Jake's desire to be his own boss was that of my grandfather and my father; the details of the situation and the solution came from me.

That was script number one.

Other scripts were written in the 42nd Street Library in the Main Reading Room, and the reason the Library became my office was very simple. I couldn't work at home. There were too many distractions, and I knew myself. If I didn't get out of the house nothing would get done. There was always something I wanted to do with the children or something to clean, or something to shop for, so I went downtown where I had nothing to do but write, and there I wrote scripts two, three, and four.

After a while I gave up the Library—not because I wanted to but because I thought I had to. A friend came to meet me there one afternoon and told me that everyone was looking at me because I was making faces. I always make faces when I write— I act out everyone's part, say their words, and become them as much as I can, but I wasn't aware that the faces I made were anything to look at. And anyway I thought all writers did it. So

I left, and I made faces at home where nobody but my own family could see—if I was going to amuse anyone, why shouldn't it be the people I love?

The first broadcast of *The Goldbergs* was in a little room in the N.B.C. studios. The control room was behind glass on one wall and the cast and myself were in the middle of the room around one microphone, and I wasn't even nervous. I told myself that I was talking to a microphone and that was nothing to be frightened about. We went on the air, we went off the air, and I don't know what I expected, but whatever it was, it never happened. In radio it takes a while for reaction to set in. It's like talking to a wall. I had no idea if we did well or badly. My family said it was wonderful, but a family is not the public. When we weren't canceled after the first show I figured we must have been all right, we couldn't have been too bad and I was encouraged.

When *The Goldbergs* started on the air it was for fifteen minutes, but we went our merry way. I had no idea if there were listeners any place, I didn't know if anyone outside the studio and my own family even knew there was such a show. I was busy and I was happy and this was before ratings.

The first time I knew that *The Goldbergs* had an audience was when I got sick. I came down with laryngitis and the show was taken off the air for a week. In those days an unsponsored show was moved from time slot to time slot to fill in the dead spaces. *The Goldbergs* had no particular time of its own. I never knew what studio we were going to broadcast from or at what time we were going to do it. Scheduling would call me and say, "This week you're on at 5:15 Wednesday and you'll work out of Studio B." I would then call the cast and tell them where and when. With that kind of schedule it's hard to build an audience, and everyone, including me, was very surprised and grateful when N.B.C. received something close to eighteen thousand letters asking about what had happened to the lady who played Molly. We weren't network at the time, just local, and the mail response was considered phenomenal.

After I had been told about the mail pouring into N.B.C. I began to feel differently about the microphone. It wasn't just an electrical gadget any more; it was like a telephone into which I could tell stories to people I knew were there listening. I began to feel responsible to them and the more I felt that way, the more the characters on the show became real. They began to react in ways that I thought the audience would like and appreciate. I found myself dealing with a family in fact and not a family in imagination. It always amazed me that people liked what I was doing. And it was hard for me to realize that I had written something that pleased an audience. I always felt I could do better for them and I tried. I wanted them to laugh and cry and live with the Goldbergs.

3 Radio Family

The Rise of the Goldbergs, as I thought of it, was a show all about "ordinary people." "Ordinary people," "little people," and "the common man" are phrases that I don't like. They suggest that, somewhere, high in an office building, is a big person, a super person, who is being very tolerant. Anyway, ordinary people liked the show—even advertising men liked it.

The first real inkling I had that the show was liked "upstairs" in the executive offices was the day I brought a friend into N.B.C. with me for a tour. She had never seen a radio show before and since I knew my way around the building I wanted to show her I knew all the ropes. As we got out of the elevator at N.B.C. a page rushed over to me and said that everyone had been looking all over town for me and, where had I been? I asked him what the trouble was and, according to him, the trouble was something. Mr. McClelland, vice president in charge of sales, wanted me to do an audition right away—and for a prospective client. They had gotten the cast together, they had taken a few scripts out of the files, the studio was ready, the client was impatient, and there was not a minute to spare.

I wasn't impressed. In radio there is never a minute to spare and that means someone wants something done yesterday so that he can have you wait six weeks before he looks at it or listens to it and then says, "It's not exactly what we had in mind." So I asked my friend to sit in the control room while we did an audition. It wouldn't take a minute—which was my code for an hour or two.

When I walked into the studio my radio family was waiting. When I got inside the soundproofed doors I became Molly and the three actors sitting around the rehearsal table became Jake, Sammy, and Rosie.

The original Jake was James Waters, an old-timer in the theater but as young as the rest of us when it came to radio. Jimmy was a short man with white hair and pince-nez glasses. I picked him for the part, not because he looked anything like what Jake should be, but because he had the voice that gave the impression of a tallish, strongish, sometimes willful, sometimes funny, affectionate man. The ear, in radio, describes the person and Jimmy was exactly right. He seemed to get taller when he was on the air and shrank to his regular size as soon as we got off. The pince-nez glasses always fell off his nose when he was himself but as Jake they stuck there as though they were glued.

Jimmy was the father of the family on the air, and when he got sick—we had been on the air for a little more than ten years —we were lost without him. I didn't want to use another voice so I had Jimmy offstage in almost a year's worth of scripts. Papa was always in another room, at the factory, downstairs talking to Mendel, his partner—he was never heard but he was there.

The first and original Sammy was Alfred Ryder. He was a little boy in knickers when he started—when he left he was a soldier in uniform—not only in real life but in the series. As a matter of fact when the real Sammy who was the real Alfred left for the real war we did our broadcast from Pennsylvania Station before the troop train left. By the grace of God, they both came back safely.

Rosie, my radio daughter, was played, at first, by a little girl, Rosalyn Silbur. She also started as almost a baby, grew up, got married, and had children, all as my radio daughter. The funny thing about having a radio family added to a real family is that they become part of your life—they are almost as real as your own and you find yourself worrying about them as much as the people at home. When you think of the time you spend with them it's not surprising. I was with them all for eight hours a day, six days a week, for almost eighteen years—and from that you can get affectionate.

The studio N.B.C. assigned to us for that first audition was just like any other studio. The bare walls were hung with monk's cloth to deaden sound and to keep it from bouncing all around the room. One wall had a glass window behind which sat the engineer, the producer, and the director. They stared out at us, the actors, as though we were talking fish in an H. G. Wells aquarium. They could hear what we were saying but unless they pushed the talk-back button in the control room we couldn't hear a word of theirs. I got so that I could gauge their reactions from the facial expressions and they got so that they discussed points about the script with their heads bent so that I couldn't see them.

Above the control was the clock with a red sweep-second hand. The clock was our calendar and we did what it said to do. We began our radio life with the sweep straight up and we stopped what we were doing exactly fifteen minutes later.

On a wall at right angles to the control room window was another window, a smaller one, that led to a little room known as the Sponsor's Booth. In this booth the fate of families, police forces, spacemen, orphanages, and the friendly barber of Hartsville were decided. If the sponsor didn't like what he was hearing not even Buck Rogers or Chandu the Magician could make him change his mind. Snip went the scissors of fate and that was the end of that.

From a sponsor's point of view dropping a show is always justified. And there's only one reason why he does: his sales show little or no increase. He's the man who pays the bills and he's entitled to reap the benefits.

From the point of view of the people on the show, the actors, the writers, the producers, Mr. Sponsor is an evil man just waiting to tear the microphone from our hands. What he's got against us artists no one has yet discovered. The fight between the men with the money and the "creative" minds has gone on since the first artist was hired to paint on the walls of some Neanderthal spear-maker's cave. The problem isn't insoluble. The gap that exists between the men who hire and the men who produce is only as big as the Grand Canyon. All we have to do is to fill it in.

Anyway, the sponsor sat in his booth with Mr. McClelland while we stood around a microphone in the studio rehearsing. From time to time I would glance over to see how his patience was holding out. Sponsor or no sponsor I wasn't going to do a show until I thought it was ready. This particular sponsor was very patient. He was an executive-looking man in a blue suit and a Hoover collar that gave him the air of a person with a broken neck. He sat in his chair, straight up and down, and from time to time would point a finger into the studio. Mr. McClelland answered his obvious questions. It was like watching a silent movie.

The studio he saw was our home and we treated it like one. Microphones were placed on a table, one was standing free about ten feet from the table. There was a sound-effects door that we walked in and out of as though it were a real one. The table was covered with pots and pans, writing paper, a pen, and somewhere a small box with tissue paper. Next to the big table was a smaller one with two pots and a knife; one pot was filled with unpeeled potatoes and the other pot was filled with water. When we all felt we had the feel of the script, one we had done some weeks before, we sat around quietly for a minute or two waiting for the signal from the control room and the red light over it indicating we were, if not on the air, at least doing a reasonable facsimile. The light went on, the director's finger pointed at me, and I started humming and being busy. The scene was a domestic one. I was peeling potatoes. Because it was the only sound we had at that time that would make the sound of potatoes being peeled and then being dropped into a pail of water. As I hummed and peeled and dropped, Sammy wrote letters. The only sound effect that sounded like a letter being written was a letter being written.

Sammy was writing invitations to everyone Molly and Jake knew for his bar mitzvah.

"How do you spell Dobrozensky?" he asks and Rosie starts to spell the name and an argument starts. Molly interrupts to ask about how far he's gone in the list and by that time Jake has come through the sound-effects door.

"Hulloh! Beezy, beezy, huh?", he says and Molly tells him the list is almost finished.

"Oy, Molly, it's going to be some bar mitzvah. In de *shuhl* ve'll be able to have everybody."

In those early days the scripts were written as spoken. Any character who needed an accent had it put on paper in black and white. I thought it gave the scripts an air of authenticity but it was a device that I gave up after a while because I found that actors didn't need me to show them how to mispronounce the language.

Molly is also in an expansive mood, but she has a few things on her mind and she has to set the stage before she can bring them up.

MOLLY: And everybody vhat vants vill come home far de supper. Oy, dat reminds me; Sammyly, go over to Tante Elka and ask she should give you de big coppernum pot, and if she's got a roasting pan she should also send.

Sammy doesn't want to go and Rosie decides she's too busy addressing envelopes. Molly suggests that he go with Mickey, Mrs. Bloom's son, and Molly calls down the dumbwaiter to see if Mickey's home.

MOLLY: Yoohoo. Mrs. Bloom! Is Mickey home? yes? Tell him he should go vid Sammy, yes? Mrs. Bloom, you'll come down so you'll help me figure out how many chickens I need. . . .

After Sammy leaves Molly asks Jake about Sammy's bar mitzvah present and Jake proudly opens a small box (there is the crinkling of real tissue paper), and removes an engraved gold watch with a gold chain. Naturally a gold watch leads Molly to considering a suit for Sammy with a vest so he can wear the watch correctly. The suit then leads to Sammy growing up and the need for more rooms and moving—and from that Molly gets around to a letter she received from Europe—from her newly married cousin Leah. Obviously something is going on because Molly starts to make Jake comfortable.

MOLLY: Rosie, bring in far papa a liddle fruit—lovely mengereens —and some pananas—just vhat you like Jake. Maybe you vhant a stool for your feet? Vhy don't you take off your shoes and be comfortable, ha?
(Jake knows something's going on.)
JAKE: Ulleright, Molly. So vhat you vhant to ask me ullready, huh?
MOLLY: Leah and her husband would like to come to Amerike.
JAKE: Dat's nice. So vhy don't dey come?
MOLLY: A question! Vhy don't dey come? If dey had money to buy tickets dey vould be here ullready.
JAKE: So Amerike will have to get along widout Leah and her husband.
MOLLY: You couldn't spare the money, huh, Jake? I'm only esking. You could take it from my weekly money, Jake.
JAKE: Molly, you always say de same and in de end I don't take off and you don't give me.

Molly tells Jake how much Leah and her husband want to come and how hard the husband says he'll work—and Jake sees the handwriting on the wall.

JAKE: De tickets is ullready a small ting. Vhat vill be vhen dey get here, vhere vill dey live?

MOLLY: Vhen ve move, so dey move in here. You said you vanted to buy new furniture, so instead to move out everything, ve'll leave it like it is, and dey'll have home for de meanwhile.

JAKE: So you got it all figured, ha, ain't you?

MOLLY: Don't you tink it's a good idea? And even de telephone ve vouldn't have to move, so she'll be able to call me and she vouldn't be lonesome. So say you're saying yes, Jake, hah?

JAKE: I didn't say yes!

MOLLY: So it means—no?

JAKE: And I didn't say no!

MOLLY: So vhat did you said? Take anodder mengereen. Rosie, close de kitchen vindow—is a draft on papa.

JAKE: Don't be so good to me.

When Sammy comes home with the pots and pans he congratulates his father on being a great man. Tante Elka, Molly's greataunt, says she is so happy about Jake having sent the tickets to Leah and her husband—and Elka has said that if Sammy grows up to be as good as his father, he'll be a fine man.

Jake is furious and Molly calms him by saying that she only told Tante Elka that Jake would send the tickets—and she says, she only said that because she was sure he would.

MOLLY: I remember how you always said dat if God helped you, you vould always try to help someone else.

JAKE: Some people always got to have help, special your relations, Molly!

MOLLY: No matter vhat anybody is got, dey got trough de help of somebody else. By ourselves ve couldn't make notting. You know dat, Jake.

JAKE: You trowing in my face vhat your brudder Joe helped me out vid a copple notes?

MOLLY: I vasn't even tinking on Joe. If you don't vant to send de tickets vid a full heart, so don't send.

JAKE: Who said I vouldn't?

SAMMY: Atta boy, Pa!

ROSIE: Oh, Papa, you're a doll!

JAKE: I'm some papa, hah?

MOLLY: Didn't I know vhat you vould do? Give me a kiss Jake?

And that was the end of the audition. Mr. McClelland stepped into the studio to ask me to come to his office and then he left. We picked up our scripts as the engineer started to coil up his cables and the sound man rolled the door to its place in the corner of the studio. A porter came in to clean up the crumpled pieces of paper and to straighten out the chairs. By the time we left, the control lights were out and the studio was neat and empty. It was as though everybody had moved to another part of town. My radio family all had appointments in different parts of the city and we were now merely four friends, acquaintances, and nothing more. Tomorrow we would be back in a studio playing at being a family again.

When I got to Mr. McClelland's office he was sitting with the stone-faced man I took to be the sponsor or his representative. We were introduced and after saying "hello" he never said another word, so I assumed he was just another vice president in charge of who-knew-what. Mr. McClelland asked me what I thought about going on the air six times a week, fifteen minutes a show, and for a sponsor. I told him I didn't think I could write that many scripts. Besides, I was in a hurry, I had a friend waiting for me downstairs and I had to go home and change because I was going out that night with Lew.

I got home and five minutes after I had opened the door, the phone rang and it was Mr. McClelland. He was not happy. He asked what I meant by saying I couldn't go on for six days a week? Did I know who the man in his office was? He was the president of the Pepsodent Company—and then he asked how much I wanted to go on the air for Pepsodent six times a week. I didn't know and I told him I didn't know. I said that he was the expert and whatever he said would be all right with me. Mr. McClelland told me he was taking me off the air for a few weeks so I could write scripts and then I was going on at 7:30 P.M. to 7:45 P.M. six times a week—and that was that.

During those first three sponsored years for the Pepsodent Company my radio family and my real-life family lived a hectic life. I saw as much of my radio relatives as of my flesh and blood.

At home I would get up at about five or five-thirty and start writing scripts. By the time I had reached the middle point of a script it was time to make breakfast for my husband and the children. After Lew had gone to work and the children to school, I finished the last half. Some days the writing went well and fast, some days it was hard and awful, and my mood for the day was determined by how well I thought the script had gone.

By noon or one o'clock I was finished. The script went to be mimeographed and I went out. I had nothing to do until about five when I had to be at the studio for rehearsal. Some days I would walk up and down Fifth Avenue going from store to store just looking. I found it relaxing and after writing all morning I felt a need to be with crowds of people. Walking around gave me a chance to think and try to solve problems of story line. Six shows a week gave me the chance to do a continuous story rather than just episodes and that meant a lot of planning. Sometimes in the street I would see the face of someone who would suggest a character and the character might then suggest a story—and I would walk blindly up Fifth Avenue writing my next installment.

Some afternoons I would spend in the studio listening to

actors and actresses read for parts. There were times that I would come across a very good voice and that voice alone might be the start of a story idea. For instance, I wanted the Goldbergs to go away for a vacation—where, I didn't know—but when Joseph Buloff came in to read, their destination seemed clear. They were going to a hotel in the Catskill Mountains that I called Pincus-in-the-Pines and that was run by Joe Buloff as Mr. Pincus. Mr. Pincus was a sly, hardheaded businessman with a heart, naturally, of gold. He had a cook called Katie who was forever quitting and just in time for supper. Pincus and Katie had running fights and the Goldbergs became their confidants. Later the Pincus Pines idea changed into another radio series called *The House of Glass* run by Barney Glass, another Pincus but with a modern outlook.

Uncle David, Molly's father's brother, was born when I heard Menasha Skulnick in a Yiddish play on Second Avenue. Menasha's voice, soft, gentle, with a squeak in it when he got mad, suggested exactly the kind of man I was looking for; a small man with a big temper and feelings that could get hurt in a twinkling of an eye. Uncle David became so popular that I moved him in with the Goldbergs. His European outlook and comments on America were a perfect foil for Molly. They would have conversations that went like this:

MOLLY: Reading the paper, David?

DAVID (*reading the paper*): What else?

MOLLY: So read me.

DAVID: Listen: A gangster shot a man in the telephone booth and left him standing——

MOLLY: Yeah? What'll we have for supper, David?

DAVID: Whatever——

MOLLY: I thought maybe noodles—soft—it shouldn't be too hard for your new teeth . . .

DAVID: For me you don't have to bother.

MOLLY: For who else should I not bother?

From a character like Uncle David, I could drift off to almost any situation. Sometimes I would examine the lonely old man who had a doctor son called Solly the Doctor and who was very successful. David would think Solly had deserted his old father because he had gotten rich and nothing could be further from the truth—it was only that David liked to feel sorry for himself and Solly was a good excuse.

Living a double life had its tensions. I had my pie, and I was eating it, but sometimes it was more like upside-down cake. When I had to give lectures to my children about things they did and didn't do sometimes I would be able to say a word or two to them at breakfast, sometimes at night when I got home, but they took advantage of my schedule. They found ways to change the subject when they saw a lecture coming. But I found a way to get to them. I put the lectures in the script and broadcast them coast to coast. One thing I was sure of; they would be listening and a little education wouldn't hurt them. When my daughter Harriet wanted to stay up as late as her older brother I had Sammy and Rosie fight about the same thing. When my son Cherney wasn't as kind as he should have been to his dear sister I used the radio to show him "What's thicker than water?" I made pigtail-pulling an object lesson on the air. I pointed out that teasing a young boy about having girl friends wasn't nice and that brothers and sisters should have respect for each other. I know the children listened because I was told by my daughter that her brother had every right in the world to pull her braids. And my son insisted that his sister could tease him all she wanted to. The one thing they both agreed on was that I must stop airing their troubles from coast to coast. I said I would but I didn't. The material was too good to lose so I always told them it was two other children down the street who had given me the ideas for the scripts.

My children grew up in thirteen-week cycles. They got used

to having me biting my fingernails towards the end of every renewal period, and they were especially good during those times.
They sympathized with me and without any prompting from
Lew. Although they never said a word to me, I know how they
must have suffered. I wasn't fit to live with during those times.
I was so caught up in worrying myself about whether the
sponsor liked the show or didn't like it that the only time I had
for philosophizing was on the air and not at home. As Molly I
could be very sensible; as me I could be very tense and irritable.
And even though Lew told me there was nothing I could do, I
found that I was only comfortable when I worried about it. In
radio and television the contract is a built-in nerve-wracker because inside the contract, not in small print, is a clause. This
clause is known as the cancellation clause and it can be used at
the end of every thirteen-week period no matter what else the
contract says. It is possible to sign a contract for five years
with a company but the five years are divided into thirteen-week
periods and you can find yourself off the air at the end of any
one of them. This clause is the cause of what we all called the
thirteen-week jitters. We started worrying about it at the end
of the first week. When we were renewed at the end of the first
thirteen, we started worrying about the next thirteen and it has
gone on that way ever since.

It is not so much a matter of being out of work or not getting
paid; it is, simply, that a cancellation means that someone
doesn't like the show—and that's harder to take then anything
else in the world. It was a very peculiar thing but even when I
knew that the show had five million listeners, fans, who loved
it, I only worried about the one person in the control room who
happened to make a face that I thought indicated he didn't like
it. I directed everything at him because I wanted him, at that
moment, to like the show more than anyone else in the world.

I always made believe that I wanted criticism. If something

was bad, I said, I wanted to know about it—and as soon as I heard it I got depressed. My own family knew this better than I did and if I asked for a reaction they always said everything was great and wonderful and waited for the right moment days later, to tell me the truth. I knew what they were doing, they knew I knew, but it was the only way to treat me in those days. In those days? I'm still the same way.

In my whole family the only person who was absolutely uncritical was my Grandfather Mordecai. To him it was enough to hear my voice coming out of the speaker. He would come to the house to hear the broadcast whenever he was in the neighborhood and to him a show could never be bad. The reason was an odd one. In one of my first scripts I said the word "pickle" and that amazed him more than anything else could. Don't ask me why. When he heard that word he poked his son, my father, and said, "Did you hear? Tillie sag't pickles!" Pickles was the first word Grandfather learned when he came to this country. So he was a fan from then on. My father was a little more critical but not on the basis of content or acting. He would come to the studio sometimes to watch the show and when he took a dislike to an actor for personal reasons that actor could never do a decent job of acting in his eyes. He was no good from then on and every time I used him—or her—I would get the same criticism: the show was no good because so and so said, maybe, five words in fifteen minutes.

Lew was a different story. He was always very careful about what he said right after I got off the air. It was only after we had supper and I had had a chance to relax a little that he would tell me what he thought. The suggestions were always constructive and after I got over my initial mood of being rejected I could see the value of what he had said, and I would take advantage of it.

As a script show *The Goldbergs* used hundreds of people—

sometimes once, sometimes for months at a time, and when an actor or an actress was coming to the end of a run there were signs along the way that they recognized. For an actress it was mostly marriage—and as soon as they were engaged they knew they didn't have long to go. For an actor, sometimes it was a cough—and when the directions said "Coughs," actors would come to me and say, "Doctor, how long do I have?" If I knew, I would say, but most of the time I put the cough in just in case I ran out of ideas for that particular character. There's nothing like a little cough to change a plot.

One of the things that could change the original was the matter of time. On the air and about once every fifteen seconds or so I would look to the control room to see if we were timing out right or not. Before the show went on we had done a number of rehearsals and a few dress rehearsals. These were not only for nuance and meaning and to make the whole script play, but they were also for time. A fifteen-minute show has to time out exactly at twelve and a half minutes. The two and a half minutes left over are for commercials and theme and credits. If the control room said we were on time then we continued as we had been. The signal for being on time was the director's finger pointed to his nose—"on the nose" was the expression. If we had to speed up he waved his forefinger around in the air like a propeller and we read a little faster—if we were too fast he put the thumb and forefinger of each hand together and made pulling motions slowly—and we slowed up. The only thing that is never cut is the commercial, so if time has to come from someplace it has to come from the script—and no matter how careful you are during rehearsal, once you get on the air anything can happen. Actors get carried away with their lines. They read them fast or they read them slowly. They give things "expression." They act, and there's nothing you can do about it. An actor can freeze, sneeze, cough, faint, forget a cue, stumble over words, or just go blank. When that happens someone else has to say the lines—ad lib them really, in terms of another character —until the actor recovers.

I remember one actress who had a speech about what happened to her in the butcher store. She was supposed to say: "I don't know where that Hazelcorn the butcher gets off saying that my Harry wouldn't know a good piece of meat if it got up and talked to him."

The actress froze, or she may have lost her place in the script —whatever it was when her cue came she wasn't there. On the air there's no time to think. You do what has to be done—what comes to you to do—and you do it. I picked up her line as Molly.

"So what did Hazelcorn the butcher mean? Nothing. If you knew him as long as I knew him you'd know when he says your Harry wouldn't know a good piece of meat if it talked to him it only means he had a fight with his wife. Hazelcorn is not an insulter but he's a very sensitive man." I kept on going as long as I saw that the actress wasn't ready. As soon as she looked at me and indicated that all was fine I led into her next line which was: "A man shouldn't bring his family troubles to work with him. . . ."

My ad libs had thrown the timing off and the control room began to signal for a hurry up. We were in the middle of a meaty exposition about why Mr. and Mrs. Hazelcorn always fought and I didn't want to rush it. So I nodded that I had gotten the signal. I kept going until I came to a place that could be cut. My radio family was used to this sort of thing so I didn't have to warn them. If I jumped lines I knew they would follow; if I ad libbed lines covering four or five speeches I knew they would be with me. So I jumped around in the last two or three speeches trying to make up for time and trying to come out on the nose. For instance, Rosie and Sammy didn't have to argue with each other onstage, so I told them that if they were going to fight they should go and fight in the kitchen where "Mama and Papa don't have to listen." They grumbled their way off mike and gave Jake and Molly enough time to say their finishing speeches and end the show.

There is nothing that can happen that can't be covered one way or another. Once, years later, during the television series, two out of three cameras went out. Something happened to their electrical insides and we had only one camera to shoot the show. Most of the action took place in three rooms and that meant three cameras were needed to cover the movements. When the floor manager indicated that two cameras were out by pulling a finger across his neck and then pointing, the idea was only too obvious. So instead of moving from the kitchen to the living room to the dining room we played the whole scene in the kitchen, making the necessary little line changes as we went along.

The whole day has been spent building itself up to the few minutes of concentrated attention that makes up the show. When it's all over and the red ON THE AIR signs go off there isn't a more lost feeling in the world. The wonderful, exciting, even glamorous, studio is now just a room dirty with coffee cartons and cigarette butts. The scripts that we all worked so hard on are crumpled and thrown away. The precise engineer, the man whose ear you rely on so much, has snapped off all his switches, coiled up microphone wires, and is putting on his rumpled coat to go home. The actress, that glamorous vamp, is just another girl with circles under her eyes. You look around to see a world dissolving into unused electrical connections. It's as though you've been climbing a ladder into a mythical land in the clouds, and when you look around, it turns out to be the basement of a hardware store. It's a letdown, believe me, and it takes a few hours to come back to the real world. The excitement that had made the whole day move so fast doesn't disappear so easily. You feel like you want to go to a party—but you know you can't.

The next morning always kept staring me in the face. There was another script to write and another plot line to think about. The whole object was to keep ahead as many scripts as possible. Sometimes I was a week ahead, sometimes two weeks, but I knew there was no margin for relaxing and for telling myself that I could stop for just one morning. I knew me too well. One morning off would stretch into two and before I knew it I would have to be writing scripts in a taxi on the way to the studio.

So what was there to do after the radio program? Go to 21? Go to The Copa? No. There's only time to go to Schrafft's for a soda, walk a few blocks, and then go home to bed. That's Show Biz, very glamorous!

If there's any glamour to radio and television it wears off very quickly. Familiarity breeds routine and it takes no time at all to walk into the greatest, biggest, fanciest studios in the world in the same way that you would walk into a drugstore. Glamour wears off. What sticks is ego. And it's the ego, the seeing yourself as you hope other people see you, that keeps every day from becoming a routine.

I think, sometimes, that I would be better off without my ego. Not that it's any bigger than anybody else's, maybe just a little more troublesome. As a matter of fact my son once wrote a poem about me:

> Committee on Molly
> headed by same,
> who's work shall consist
> of repeating her name.

Is that nice? Especially since it's close enough to the truth to make me a little annoyed.

But, like it or not, ego is something that a person needs even if it has a way of making things harder than they have to be. Especially if you happen to be like me, a person with two kinds of ego, forward and reverse. When things are going the way I want them to go I am in forward ego; when they aren't going the way I want, I'm in reverse. And reverse means a pretty black sort of mood. Lew tells me to take stock of myself and count up all the good days and all the good things, and when I do I feel ashamed of myself—but still I can't get away from feeling that I'm absolutely no good.

On the other hand, when I'm in a good mood, hardly anything can touch me. I feel so good that I make life harder for myself.

I remember, in the early days, when I had just started and the show was first a success, I was offered a two-week engagement at the Steel Pier in Atlantic City. Now, playing the Pier was a chance that didn't come to everyone and I took it. It was the height of personal appearances; there just wasn't anything better. Flattered is not the word for the way I felt, and when I told the cast the four of us acted as though our faces were going to be carved into the side of a mountain.

The Pier is a movie theater that juts out into the Atlantic from the boardwalk at Atlantic City. It's a big and very gaudy place. When we got to Atlantic City they were just taking down the electric lights on the marquee that read IN PERSON! AMOS AND ANDY! and they began to put up, LIMITED ENGAGEMENT! DIRECT FROM RADIO! "THE GOLDBERGS" IN PERSON!! That was very pleasing, especially at night when the yellow border lights chased themselves all around our name—and when the broadsides went up with our pictures. And it was also very pleasant to walk up and down the boardwalk smiling to people who smiled at me and stopping to sign autograph books.

Before we opened I talked with the manager of the theater,

who told me that *Amos and Andy* had done capacity business and that they had played six or seven shows a day. That's all I had to hear, my ego started to act up, and, naturally, I wanted to do better—but it wasn't up to me. Either people want to see you or they don't. There's no way to fill up a theater if audiences won't come. At first I was worried that people didn't want to see us. I conforted myself with the thought that if nobody wanted *The Goldbergs* we wouldn't have been asked to play the Pier because it was a big theater and one of Atlantic City's great attractions—and it wasn't the sort of place that took chances with acts.

The first day, playing five shows a day, we did very well—as well as *Amos and Andy*. The skit ran for ten or fifteen minutes. As always, I enjoyed myself but I got carried away. I went to the manager and told him if he wanted us to appear a few more times a day, all he had to do was ask. We'd be very happy to please. Well, the manager was no dope—we were playing to capacity—so he took off the main feature, kept the newsreel, and increased our appearances to ten times a day. We started at noon. Newsreel, *Goldbergs*, Newsreel, *Goldbergs*. We were on the stage all day until midnight. The only rest we got was during the newsreel. But we broke records—and that felt good. We didn't even get paid for the extra performances. We could have been, but it was more important to make the ego feel right than to ask for money.

When the ego makes you feel big, there's nothing bigger, but when it makes you feel small, you're infinitesimal. After the big successes Berg's law—"Watch out!"—comes into effect. The show had been on the air for the Pepsodent Company for three years. We had done well. We had an air audience of many millions of listeners. Our mail ran to six or seven thousand letters a week, and when Pepsodent ran a premium offer they were swamped with takers. For one label from their mouthwash and ten cents the company would send a Beetleware glass and they ran four to five months behind filling the orders. We knew we were popular, even by accountants' figures, and it came as a shock when I was told Pepsodent was canceling. It wasn't the show, they assured me. It was just a matter of shortages of material that went into the making of the glass mouth wash bottles. It sounded impossible and I thought they were trying to let me down easy. But it was the truth. I waited to see what show Pepsodent was going to put on the air after me but there wasn't any, and that meant more to me than the money. At least my pride was salvaged.

Yet, there's only one way to feel when you get that kind of news: terrible. And you know, no matter who says what, that it's all your fault. I tried to feel better by telling myself that things could be worse but I couldn't really make up anything that could be worse as far as my profession was concerned. The show wasn't out of work—we still had personal appearances and we could have them any time and any place we wanted. But that wasn't the point—we had been dropped by a sponsor and the only cure for that is another sponsor.

I started to think about a different sort of radio show. I was determined to get back on the air—if not for me, then for my family, because I was beginning to drive them wild. I thought and I thought and I came up with an idea that I called *The House of Glass*. It was about a man called Barney Glass who ran a hotel. I jotted down notes for a first script and I started to get excited. I went to the phone and called Tom Revere at Benton and Bowles, the agency that had sold *The Goldbergs*. I read the notes I had for Tom and he liked it. And when Tom Revere likes something, it has a chance. The show was sold inside of a week and a month after that it was on the air for Palmolive-Peet as a half-hour show once a week.

Now I was happy. My ego was satisfied for the time being

and all I had to worry about was the thirteen-week renewal cycle, whether people liked the show or not, or whether the sponsor was happy.

I was having fun with *The House of Glass*. It was Fleischmanns all over again—through a ribbon microphone. Barney Glass was my father. The hotel was full of guests, all of whom I had known. I used what I could remember of their stories, and where there were unhappy endings I added happy ones. The radio hotel always solved its problem with a laugh, and as far as reality was concerned all I had to do was change the names of the guests and I had my story line.

I would have been happier except for Burns and Allen. They went on opposite us after one year and they knocked us off the air. They were new, fresh, original, funny, great. There's nothing you can do against that sort of competition; even the ego will admit that. Palmolive took us off—and I was back home making trouble. But not for long. Tom Revere and Palmolive then asked if I'd go on for them across the board as a fifteen-minute show. If I hadn't said "yes," my family would have. So that's what I did.

The Goldbergs were on for Palmolive for two years. At the end of two years I took a break. I was trying to develop another idea for radio and it involved going to Hollywood. The trip was planned for three weeks—it lasted for nine months and the radio idea got turned into a movie.

While I was on the Coast Procter and Gamble decided *The Goldbergs* was for them, and after I came back to New York we went on the air. We stayed together for ten years and that, I think, is some sort of a record. Procter and Gamble were very good people to do a show for. We kept in our separate worlds. I wrote shows that sold soap—they made soap and never once made a single suggestion about what I should say or what I shouldn't say. Our ten years together were very agreeable and

I became superstitious about them. To me, the sight of P & G soap was always a good omen.

During those ten years everything about *The Goldbergs* changed but the theme song, "Toselli's Serenade." For instance, Jake's business failed in New York and we all moved to Lastonbury, Connecticut, where there was a deserted factory. The town was on its last legs and Jake and the citizens got together, pooled their money, and opened a dress business there. The stories in Lastonbury were also soap-operaish. Everything went along each day very smoothly and led up to the Friday cliffhanger. The family, in one episode, was held at gunpoint by an escaped criminal who was rude enough to keep refusing Molly's offer of hot tea. He was foiled on a Monday by Sammy calling to say he would be home late and Molly bawling him out for going with that terrible boy, Tom. Sammy knew there was something wrong because he had never known anyone called Tom—so he came home with the police.

Another story that took a few weeks was one about Mike Machuchak, a character based on Conrad the dishwasher. Mike was in love with a girl, a gold digger, who was after his hard-earned money. When Mike found out he said he didn't care because he loved the woman—and by that time she also loved him. It had a happy ending with everyone getting what they wanted: Mike got the girl, the girl got Mike and the money, and *The Goldbergs* had two more good friends.

During the ten years with Procter and Gamble Sammy and Rosie grew up. And when war was declared Sammy went off to the army in both lives, radio and real. We didn't have him on the show but we had letters from him and we did a story about a girl who came to the Goldbergs and said she was his wife. Of course she wasn't. She was found out in the end and there was a time there I played with the idea of really getting Sammy married. I didn't do it because I didn't want to encumber the family with another character at the moment. It was only when we got to television that Sammy finally got married.

Rosie, of course, went with boys, none of them suitable to her tastes but all of them with good points appreciated only by Molly, Jake, and Uncle David.

Gradually *The Goldbergs* became a situation comedy and the tragedies we dealt in before were treated with a different eye. Uncle David didn't want to become a burden to the Goldbergs or to his son—a human sort of problem—so he took up salesmanship. He sold graveyard plots to all his nearest and dearest friends and relatives. He ran into a snag when Tante Elka refused to be buried next to Cousin Simon, the skinflint of the family. Since those were the only two plots left and there was no real solution—no one else would want to "lie down by Simon"—David gave up selling plots.

Essentially the family remained the same. They changed with the times but they still looked at the world in their own way. Jake made dresses with long hem lines when the fashion decreed and shortened them when the word came from Paris. Molly took her friends where she found them and that included a kleptomaniac on a bus. Sammy went to engineering school after the army and Rosie kept on playing one boy against the other. David argued constantly that his cousin's son, a dentist, wasn't a doctor; Solly the Doctor was a doctor, but positively a dentist isn't a doctor.

The mail that we received—sometimes thousands of letters a week—served two purposes. It showed the sponsors that people were really listening, and it gave me a feeling, a relationship, with an audience that I never got to see. Letters came from all over the country, and, contrary to everyone's belief, the majority of the mail didn't come from the Jewish population. *The Goldbergs* cut across religious divisions. The audience refused to be typed and from the mail I learned a great lesson:

There is no way for anyone to predict what the American public is going to like, going to do, or going to say. I've gotten letters from priests, ministers, and rabbis, and from millionaires and paupers. Letters have been signed by every possible sort of name from Arajibian to Zelinowsky, and I'm proud of it. I didn't set out to make a contribution to interracial understanding. I only tried to depict the life of a family in a background that I knew best. The reactions of the people who listened only showed that we all respond to human situations and human emotions—and that dividing people into rigid racial, economic, social, or religious groups is a lot of nonsense.

PART FOUR

TILLIE BRANCHES OUT

1 *"Broadway"*

In 1948 I was off radio and looking for some way to make the transition to television. I had more time for myself than I knew what to do with. I had always been in the habit of waking at six in the morning to write scripts. Then all of a sudden I found myself waking up early and having nothing to write. That's when I decided it was about time to get to my play. It didn't come out of the blue because I had had the idea for some years but I had never seemed to be able to find time to write it. In 1948 I had the time. The only thing I needed was someone to tell me I was doing the right thing. I knew it was going to be a tough job but I wanted encouragement, especially from my family.

The first person I asked was Lew. His reaction was more than just encouragement; he practically made up the first-night reviews for me. He saw the future like a kindhearted fortune-teller—everything was going to be great, nothing could be bad, and there wasn't a critic alive that would dare say one bad word about me or my play. I was flattered that when it came to me Lew forgot about freedom of the press.

My daughter's reaction was also that a play would be a great idea and she started to bring me books about the Elizabethan theater, a college speciality of hers, and books on the theory of playwriting, and copies of Strindberg, Ibsen, and Bertolt Brecht. When I told her I thought I was going to do a comedy she then started to load my night table with Karel Čapek and Bernard Shaw. Well, she was a Barnard girl at the time, discovering what had never existed before, and I never dared tell her that I put away the books until I had written the play. It was going to be a hard enough job without competing with the masters.

My son was no longer living at home. He was going to graduate school and was writing very modern music. He was also engaged. So the only time I ever got to speak to him about anything was on the phone. I called him to find out what he thought about my writing a play and his reaction was simply, "It's about time!"

My reaction to his reaction was, "When are we going to see you? Come for supper?" Cherney told me that if in the midst of art I could still talk like a mother the least he could do was to act like a son and come see the old folks at home. He even promised to get a haircut, and for him that's the height of filial devotion.

The last person on my list to call and tell was a famous producer who had been asking me to write a play for a number of years. He had even given me an advance, so when I told him that, finally, I was setting about writing the play, he wanted to know the exact date I could deliver it to him. I said I didn't know but that I would like to spend a few sessions talking to him about it.

Ideas take so many different forms before they finally hit their final, workable, shape that talking it out is always a good plan. That was the producer's idea and mine at the time. The only trouble was that we hardly ever got to talk about the play. Our meetings took place in Sardi's, and Sardi's is a place where mostly theater people gather. My producer friend was a theater person of some importance and he knew everyone. So as we sat at our table the theater world would pass by and stop to spend time discussing this and that. If I had been a gossip columnist I would have had enough information from one lunch to fill twenty columns. I heard that so and so's play, due to open in a few days, was not only having second-act trouble, but also first and third. The leading man was getting divorced again and the leading lady, playing the part of an eighteen-year-old unmarried nice but frigid virgin, was showing her pregnancy a little too much—and to add to that trouble, her husband, a doctor, refused to let her wear a corset—and the lawyers were getting nowhere. It was very obvious, my producer told his friend, that the play was going to be a hit. He explained when I sympathized with the troubles that it was only when things ran smoothly that you could expect trouble.

People would run up to the table and say, "Hello there!" or women would drop by to say, "Hello, darling!", and he'd always smile and say hello back. After they passed by he would say he'd never seen them before in his life but if it made them feel better and more important he didn't mind. The theater was one place where ego and childish behavior were assets. If an actor didn't act as though he were the most important person in the theater he wouldn't last ten minutes. An actor has to have a big ego to put up with what he must put up with. His life was terrible, according to the producer. First of all, to be an actor you have to study, take voice lessons, acting lessons, dancing lessons, fencing lessons, because it's possible to have a part in a Shakespearean play or understudy Errol Flynn. Then the actor has to make his rounds. That means going from production office to production office and being told there's no work. Even broke, an actor has to look neat and prosperous—as though he had just finished fifty-two weeks with a hit play. Finally when he does get a job, who knows if the play is going to be a hit or a flop? Even if it's a hit and the actor starts to make a steady salary—a high one according to weekly wages in other jobs—he's been out of work so long that he averages thirty cents a day free and clear, because his salary is used to pay debts. My producer friend said he couldn't understand why anybody would subject himself to such a profession—but he understood all right.

As I sat around Sardi's I began to understand a little about the theater and what makes it go. The secret is that no one feels inferior. The actor says his job is the most important. An actor doesn't need a playwright, all an actor needs is a stage—he can say what has to be said without a script. The playwright knows that's wrong. He's the most important. The last thing he needs is actors. His words have meaning, if they're read or if they're spoken, and without him there wouldn't be a theater. The director can prove that this isn't so. Without him plays wouldn't make sense. Writers need his advice and actors need his guidance, so there's no argument. He's the most important. The set designer doesn't argue. Just let someone try a play against a dirty brick wall and they'll see he's the one who makes or breaks it. The producer is really the theater according to the producer. Without his ability to raise money, his astute judgment about what makes a good play and who the best actors are for it, there would be no theater at all. There are people who will argue with him but they're all working in plays at the moment. The stagehands have their own view, they won't even discuss the matter. They have a very strong union so they don't have to. If any one wants to argue they can always strike to prove the point.

If you ask about the audience and want to know how important they are to the whole of the theater, the subject changes very quickly. An audience is a necessary evil in spite of the fact that they are the very ones that all this ego is directed at. And they are the ones who ultimately decide—hit or flop.

Anyway, the producer and I talked. We discussed anything and everything, but not the play.

I knew nothing about writing a play but I did know that first things came first and when first things (gossip) were all finished, maybe then we would talk about it. So I kept meeting the producer and then going home to keep on writing.

When the play was finished—according to me, finished—I brought him the manuscript. I didn't know about length. I had three acts, a plot, a good beginning, middle, and end. The producer took one look at the play, weighed it in his hand and asked me what it was, *The Iceman Cometh?* He took the play with him and we kept on meeting at Sardi's. We also kept on talking about everything but the play. I was getting restless and I kept asking about my play. The producer kept saying that there was time, and there was except that I was restless and I didn't want to wait—but I had to. I didn't know what else to do.

I was learning something but I didn't know I was learning. In the theater there's always time. Things get done but they get done in their own way. I was told that the producer would get around to me and my play but I had to be patient—and I'm not the patient type.

I went to visit my daughter that summer. Harriet was in the stage-struck phase of growing up and she was working as an assistant apprentice stage manager at a summer theater in Connecticut. From her letters I knew she was enjoying herself. She wrote about all the excitement and glamour of the summer theater and invited me to come and see. I went and I saw, and all I can say is that the summer theater is for the young, the strong, and the healthy. I thought I had brought up my daughter to be a lady, but there she was lugging scenery from the shop to the stage; standing on ten-foot ladders and painting backdrops; staying up all night drinking coffee and discussing whether or not the gelatines over the spotlights should be blue or magenta. And which color was true to Strindberg and which wasn't. I suppose glamour is a matter for definition. To me it looked like hard work.

But she was doing fine and enjoying herself, and, being my

daughter, she was also talking. She mentioned to one of the young men who ran the theater that I had written a play.

Part of the business of a summer theater is to find a play that will be suitable for the winter theater, Broadway. Also, during the winter, part of the winter theater's business is to find a play that will be suitable for the summer. The whole object is to have as little time not working as possible. In the theater there are no vacations—time off is called "between projects," and that's really what it is because there's no peace unless something is going on. The most restful times are the days after good reviews.

The fact that I had a play and the fact that one of the men at the summer theater was looking for a play, would, in any other sort of business, mean something. In the theater it usually doesn't mean a thing. Theater people have a habit of optioning anything from a three-page outline of a saga in blank verse to the telephone book just in case they happen to think of something to do with it. Sometimes they even think of buying a finished play but not often.

This time my play, *Me and Molly,* was read and liked. But that means nothing even though it sounds like something. For every producer who doesn't like a play there's one that does. It's not just that opinion is divided—it's all mixed up. If one producer likes a first act then the second producer doesn't but he's crazy for the third act, and if they ever agree then the director hates the whole thing but he sees a little hope in the stage directions.

So, the play was liked by one man and he wanted to show it to Oliver Smith, a producer and designer of great talent and imagination.

Oliver Smith read the play, loved it, and wanted to do it. Was that a step forward? I was naive enough to think so. But I had a commitment with John Golden and I didn't know what to do.

I returned his advance and told him, right or wrong, I wanted to put the play on. He agreed with me, said he still wanted to do it, but he couldn't promise me any definite production date. Oliver Smith got the play, but—first he had to attend to another project, *The Big Bonanza* which was opening in Philadelphia. After that would come my play.

I went to Philly for the opening of *Bonanza* and then I rode back on the train with Oliver Smith. Now that *Bonanza* was on I thought it was my turn. On the trip back I kept asking what was going to happen. I wanted to know when—I didn't care about where or how. That wasn't my business. But, again, I kept getting "buts" and "Gertrude, there are a couple of things you have to understand. . . ."

By now Gertrude was beginning to understand. I started at the beginning. I asked Oliver if he liked the play. He did. I asked him if he wanted to do the play. He did. I asked him what the trouble was and again I started to hear a whole set of explanations that explained nothing. So I asked him if it was a matter of money. He said it was—that's exactly what it was.

The problem of money was nothing, I thought. If the producer liked the play and wanted to do the play that was all I wanted to hear. There had to be a way of getting money. Up to then I had always thought that a producer who wanted to do a play wrote a check and that was that. But that's not the way it is. A producer has to raise the money from everyone and anyone who is willing to take his word that he has a "great" play in his pocket.

I sat down to think of who could help. And when I sit down to think about people, I sit down with Fanny.

Now Fanny Merrill is someone I have to describe but I'm sure I can't. She's more than a friend, more than a business associate, more than a right arm. She's closer to me than a sister and she knows more about me than I do myself. We've been together for a good many years. We've been mothers together and grandmothers together and we knew each other when— from black hair to gray—and we've told each other things that sometimes we don't even say to ourselves.

I met Fanny by mistake. I thought she was a radio critic from Philadelphia, but instead she turned out to be a friend, and a person I came to rely on for everything. In my dressing room, at Sardi's, at home, at the studio, it's always Fanny I turn to, Fanny who knows everyone and everything. Fanny could be on a desert island and she'd know the visiting cannibal chief. She'd know him from when he first started out as an extra at the old Fox studios in the Bronx.

Fanny never forgets an appointment, she never forgets a name, and she almost never forgets a phone number. The only ones she doesn't remember are the numbers of people she doesn't like. As far as Fanny is concerned those people don't even exist. It's lucky for the world that there are a very few of them.

Fanny has a method of filing that would make IBM change their motto from THINK to HELP! She writes things down on little scraps of paper and stuffs them into a clasp envelope. When she has to look something up, she empties the envelope and goes through each piece of paper. That's one reason why her memory has gotten so good—it's easier to remember than to go through the envelope.

Together, Fanny and I went through each scrap of paper and we made lists of lists of "who do we know." I was going to get the play produced no matter what and Fanny was just as determined. There must be someone among all the people the two of us knew who could help us raise money for such a simple thing as a play.

We came, finally, to the most wonderful, generous, and logical person in the world, George Gershwin's mother. Rose Gershwin was one of those people who is always ready to help—no matter what and no matter who. I asked her if she knew anyone who would be interested in backing a play—and Rose knew. How many did I want and where did I want them, she asked. I didn't know how these things were done so I said I would have a little party for her friends—and then I would read them a few scenes from the play.

I was working in the dark. At the time I didn't know that this was the way things usually are done. I called Oliver Smith to tell him what I was doing and he didn't say a word except that I was to call him when it was all over. So I had the party. I figured that since I was asking people for money, the least I could do was to feed them. I fed them first and then I read to them and by the time the party was over the play was financed.

The play was the story of Jake and his family set in 1919 just after the First World War. Jake was a man with ambition and a conscience. He wanted to go into the dress business as his own boss—sound familiar?—because he didn't want always to be the last sewing machine near the window. He said, "I wouldn't rest in my grave if I didn't die a businessman." Jake persuaded a friend, Mendel, who worked with him in a dress factory to become his partner in a new venture. The whole plan hinged on Molly's rich cousin Simon, who was also in the dress business. Simon was always the villain in *The Goldbergs,* and he stayed the villain in the play. He refused to help Jake —and that meant that Mendel wouldn't be Jake's partner. Mendel didn't want to be a businessman anyway—his ambition was to be a druggist, because it was the closest thing to a doctor that he could be at this late time in his life. Jake began to feel worse and worse but not bad enough to give up hope. He took in as new partners two men who lived in the apartment building. They pooled their life savings and Jake took a lease on a loft, rented machines, and bought dress silks. The wives of Jake's new partners objected. They went to see Molly and told her that they weren't willing to take a chance with all their savings—they told Molly to tell Jake that the partnership was off. Molly, who understood how they felt, promised that Jake would return the borrowed money. When Jake came home full of hope and plans Molly told him what had happened. Jake was willing to return the money but it had all been spent and Jake's savings had gone also—and he couldn't pay back the money from week to week because he had just quit his job. There was no hope. There wasn't even a chance of a business reconciliation with Mendel because Mendel was willing to be a friend, not a partner. Jake borrowed on his life insurance, paid back his loans, and looked forward to a very bleak future. Molly, meanwhile, had been playing with an idea that she had had for a long time. Manufactured dresses didn't fit her and she wondered about why there weren't the odd sizes—"half sizes," she called them. Without Jake's knowing, Mendel made Molly a few sample half-size patterns and Molly sewed dresses for neighbors with the same problem she had. It worked fine. Simon knew a good thing when he heard one. He offered Jake a corner in his factory, a machine by a window, where he could experiment with half sizes. Jake was willing but Molly wasn't. She didn't care for Simon's attitude and the way he said that he would revolutionize the dress business. Jake was still going to be a hired hand and that's not what Jake wanted. Simon was insulted and again Jake saw his hopes blow away. Molly told him that once he had been able to raise money for a business without an idea—and now he was a man with an idea and nothing should stop him. In the meantime, even though he had no job and no regular payday, the family would get along because finally Jake was going to be doing what he had always wanted to do. Curtain.

The play went into rehearsal not long after my money-raising party—and it was an experience. I had been going to plays all my life and I found out, on the stage, that I had never really been to one. It's a strange new world that no one can tell you about—it has to be discovered by yourself, all alone on the stage. First of all, there's a new language that has to be learned. I could talk radio very easily, but stage talk was a foreign tongue. I had to get used to stage right, which is on my left, and stage left, which is on my right. When you think of it from the audience's point of view it makes sense, but to a newcomer it was an upside-down world. Scenery flew and the wings stood still. A stage that looks tremendous from an orchestra seat gets smaller and smaller the more you work on it. Canvas flats become brick walls with a little paint and a lot of talent; wine is cold tea and hot coffee is colored water. The only real things on the stage are the actors—and your husband, son, and daughter are strangers backstage and your nearest and dearest as soon as the lights go up and the curtain rises.

By the time we were ready to open in Philadelphia I was ready to give up. I had started out with a play and I had begun this new part of my life with confidence. I had worked hard and everyone else had worked hard. We all had a goal but I didn't have a perspective. I had been working on both sides of the stage. On the stage I was an actress, on the other side, sitting with the director in the empty orchestra, I was the writer. Oh, I had to argue with myself. As an actress some speeches pleased me very much. As a writer I could see that they had to be cut or taken out completely because they stopped the action of the play. I had to be brave when I told my actress self that her favorite lines would have to go—and I had to be ruthless as a writer in cutting juicy, well-written lines. And that wasn't all of it. At two in the morning Ezra Stone, our director, would call me on the phone and say, "You know, just before the second-act curtain where Jake and

Mendel argue? I think Mendel's speech has to be much stronger. It would play better ..." Then I'd get out of bed, go over to the desk and look over the scene and try to do what I could to make it stronger. I kept wondering if there weren't easier ways to become a nervous wreck.

Curtain time came closer and closer. During rehearsals I listened to every line that was said and wondered if it should be changed. Ezra Stone kept trying to make me feel easier and confident. Oliver Smith tried to soothe me. But nothing helped. It was like telling a condemned man to eat his oatmeal before it got cold—that's all he's got to worry about.

The time came. The curtain went up, I went on, and I found myself in the middle of a three-sided, union-built, canvas apartment—and I was still nervous. I wasn't worried about the play any longer. It was too late for that. I was worried about the audience. But when laughs came in the places I had thought they would come I began to feel a little better. It was only after the curtain fell on the third act that I could relax for a little bit. But even that respite didn't last long. When someone said, "They'll love the play in New York," I began to worry all over again. I had almost forgotten we had another opening night to go through.

After we opened in New York and received excellent reviews, everybody said that I had been foolish to worry. But I knew better. I'm a firm believer in anxiety and in the power of negative thinking. I was sure that if I had said to myself that the play was great, it would have turned out to be terrible— and if I thought, even for a minute, that the reviews were going to be wonderful, they would have been pans. That's my theory, but I'm never going to test it out by saying that a play is going to be a success. Its better to be a coward and run for a year than to be a brave and close in a week.

2 "Life Among the Electrons"

It was during the time that *Me and Molly* was running on Broadway that I saw somebody was writing on the wall. The translation was simple: all the writing said was, "Television!" It was easy to see that radio was on the way out. There were lots of people in radio who didn't want to believe the moving finger and every control room was a little replica of a Hollywood movie studio when somebody mentioned sound. It couldn't happen, it wouldn't catch on, and it was a trick. But as they talked they began to make other plans. It didn't take long for the halls, the corridors, and the studios of the radio stations to lose that feeling of excitement that made radio what it was.

Getting into television was the next step for me. I threw the whole problem into my agent's lap because an agent is a person who's supposed to be able to do anything. The truth of the matter is, he isn't. He's human, too. Most agents don't like to admit it but it's so. An agent is what he is because of the people he represents. He's a business manager, an adviser, a man who gets you work, and he's the man who knows everything that is happening everywhere in the entertainment world. And he's the man you blame when things go wrong. There's nothing better than a good agent and nothing worse than a bad one. My agent was good and so I felt that everything was going to be all right and I'd be on television.

What I didn't know was that there were people in the business that could only see out of one eye. To them, one thing was one thing, and another thing was another and never the twain shall meet even if they asked for an introduction. *The Gold-*

bergs had been on radio for almost twenty years and there were people who just couldn't see it as television material. "It wouldn't translate," was the way they expressed it. The reason it wouldn't translate was because they couldn't speak the language.

My agent would call me one day to say that N.B.C. didn't think *The Goldbergs* could be a television show. Well, that was *their* opinion. I knew different. So I told my agent to get to work on C.B.S. He did and he called back a few days later to say an audition was all arranged. Good! I started to think about a script. Then I got another call from my agent—the audition was off. They also thought that the show wasn't for TV.

I got annoyed. I was also worried. If you're turned down by N.B.C. and C.B.S. then you're out of business, and that was something I decided I wasn't. That night I couldn't sleep. I tossed and I turned and I burned. About three in the morning I tried to wake up Lew and tell him about a decision I had made, but he was already awake listening to me fuming. I said I couldn't and I wouldn't take this lying down, that was my decision. Lew said I should relax, it was three in the morning, there wasn't anything that could be done. I couldn't even call my agent at that hour. So I tried to relax until daylight. At nine-thirty I picked up the phone. I had decided I wasn't going to talk to "executives," I was going to talk to their boss. A Boss is a Boss and if you're a boss it's not by accident. William S. Paley was the boss so I called and asked for an appointment. I was told that Mr. Paley was leaving to go on a cruise and he didn't have much time. I said I didn't need much time. The secretary said would ten or fifteen minutes be sufficient and I said three minutes would be plenty.

I went to see Mr. Paley. I had never met him before and the only thing I knew about him was his reputation and the fact that he had a very beautiful wife. I knew his time was short so

I said "hello" and got down to business. I told him that I was supposed to have had an audition of *The Goldbergs* for television and that it had been canceled. I said that I thought he should know about that. Then I told him that the show might be a flop on TV—or it might be great. I had been on radio for twenty years, fourteen of them on C.B.S., and I said I thought I deserved an audition.

That took two minutes. The third minute was Mr. Paley's. He got up from behind his desk, came over to where I was sitting, put a hand on my shoulder and told me that I would have my audition. That was that and I left.

By the time I got back home the phone began to ring. There were apologies from various quarters at C.B.S. and an audition was planned. Believe me, there's nothing like three minutes with the boss.

I began working on the audition script. I wanted it to be simple, funny, and to show what the series could be. An audition script is a very peculiar form. It's probably the hardest of all scripts to write because it has to show the past, the present, and the future of all the characters. It has to project in one half hour the possibilities of thirty-nine other shows. And it has to convince the network, the advertising agency, and the possible sponsor that the show is exactly what they want and what they need. And that's not so easy, believe me, because what they want and what they need may be two entirely different things and either or both may be determined by what they see. If what they see is a good show, then usually that's what they may decide to take—nothing is ever definite. That's why writing an audition scrip is so different. Believe me, writing a script for an audience is much easier. You're writing for their enjoyment and not because they're possible sponsors, and the problems you have to solve are dramatic ones. The audition script has those problems also but in addition it has the added ones of exposing characters and situations in a way that's unnatural to them because they are being judged, not enjoyed.

Of course, *The Goldbergs* had been on radio for a good many years and everyone knew about them. But during their radio days they had been a little of everything. They were a real make-believe family with heart-tugging emotional problems, and they had been a situation-comedy family with funny but human problems. What were they going to be on television? It seemed natural that the comedy format was for TV. The radio show had developed into a comedy out of afternoon tragedy and I wanted to keep it that way.

Nobody really suggested that the format of the show as a situation comedy should be changed, but also, nobody really stood up and said that that's exactly what it should be. Television was still a baby. The studio was being built around us as we rehearsed and there were no experts who knew what some other experts told them a survey said the public wanted. Mr. Paley had ordered an audition. Mr. Paley was the boss. So, there was going to be an audition.

In those days a television show was done live. There were no kinescopes, no tape, nothing but cameras and actors, writers, producers, and directors. It took five days of hard work to put a half-hour show on the air. If you didn't see it when it left the transmitter, you missed it.

The audition show was to be done for an audience of agency representatives and network officials. They were to watch it over studio monitors, and they were going to make up their minds about what they saw as soon as they saw it. The only thing we could do, the actors, the director, the cameramen, the soundmen, the floor manager, and the stagehands, was to learn our lines, pay attention to the floor marks, and do the best we knew how.

We all knew that there was going to be one chance and no

more. Our audience was going to be ten men and as the time for the show came closer I kept feeling like saying to them, "We who are about to audition, salute you."

It was a very serious business but even in the middle of such concentrated and painstaking work of rehearsal I felt like giggling. Again I was a fish in an aquarium being watched by divers who had descended from "upstairs" in the station and some who had traveled all the way from the agency for this performance. The men all wore dark suits, conservative British regimental-type ties, highly polished shoes, and they all carried gold cigarette lighters. A gold lighter is to television people what the handcuffs are to a policeman. Without them a man is out of uniform. They wore everything they were supposed to wear because they were victims of their own brilliantly thought out fads and diseases. They wore hats because the ads said women went for men in hats. They wore garters because their ads showed men who didn't wear them being fired by bosses whose socks stayed up. And from time to time they would chew on mints full of secret ingredients for their stomach's sake.

In contrast to the executive type were the worker types. The cameramen in slacks and shirts had their eyes glued to their finders. They wore earphones and mikes through which they could hear the director's orders and could talk back to him when it was necessary. Cameras would push into the set and their three-lensed turrets would look in at you very inquisitively. As soon as you started talking a mike on a long boom would drop to a few inches from the top of your head and as soon as you stopped talking it turned like a scared fish and scooted overhead to where another actor was starting to say his lines. It was just like having Big Brother and his whole family watching.

After the dry run in which we worked through our positions and places, the cameras were warmed up and the hard work began. We had just a few hours to put all the elements together and in that first audition we had to become veterans in five hours.

The cast of the first show had done very little TV. In those days, 1948, there was very little TV to do. But they were all veterans of radio and the stage, and they knew how to make believe. Sammy was played by Larry Robinson—he was Sammy at seventeen. Rosie was played by Arlene McQuade—she was supposed to be my fourteen-year-old daughter. I had known Arlene for years. She played a neighbor's child on radio when she was five and couldn't read a line. I would read her part to her and she would memorize it, cues and all. She even memorized everybody else's parts and could prompt them. When we were on the air I would have her stand next to me so that I could put my hand over her mouth until it was her turn to say her lines.

Jake was played by Phillip Loeb, a veteran of Broadway and the movies, and Uncle David was played by Menasha Skulnik.

Finally the time for a dress rehearsal came and after that there was nothing more to do except the audition itself. We took our places, waited for the floor manager to give us our cue. The theme was played, the opening titles went on camera, dissolved slowly, and the floor manager pointed a finger at us—and we were on.

We went through the audition script forgetting that anyone was watching us. We had no time to worry about anything except our lines, our movements, and our places. It was only after the closing credits passed across the screen that it occurred to me that we had finished our audition. So far as I could tell from the inside, it had been a smooth performance. But sometimes that isn't enough.

The result was immediate acceptance. The agency said they wanted the show and General Foods bought it and we went on the air Monday nights at 9:00.

It didn't take long for us to become veterans. After one week we were telling one another what every piece of equipment was used for. When someone used a technical word such as "aspect ratio" the rest of us would nod in agreement. Actually we were completely in the dark.

After a few months, we stopped fooling ourselves and left electronics to those who really knew. That was when we really became veterans—able to settle down to the five-day routine needed to put together one live half hour.

The first day of the five was one in which the actors read their lines and I made whatever corrections were needed. Sometimes the script timed out too long and sometimes too short. With experience I was able to tell from the number of typewritten pages just about how a script would time, but for the audition I didn't know a thing. Sometimes lines would have to be changed to suit the actors and sometimes new scenes would have to be written or rewritten completely in order to revise the sense of the script.

On the second day of rehearsal the bare floor of the rehearsal hall would be taped out with masking tape to the exact dimensions of the floor plan of the set. Folding chairs and card tables would take the place of overstuffed chairs, sofas, doors, stoves, statues, and then we would walk through the action the director had planned. On the third day the technical director, the man in charge of the cameramen and soundmen, would come and watch us go through the script. He would then make out "shot sheets" with the director for the use of the cameramen. The "shot sheet" is a map of which camera goes to what set, when, how long, and who is in the shot, and then it tells the cameraman where he goes next. The fourth day is just like the other three except by now all the actors must have memorized their lines and movements. Also, time is taken with costumes and a last-minute run down of props is made. Some scripts would call for a complete ten-course meal, some would need a car, some would need a rainstorm, some might need a pool table or the interior of a Greyhound bus. Whatever was needed was gotten. In one script a baby grand piano was needed. It was going to be hoisted through an open window and to the technicians in the studio it was a minor problem. The only problem they couldn't solve was bringing an elephant up in an elevator to a variety show. The elephant was too heavy and too scared. So they did the only thing they could do—they didn't ask for the script to be changed, they brought the whole studio, sets and all, down to the first floor so the elephant could just walk in off the street.

All this time the producer is making sure that whatever is needed is being built or purchased; that the costumes are right; that all the personnel and equipment are ready for the big day; that the contracts are signed, and that the actors, technicians, ad men, studio executives, are happy. The producer knows where every nail in the set happens to be. He inspects and approves everything and no matter what is asked for he makes sure that there's a way to get it.

The fifth day is camera day and the day the show is broadcast. It is also the day when the sets are brought in from the workshops and set up. The furniture and set dressings are put in place while the lighting director starts to hang his equipment and to get ready for the final lighting. It's a process that goes on all day long. The sets are all up and dressed by the time the actors come to the studio and that's about ten in the morning. The next process is called "dry rehearsal" on the set. No cameras are used but the cameramen and other technicians are now present. As the actors go through their lines and movements they follow with their shot sheets and make themselves familiar with the show.

These technicians were always my best audience. If they

laughed I knew a line was really funny—if they didn't laugh I wanted to know why and they never made any bones about telling me. ("That punch line has no punch, Mrs. Berg!") They worked hard and well and they had as much pride in the show as I did. I never met a technician yet that said something was good enough when he knew he could make it a little better. Everybody was part of the show and we never had to worry that camera number one wouldn't be where he was supposed to be at the exact moment he was supposed to be there.

Everything come together on the fifth day and from the actors' point of view it looked like chaos. From the control room's point of view it was organized confusion. The director would be ordering his cameras to move from one set to another; he was setting up shots so that he could catch the action in the best possible way; he was making sure the microphones were exactly where they should be so that the words could be heard—and everything was supposed to be timed down to the split second. And while he was doing all this, he would be dictating notes to his assistant so that he could correct the actors, not only as far as their position was concerned, but also as to interpretation. The control room always reminded me of a place where one man with twenty hands lived.

As soon as we would finish a run-through we would break for ten minutes and then start in again until everyone knew exactly what he was to do when the show went on the air.

After all the technical obstacles have been hurdled and the show goes out over the air, the big test is yet to be passed— the test of being liked by the audience. Our ratings, fortunately, were high. We were in the top ten on all the scales and because we were so high I defended the rating services. There was nothing wrong with them. It's a funny thing about ratings. As long as you're on top they're wonderful, but if you ever begin to drop they have no meaning. It's like critics—if you get good reviews they're important to the theater. If you get bad ones, then the critics are ruining the American stage. Because it's not a matter for logic, it's a matter of being liked.

If I say the show was well-liked I'm only being grateful. We had very loyal audiences who followed us from C.B.S. to N.B.C. and on to film. It was always a wonderful feeling to know that there were people at the other end of the camera who didn't think of us as a television program but as friends. We felt the same way about them.

But, as in everything else, there's a backstage and an out front. I've often wondered what our audiences would have thought of us if they could have seen us getting ready to make believe. Take Eli Mintz who replaced Menasha Skulnik in the part of Uncle David as an example. Everybody who saw the show thinks of Eli as a kindly old sensible gentleman. He is when he puts on his mustache and his Uncle David costume, a frayed, much too large suit that was never pressed by the dresser on purpose. But the real Eli is a much younger man, quite fashionable, and very self-assured. It was almost a frightening experience to watch him become Uncle David as the camera day went along. Eli's make-up took a long time and he did it himself gradually during the day. First he would appear with powder in his hair; then one half of his face would be pancaked, and later the other half. Next he would appear in the baggy pants and the old-fashioned shirt and collar, then the mustache, and finally he would come out complete. The stagehands and cameramen who had been joking with Eli all day long would start to treat him with the respect due an elderly uncle.

Working with actors and actresses almost every day in the week means that you meet every possible variation in human behavior. We had an actor who hired a lawyer by the hour to negotiate contracts for him. He didn't work that often so he said that he didn't need a full time counselor. We had an actress —no names because she won't believe it anyway—who was very stubborn. She took direction very well and understood exactly what the director wanted her to do and could even do it for him whenever she was asked. Her only trouble was on the air. Then, when she thought no one was looking and because she knew she couldn't be stopped right then and there, she did her part her own way. We would never have used her again after that first time except for one thing: She was a wonderful actress.

Then there was another actress who was just fine during rehearsals. We all expected a great show, but when camera day came around she didn't show up. We called every place we could think of including her own home—but there was never an answer. Finally we sent someone over to where she lived and there she was, happily drinking and rehearsing her part. The studio doctor went over to see her but medicine hadn't progressed far enough yet to make her sober. Time was running out. We had a seven-thirty show to do and obviously we had no actress. We called in a few women who we thought could do the part on practically a minute's notice but it was too much to ask. There was only one thing to do and that was to call the sponsor in Chicago and ask for permission to put on a show we had done before, one that had been recorded on film. We were given the go ahead, the agency was notified and reluctantly approved. It was all right with everyone but the cast and the studio crew. We had worked ourselves into a state of excitement for the show and at five in the evening we were told we could go home. It was like being out of work. We didn't know what to do with ourselves so we stayed in the studio to watch the film. Everyone looked but me. I sat in a corner and listened. If there's one thing I can't do, that's watch myself act. I never have and I hope I never will. Maybe it's because I'm afraid I won't like myself or maybe it's because I feel that once I do see what I've done I'll become self-conscious about my acting. Whatever it is, that's the way it's always going to be.

Everybody thinks actors are characters, but if you ask an actor who he thinks is a character he'll say the directors. They're the character's character. They all come with their own special brand. One director we had wouldn't speak to the actors until they all chewed chlorophyll gum. Another one gave us antihistamines as soon as the temperature dropped and he saw that winter was coming. Another director loved scenes with thunder and lightning and sometimes a little rain, provided he could use real water and not the special-effects machine that just made it look as though it was raining. When the time came to give the cue for lightning he would stand up in the control room, point a finger towards heaven and shout, "Let there be lightning!" He would call for rain by stretching his two hands out over the control table and saying, very gently, "Pour forth." For thunder he would point a finger at the sound-effects man and yell, "Boom!" He said that these scenes gave him a feeling of power and that he liked to pander to his megalomania now and then.

A television studio is a great meeting ground but it's not a melting pot. It's more like a kitchen shelf where everything and everyone has a place. This can be seen during the ten-minute break that comes once every hour. The director is in a huddle with his group of helpers. The technicians gather together except when there's a pretty actress on the set, then they gather wherever she is. The actors mostly go off by themselves to mumble lines. There are only two things that unite these groups. The show is one and the advertising agency is the other.

Every time a live show is done the agency sends down a representative who speaks for them and for the sponsor. Sometimes it's a man and a girl assistant—sometimes it's a woman with a man assistant. They arrive about one hour before the show goes on to time the commercials and check the sponsor's message to the public. Their job is to make sure there has been no tampering—as though anyone would dare. All these people have eagle eyes, sharp ears, and they all carry stop watches. As soon as the commercial begins the click of the starting watches raises the sound level in the studio. As soon as the commercial has been timed and O.K.'d for expression and interpretation, the stop watches are put away until showtime. Then they time the commercials all over again.

Sometimes they have suggestions to make about the show. One agency man objected to a teapot in the kitchen set because the sponsor manufactured coffee. It was a very good point and it showed that he was paying attention because a microscope was needed to spot the tea pot. I will say that this kind of suggestion was very rare. For the most part the sponsor and the agency hardly bothered me. They would send me the points they wanted incorporated into a commercial and I would write them. If there were ever changes they were minor. I have always had amiable relationships with my sponsors. Their products sold—even to me. I still use the toothpaste I first started to advertise on radio. I still drink the coffee without caffeine before I go to bed—and in the morning I use another coffee I advertised but this one has caffeine. The sewing machine I use once sponsored me. I haven't changed my floor wax since I had one as a sponsor. And I'm sure I'm healthy because of the vitamins I once sold and still use.

I'm loyal but sometimes I've laughed at what went on and I've often thought of doing a show from three points of view —from the actor's, from the writer's, and from the sponsor's. The show would be in three acts. First we would see what the actor thinks the show is all about. It would be just close-ups of the actor. When he wasn't saying his lines and other actors were talking, the sound would be turned down very low so that it would be almost impossible to hear them. When The Actor had lines to say the sound would go back on very loud and very clear, perhaps with just a touch of echo for the cosmic touch.

The writer's scene would have no actors, only beautiful colors on the screen and the lines would be read by Sir Laurence Olivier and Dame Judith Anderson.

The sponsor's view of the show would be just a blank screen. The only sound would be the sponsor humming to himself impatiently and tapping his foot. Only when it was time for the commercial would anything be seen. Then the sound would be turned up and the picture would be in color. After the commercial the screen would go blank and the only sound would be the sponsor applauding.

But working with this complex of studio crews, actors, directors, and sponsors has never been a real problem. We all worked in order to make a show that was as good as possible. We all felt responsible to our audience. And even when the show was over for that week, responsibility to the audience didn't stop.

Some of our audience thought we were really a family that lived on East Tremont Avenue in the Bronx. We would get letters asking us what had happened to the apartment house. Some viewers had gone there to look us up and there was no such place and their letters sounded as though they felt cheated. Some felt we had a very good effect on their children and letters would come asking me to say a few words on the air so that Junior would behave. One letter came asking me to, please, keep the son of the house in the pool room. It started:

Dear Mrs. Goldberg:
Say a few words, please, to my son Harold. He's hanging out and my husband is worried he will fall into bad hands. Every time he

comes home his father, my husband a second-time marriage, hits him good but it don't help. Harold calls him bad names and again he goes to the pool hall for a little snooker. Personally, what's wrong with pool? So if you say a few words maybe my husband will listen. Harold is never home when you are on the TV but my husband is. If you say pool is all right I'm sure he'll leave Harold alone.

Very truly,

There wasn't too much I could do for Harold but the letter gave me an idea for a show about pool. Uncle David just happened to buy a pool table and went for lessons to the local pool hall. He fell into company, if not bad, then at least smart enough to know that on Uncle David's pool table they could play for free. The house crawled with shady characters until Jake put his foot down and Sammy taught his dear uncle all he knew about pool.

The Goldbergs were on television for almost ten years and there was hardly a subject we didn't touch. Our limits were simply what we thought our audience would believe we would do. That left out murder, theft, arson, and divorce, among other assorted vices and reverses.

Plotting and writing the shows started early in the morning at about five or six A.M. If the idea was good, the script was written very fast. If the idea had holes in it, the writing could take hours. But before I got down to the writing, I had to start the thinking. And the thinking began with shuffling papers, moving pencils, looking at the morning papers, and doing everything I could do to delay starting. I really always wanted to get at the script but I had to get myself into the mood. I would start biting or chewing on a pencil and then there would come a soft knock inside my head and a voice, a very familiar voice would say:

MOLLY: I could interject?
ME: Where were you?
MOLLY: Visiting upstairs. Stop biting the pencil.

ME: I'm thinking. Whom were you visiting?

MOLLY: Whom? Very fancy. Don't chew the pencil! You'll get an ulcer from eating wood. I was by Mrs. 4 B. We chatted a little back and forth. So stop with the pencil! (*Put it down.*) You know she has a son?

ME: I didn't know.

MOLLY: How many years are you in the building already?

ME: I don't know everybody. (*I pick up the pencil again.*)

MOLLY: Mrs. 4 B's son everybody knows. He's a doctor almost. Third year Med. You know what Mrs. 4 B said? She said her son, almost the doctor, said that chewing pencils absolutely gives ulcers. You know him?

ME: I told you I never met him. (*I put down the pencil.*)

MOLLY: Can you imagine! He's a very good-looking boy. You didn't bunk into him on the stairs?

ME: No. Why?

MOLLY: I thought if maybe and perchance if you had made the acquaintance of the aforesaid . . .

ME (*interior monologue*): There's a plot here someplace. (*Aloud.*) What's wrong?

MOLLY: Did I say? What should be wrong?

ME: I know you, Molly. . . .

MOLLY: It's nothing.

ME: You're not talking to a stranger.

MOLLY: I made a promise.

ME: All right, don't tell me.

MOLLY: Well, if we're talking already, so let's talk. You know why Mrs. 4 B is crying out her heart all the time?

ME: Is it a good reason?

MOLLY: For her it's good. The boy is running with a girl! Can you imagine?

ME: What do you want me to do?

MOLLY: Did I say? But if you're asking, my advice would be he should get married.

ME: You think so?

MOLLY: Positively! you want to know why?

ME: That's a reason?

MOLLY: That's not a reason? Listen, with the eyes he's got, better he should marry a girl. Especially her. She's blind.

ME: Blind?

MOLLY: She's in love and who can't see except those that don't want to? And who doesn't want to? A person in love.

ME: So what can't she see?

MOLLY: She can't see he's crossed a little in the eyes.

ME: You said he was good-looking.

MOLLY: He's not bad but good he's not neither. And if he doesn't get married to the girl while he has a chance I'm afraid of what'll be in later years. Mrs. 4 B'll cry then because he's not married and since she's already in the midst so let it be already.

ME: So what can I do?

MOLLY: Well, since you're asking and if I'm answering so I'll tell you. . . .

Rest assured that Mrs. 4 B's son is practically a married man. In twenty-six and a half minutes of air time the lady upstairs is going to have a daughter-in-law, and she'll even be happy about it. All that has to be worked out are the details, and for that I don't need Molly.

3 *Bedford*

The people who work in radio and television are a very restless group, and there was a time, at the end of the thirties and the beginning of the forties, when being a country squire was what caught their imaginations. Everybody wanted a house in the country but it couldn't be just any house. It had to be near enough to New York so they could still work there but it had to be far enough away from New York so that it was in the country. It had to be small enough so that the upkeep didn't become a hardship; it had to be large enough so that guests would be comfortable. What everybody wanted was a dream house and that's not so easy to find.

I had a very dear friend in those days. He was a cellist who became absolutely convinced that the country was the only place to live. His name was Nicolai Brantchik and from his name you would expect to see a Russian with a fur coat and an astrakhan hat. What in fact you saw was a short, bald, stout man of about fifty who stood only a little higher than his cello and dressed in the fashions that would catch on tomorrow. From the way Nicolai talked about the country it seemed reasonable that he had been brought up on a farm. He hadn't been north of 57th Street in his whole life up till the week he decided that country life was the only life.

One day I just happened to say to Nicolai that we were looking for a place in the country. We had been looking for one for five years and we hadn't found what we wanted. That's all Nicolai had to hear. He told me of the most wonderful place in the world, a village forty miles from New York City called

250

Mount Kisco. There were houses there, and what houses! He guaranteed satisfaction. And when we decided to go for a ride he asked me to drive to his place and he'd show us around.

Because Nicolai could make anything sound interesting, the next weekend we went to Mount Kisco and started looking for Nicolai and his house. Nobody knew of him, nobody had even heard of him.

My father, who was driving, never gives up. While we were in the neighborhood we might as well look around. I agreed. We went to a lady real-estate agent and explained what we wanted. Real-estate agents are always deaf. I wanted to see something with six or seven rooms and she took us out to see something with fifteen or twenty. I kept asking for small and she kept showing us big. One house, in Bedford Hills, a few miles from Mount Kisco, was one of the most charming places I had ever seen. I liked it. My father loved it. It was too large so I didn't even inquire about price. My father did. By the time we left he knew everything there was to know about the house. What I should not have forgotten, after all these years, was what didn't even cross my mind. When Jake fell in love with something, it was as good as his!

When I got back to the city and saw Nicolai at the studio I told him we had driven up to see him and couldn't find his house. Well, he said, it really wasn't *his* house. It belonged to the lady he happened to be living with at the moment. Nevertheless, he said, it was a charming house even if it wasn't his. The woman, he said, was also charming. I didn't know whether he was recommending a house in the country or love in the country.

A few weeks passed without any decisions being made. I wanted to look at more houses, my husband suddenly decided he was going to get interested, and my father was worse than the real-estate agent. He was selling us Bedford, day and night.

We went back to go through the motions of looking at a few

more houses and our real-estate agent brought us back to the house at Bedford again. It *was* a lovely place and between Jake's recommendation, the not-so-stratospheric price, and my husband's agreement with his father-in-law there was nothing else to do but buy the house.

During a rehearsal I told Nicolai that we had bought a home in the country and we were going to be neighbors. Nicolai shook his head at me. The country, he decided, was no place for people in our profession. Traveling back and forth was very wearing and he had given it up. He had refallen in love with the city. The reason was simple when I finally got it out of him; he was in love with the city because he wasn't in love with the woman any longer. He had become a cosmopolite and if I wanted to know he would tell me the best place in all of New York City to have an apartment—Gramercy Park. Why Gramercy Park? He had fallen in love with a woman who had a duplex down there. Why didn't I look in that neighborhood?

The Bedford house hadn't been lived in for seven or eight years when we bought it. That's a little detail that never crosses your mind when you buy a house. It's like falling in love. Faults can be cured later. Well, we were faced with faults. The outside had to be scraped and painted. The house needed new foundations and supporting beams. The roof needed shingling, new screens had to be put up, the porch had to be rebuilt and the grounds had to be put in shape. Inside, some floors needed repairs, the whole interior had to be painted and a hundred other things had to be done. We all made guesses as to how much it was going to cost. My husband's estimate was high, mine was in the middle, and my father's was the lowest. It turned out that my husband was right and my father was very wrong. His excuse was that if I was going to use expensive wallpaper, naturally the cost would go up. The wallpaper was what did it and nothing else—not the new oil furnace, new stove, new refrigerator, or even a whole new roof—the wallpaper was it. The biggest expense we had in the whole house was me. I furnished it. It was no problem because I knew antique dealers and the dealers I didn't know knew friends who knew me. Furnishing the house was something I loved. I covered Pennsylvania and New York State looking for Early American furniture, and with my luck I found everything I was looking for. I had fun. And the furniture I bought, I bought because I liked it and not out of any relationship it might have had with historical events. I found an old cobbler's bench in Pennsylvania and brought it to Bedford with absolutely no idea of what I could do with it. It turned out to be a coffee table for the living room. In upper New York State I found two very old tin-lined cabinets that were once used as sinks and I now use them as boxes for plants. Naturally, I use a cranberry rack as a magazine rack, and I found an Early American dining-room table which—only because my imagination ran dry—we use as a dining-room table.

After a while I found I was mixing periods and enjoying it. My husband and I have a canopied English bed and on one wall is a French dresser, in front of the fireplace are two Biedermeier chairs from Fleischmanns, and the rug on the floor is authentic Sloanes. The sun porch, off the bedroom, is where I write and it's furnished in authentic Me. There's a card table from the apartment in New York, a daybed from heaven knows where, a bureau from storage, and a hooked rug from an auction. The only real piece of Americana in the room is a hope chest dated 1780 in which I keep old scripts and a warm blanket (Saks) for cold days. And on the window sill is a pencil sharpener that I've had since I first began to write years ago.

When I say to people that we like Bedford I can hear my father saying back, "It's a sacrifice but it's home." Of course he's right. The house is a large one. The original and main part was built in the 1700s. It's two stories high with a tremendous attic that runs across the whole house. On one side is a large screened porch and the whole building is shaded by three huge horse-chestnut trees. The new wing of the house, built in the late 1800s, is an exact copy in style of the original building. Together they make an L and to my eyes they are perfectly proportioned.

The grounds around the house roll. There's a lawn and a garden in the back. Looking out from the screened porch you see another lawn that goes downhill to a small lake stocked with bass for my grandsons and across the lake is a long ridge and beyond that a field. Across the road are five acres of land that my father, his democratic principles slipping a little, insisted we buy in order to keep the privacy of Bedford intact. A little distance from the main house is a barn in which we all keep things as a storehouse. I have old scenery and furniture in there. My daughter has play pens and toys, my son has a baby carriage, a few tennis racquets, and odd musical instruments long ago discarded. It's a history of the family in a way and we all go in and out of the barn putting away one thing and taking out another. It's a grab bag of interchangeable parts for us.

A gravel path leads from the barn past a chicken coop and washhouse to the flower garden and a vegetable garden, and finally the greenhouse. Inside the greenhouse is a fig tree and grapevines, hibiscus, poinsettias, African daisies, and orchids that my son has decided to grow. It's his hobby and if I had a hobby that caused me so much grief, I'd give it up. But not him. Every time I turn around he and his son, Adam, think they've found another way to beat nature.

Bedford is a house that keeps changing with the family. The back porch is full of toys in the summer and the laundry room next to it is full of toys in the winter. There's always a sled or a bicycle someplace that is as much a sign of growing and life as the buds on the trees. Bedford gives me the feeling that nothing ends, there's a continuity of seasons, life, children and grand-children, and when I talk like that my children call me Dr. Schweitzer and poor Bedford becomes Lambaréné. It makes me sentimental. I can't help it and I tell them when they get to be my age they'll speak differently. That's when they call me Mrs. Proust.

It might be said that my life, up to now, has been one long hotel. I have no complaints, because the pleasure has always been mine. Most of my younger years were spent at a hotel—and when there was no longer a hotel to spend my time in, the house at Bedford became another hotel. Guests came and guests went—just as in Fleischmanns—except they didn't pay and they stayed for weekends, not two-week vacations.

Guests came in pairs, guests in family groups, and guests by the dozens. When there wasn't room in the house for people we would rent rooms in the village for the overflow. And the guests that came over a period of years were a constantly chang-ing group. They changed as the times changed or as I changed, but there always remained a foundation of friends and family that they revolved around.

In the beginning, when the house was finally finished, there came a group of people that my father decided to call "The Cream of the Cream." Mostly they were professional people, friends and acquaintances I had met in my work. They were writers, artists, performers, agents, theatrical and literary peo-ple. Jake called them "deep thinkers" and complained there was culture in every room and deep discussions on the lawns. He wasn't impressed, but I was. Some of the people in this group became very dear and very close friends—others were exactly what my father said they were, "deep thinkers." To understand what he meant you'd have to hear him say it. My father re-spected knowledge—what he didn't respect was the extreme positiveness of some people who thought they were just a little too smart for ordinary folk. He would listen to the various discussions and then take me into the kitchen to ask me what it all meant. Everybody, he said, had an opinion—they were all against crime as far as he could tell. He was against it, too, but did that make him an intellectual? What he resented most was the attitude that they were right and everybody else was wrong. He took it personally and I couldn't blame him. Each time he came back to me to report another discussion he would be angrier. "Now," he would say, "the big thinkers don't like Hitler! Is that something to talk about? Who likes him? Me they have to convince? I didn't like him five years ago. Maybe I'm a genius."

My father could hold his own with anyone. Maybe he couldn't discuss Gide but he could tell if the speaker discussing Gide was a snob or not—and as soon as he spotted one, no matter what the man, or woman, said, it could never be right.

There was one guest, a writer, Jake really had it in for. Normally, he would have liked the man, for Jake had great respect for men of letters. But when the writer first walked into the house Jake said, "A fake!", and he never changed his mind.

My reaction was, simply, "Pa, don't make any judgments. He happens to be a very respected man."

"Not by me," was all he said.

He was right. According to the writer, nothing in the whole world was right and life seemed to be a losing battle, from childhood on it was a downhill fight that we were all in except himself. He was above the crowd, a lonely observer, born too soon or too late or something.

The writer was a short man, a little too stout, and every time he "drove by" the house it was in a different car with a different woman. The cars he borrowed from friends, who, it seemed, couldn't say no to him. The women he borrowed also. They, too, couldn't say no, but they were all of a pattern. They were disappointed modern-dancer types who wanted to study with Martha Graham but never quite made the grade. They wore dirndl dresses, peasant blouses, and when they weren't barefoot they wore sandals. When the writer talked, they sat at his feet, also in sandals, and listened. Jake called them "glasses of water" and forgot them. They didn't have enough life for him. But it was the writer that took up his attention. Every time Jake passed him he had another story to tell me. "You know who he doesn't like today? Shakespeare!" I didn't want trouble so I would tell my father that the writer was entitled to his opinions and Jake agreed. "Sensible opinions, yes," he would say, "but opinions like that, no! You know what else he said? For *Othello* he gives Shakespeare A for effort. That's an opinion?"

Jake took great pleasure in making sure the writer never got what he wanted. The writer's favorite drink was Scotch and when Jake saw him drive up he would hide the bottles. Then, pleasantly, he would ask the writer what he wanted to drink.

"A little Scotch, please," the writer would say.

"We only have gin," my father would tell him.

"A little coffee then . . ."

"Tea? The grocer didn't deliver yet."

In an effort to make peace I told my father that the writer had written a number of books, but I made the mistake of saying they were mysteries. That's all he had to hear. "Such a big philosopher and he writes he kills her and she kills him? From that he has the right to give marks to Shakespeare?" He relegated the writer to the lending libraries and called him "Killer."

As with everyone he didn't like that person's days at Bedford were numbered. In some way either Jake or fate would catch up with him. The writer, a man with too much ego, never suspected that Jake didn't like him. He even took to calling him "Pop" thinking it was friendly. Jake's reaction was to tell me that, "Something's going to happen to that man and if I liked him I'd tell him but I don't so I won't." Something did happen. A husband who didn't agree with the writer's views on sharing the wealth (car and wife) manhandled him one night and the writer left New York for the coast. Jake's only question was, "How far is California? Three thousand miles? So we'll have a little peace and quiet."

"Pa," I said, "he wasn't that bad. . . ."

"I'll give him E for effort," my father answered, "but I wouldn't pass him."

At one of the Bedford parties, I'm not sure what the celebration was about, we served nothing but champagne. The party went on for hours and my father took charge of everything— including the drinks. The group wasn't one that he was fond of —but he was an old hotelman and guests were guests. Late in the evening I found him in the kitchen pouring ginger ale into some empty champagne bottles and I got very annoyed. He told me to calm down, he knew what he was doing. He pointed to the living room and said that the deep thinkers were a little high, it didn't make any difference what you put in their glasses any more—and, besides, he wanted to save the real stuff for when we had friends at the house. It took a lot of talking but I finally convinced him to open a few more champagne bottles.

People met at Bedford and I'm happy to say a couple of marriages developed. We even had an almost tragedy that started like a television drama. It was late, it was raining, and it was cold. That alone is a mood setting in the country. And when there's a knock at the door at two in the morning you know there has to be a story. The story was—and it's not such a simple one—that a dear friend of mine had fallen in love. Falling in love is wonderful except that the lady in question was married, almost middle-aged, and had a few children. Her husband was a good, kind, and I thought charming man, but once a person gets infatuated you might as well forget about reason. The woman had fallen in love with a headwaiter, but not even a headwaiter with snobbish Continental manners. He was a crude man, not even good-looking. Maybe he'd be all right for Lady Chatterley but not my friend, who was also a lady.

I opened the door and there she stood with her headwaiter. They were eloping and could they stay the night? What could I say? Of course they could stay the night—but in separate rooms. So they stayed. They had to. The woman had told her husband she was coming to visit me. In the morning I had a talk with my friend. Most of the time things are none of my business but this time it was. I don't like to be a moralist but there is right, there is wrong, and there is foolishness. This was foolishness and I told her. I told her to stay at Bedford for a while—think things over, then make up her mind—but I said I didn't think she should rush into such a thing. She agreed to stay—and that was my cue, because if she had refused then I would have known that she was really in love. But you're not in love if you say you'll think about it.

The headwaiter left. At least he had a job and had to be somewhere. The lady was going to follow a little later. She stayed for one day, then she stayed for two days—and every time I saw that she was getting ready to leave I would have another talk with her. If my talk didn't work and she still was ready to leave, Fanny would have a talk with her. We alternated talking for almost a week. Every night I would call her husband and tell him that his wife wanted to stay at Bedford for a little longer and was that all right? It was all right. He wanted her to enjoy herself. At the end of the week, Fanny and I, between us, managed to send her back to her family. Fanny and I glowed for days afterwards, feeling ourselves part Dorothy Dix and part girl scout.

My husband, my father, and myself all hoped for things when we got the house. My father got an idea in his head that a house in the country should have pigeons. Where the idea came from heaven only knows. There was no sense in even talking about it with him because he had his own way of deciding what should be what and any argument about pigeons always ended up the same way: I would say "no," my husband would say "no," and Jake would say, "How can you have a house without pigeons?" The way he said it made it clear that only ignoramuses didn't know the facts of life. He had a natural talent for translating from English to Jake. He got it from his father, Mordecai. Anyway, our noes went in one of Jake's ears and came out of the other yes.

Jake could never be subtle when he tried to hint at things—he wasn't good at it. Lew, Jake, and I would be walking around the grounds and from out of nowhere would come, "You know what's a very nice bird? A pigeon. Very friendly bird. You notice how they eat out of your hand in the city? They even fly. My favorite bird."

"Pa," I would then have to say, "I don't want pigeons." And Lew would tell him that there were pigeons in the city only forty miles away. He could see all the pigeons he wanted to during the winter.

Jake would shrug his shoulders and we would go on walking but ten minutes later he would be at it again. "You know what I heard? I heard that pigeons eat flies. There's lots of flies here."

"Not at all," Lew told him.

"I just saw one."

"It was a bee."

"They also eat bees."

A few weeks passed and I had forgotten all about pigeons. My father was waiting for that—he knew it would happen. I went away for the weekend and when I came back to Bedford I didn't see that anything had changed except that Jake kept looking out of the windows and taking a few more walks than he usually did. Also, when I walked with him, he would keep pointing out the flowers to me. I like flowers, he liked flowers, but I couldn't keep looking at the ground all the time. I just happened to look up at the sky and I saw birds. I followed their flight and they landed on top of the barn where there was a little cupola—just perfect for pigeons.

"Pa," I said, "do you see pigeons?"

He looked at me, startled. "Pigeons? Where?"

I pointed to the top of the barn.

"Looks like swallows, I think."

If there's one bird I can recognize, it's a pigeon and I told him so.

"Not chicken hawks? They have a lot of chicken hawks here," he said.

"Pigeons!" I said.

"They must have flown in from the city."

"That must be it. I can't imagine any other way they could have gotten here."

"Nature!" he said. "Amazing!"

I agreed with him and he asked what I wanted done with the pigeons. "If they're homing pigeons," he said, "it won't be so easy to get rid of them. They look like they like it here. . . ."

With my father, nature, and the pigeons pitted against me, what could I do? My father, all by himself, was trouble enough, but now he had help. "If they're here, so let them stay," I said.

"The poor things," he said. "Maybe I should feed them a little something?"

"I guess so," I told him. "Now that they're guests maybe you better."

"Whatever you say."

Jake acted reluctant about the pigeons for one whole day but he didn't overdo it. It took a little while before he finally told me that he had gotten the pigeons from a dealer in Yonkers who specialized in breeding ordinary city pigeons. The man wasn't interested in improving the breed, all he wanted was to breed pigeons and sell them. My father was exactly the kind of customer he was looking for. I wonder if he ever found another.

We went through almost the same process with chickens. One day there weren't any, the next day there were hundreds. Jake was always trying to find a way to make the land around the house productive. Over the years we had the most expensive corn, peas, and tomatoes in the county. The carrots were our present to the rabbits. We grew them but we never saw them. We had a cow that never gave milk and we almost, not quite, had mink and chinchilla. I wanted to rest, my husband wanted to read in peace—but Jake always had a scheme. The zoning finally made him give up mink and chinchilla. I'm very grateful for zoning.

Things are different today. There's no Jake. He died in 1945 in his own way. He had a heart attack and was brought to a hospital in New York City. It was the first time, in all those years, that I can ever remember him sick. Sickness was something he hated—it wasn't for him. He got better and I had him stay with us at our apartment in the city. He had a private nurse. He didn't want her but he had to have her. When he gave in I knew he was sick. The doctor told him he couldn't smoke —no pipe, no cigars—but smoking was something he refused to give up. He smoked when no one was home and when the nurse was in the kitchen fixing his meals. He figured that if no one knew about it, it couldn't hurt.

Jake was alone in his room. He was getting bored with being in bed. I don't know how he managed it but he sent the nurse out of the room for something. A little bit later he called for us. When we got to his room he was sitting in a chair wearing a nurse's cape and one of her hats. He began joking and we began laughing and then—in a second—it was all over. There wasn't any Jake any more. He just stopped in the middle of a joke.

You don't forget the people you love, especially when they have left you with only happy memories. That's why the houses, the apartments, the places, you've been with them are so important. Jake isn't at Bedford and yet he is. When the family is up there, every once in a while someone will say, "remember what Jake did when . . ." or, "Grandpa used to do this or that . . . ," and then we all laugh about whatever it was just as though he was still there with us. Sometimes it's very lonely without him but it would have been much lonelier if we had never had him.

We can laugh about Jake and the Brandts—a very charming, happy family with their own kind of craziness that especially appealed to Jake. Mrs. Brandt was a health fiend. She made her whole family into health fiends and they would arrive at Bedford in the coldest weather, change into bathing suits, and go for a swim in the pond. Nobody minded, nobody cared, it was their way of living and if they wanted to freeze, good luck. What we appreciated most was that they never tried to persuade us to join them. Now, in cold weather, we look at the pond, hear Jake cluck to himself, and almost see him marching off to the kitchen to make another pot of hot coffee to unfreeze the Brandts.

I remember the first time my daughter-in-law ever visited us. Jake used to say to my son that when he got married make sure it was to a pretty girl. When Dorothy walked into the house, Jake took one look at her and made her pick a pin or a ring from his private collection of jewels. The jewels had little value on the market—they had great value in friendship. When he let Dorothy have her pick, she was a member of the family right there and then.

4 *A Majority of One*

The business of being an entertainer is a very peculiar one. If you have been in it for any time at all you find yourself being identified as one kind of person because of some of the roles you've played. And, because of professional pride, there comes a time when the actor or actress tries to rebel. I know a very nice, sweet, family man—an actor—who started out in the theater thirty-five years ago playing a juvenile villain. As each year passed and as he got older he found himself playing twenty-year-old villains, thirty-year-old fiends, forty-year-old murderers, and today he's playing fifty-year-old psychopaths. All he wants from life, he says, is just once to be a hero. He doesn't want to be caught by the police in the third act any more. It's gotten so that when he walks into a room full of people he gets booed. He's not the only actor in that position. Another actor I know always plays soldiers—corporal or sergeants. He wants terribly to be a captain in his next play but I don't think he'll get promoted.

Actors and actresses get hired by producers for what the producers think they can do. Plays cost a great deal of money to produce and producers don't want to take chances. If they have a play with a neurotic in it they'll say, "Let's get Howie, he's got a good twitch," or if they have a part in a play that calls for an overly protective mother with suicidal tendencies they'll say, "See if Sally can do it; she played the same part in *Oedipus Under the Elms*." And Sally gets the part, does very well, and is in demand by every producer in the country for exactly the

264

same part in a different play. It's as though a musician played Beethoven very well and because of that nobody would give him the chance to play Chopin.

Actors and actresses try to break away from "type casting" but it's difficult. If a producer calls an actor's agent and asks for a young idealist-type actor, the agent sends down six young men —all of whom have at one time or another played young idealists. If the agent sends a man who just happened to have gotten a good review as a comedian, the only thing he gets to read are the magazines in the waiting room.

It's not only actors who get typed. Writers, in their own way, have the same problems. Harry is good for mysteries, Charlie writes a funny script, and Douglas is very good on war stories. It doesn't make any difference what any of them think they can write or want to write—it's what they have written. This is called "the track record," and it may not mean a thing in the long run. Posterity might very well remember a mystery writer for a funny play. But posterity isn't now, and it's in the now that he won't get his chance unless he pushes and tries to convince the powers that be.

The wonderful thing about all this is that the rules of the game can change overnight. Suppose a producer gives an actor a chance. Suppose the actor is a comedian and he's given the part of a serious Latin student caught in a web of circumstances in the Balkans just before World War One. And then, because we're supposing, let's say the play is a taut drama written by an author who never wrote anything but farces before. The producer is famous for his musical comedies and girl shows; the director just came from Off Broadway where he directed ten experimental plays—five English with two characters apiece and five French with just a man and a dog in each. A few backers are found who don't know much about the theater but like the play.

Now, it's the morning before opening night. The people in the know, the readers of *Variety* and *Billboard*, the wise money, and everybody else on the fringes of the theater hear the play is no good. "A bomb" is the expression. If the decision were up to them the closing notices should be hung backstage. But it's not up to them and the play opens. Somehow, between the morning and the evening a miracle happens. The critics rave about the play, the audience is ecstatic, and there are fifteen curtain calls—the play is a hit. Now, what happens? The comedian is in demand by every producer. He's in their files as Student, Latin, idealistype. The playwright is asked to do another war drama and if he comes up with another comedy nobody will listen to him. The director gives up experimental plays and the producer is hailed as an intellectual—and he's laughed at when he says the next thing he's going to do is *Blackouts of 1961*.

Because of the type of role I played for years on radio and television it was only natural that I should be cast as a mother in the things I did outside of *The Goldbergs*. However, like other actresses I yearned for different parts to play—maybe an English countess, a Southern belle, a lady Raffles. But what I wanted I never got except for one season in summer stock when I played the matchmaker in Thornton Wilder's *The Matchmaker*. But summer stock wasn't Broadway and I wanted Broadway. I had been there once and I wanted to go there again. In the summer of 1958 I began to write my own play, and even though it was my play, I went and cast myself as the mother. I was my own victim. I kept telling myself I wanted to play a part in a Greek drama, a French farce, or even *Angel Street*. Here I was writing a play that was about a mother!

I was at Bedford writing when the Theatre Guild called. It was Lawrence Langner, who said he had a play he wanted me to read. And when Mr. Langner of the Theatre Guild says he has a play he wants you to read, you read, immediately if possible.

They sent the play. I read it but I wasn't convinced. I gave it to my husband to read, then my son read it, and then we sat down to discuss it. The play, *A Majority of One* by Leonard Spiegelgass, was, again, about a mother. A Jewish widow with a daughter, a son-in-law, and an accent. The play had a Japanese industrialist—that was a switch anyway. I didn't feel that I wanted to be a mother again in a play. The mother, Mrs. Jacobi, seemed to be a nice enough woman. She was from the Bronx and a very familiar character to me. The daughter I had also met, the son-in-law, too. My first reaction was that the play wasn't quite what I wanted.

I had been a Jewish mother for too many years. I wanted to break away from my self-imposed environment and move into a different world as a different person. I wanted to talk English without an accent, I didn't want to be predictable, but here was a chance to be on Broadway. I didn't know what to do. I just wasn't in my Bronx mother mood. I was feeling more like a British heroine, a Mrs. Miniver on the white cliffs of Dover.

But, even before I had a chance to say "yes" it began to look as though I wasn't going to have a chance to make up my mind. Somebody someplace who was involved in the play said they thought my playing Mrs. Jacobi would remind people too much of Molly Goldberg. I figured that that was their problem, not mine, but in spite of philosophy and in spite of not even having agreed to do the play I felt bad, rejected, even annoyed.

The theater has a grapevine that spies could take lessons from and rumors filtered out to me in Bedford Hills. The casting of Mrs. Jacobi, an undeniably Jewish lady, was going through a reevaluation. This high-sounding phrase meant that someone was looking for a non-Jewish lady to play the part. That didn't bother me. There's no law that says an actress has to be of the same religion as the person she's supposed to play. Not even Stanislavski would insist on such idealism. Lloyd Nolan who played Commander Queeg didn't have to join the Navy for thirty years before he got the part. The only disturbing thing to me was the thought of being rejected because of my past. As I saw the problem it was too late for me to change my religion.

I was recasting the play one morning when I had a call from Garson Kanin. I've known Garson for years, since he was a child actor on *The Goldbergs* who played the part of a neighbor's child called Malcolm. Malcolm had a habit of asking me for a banana every time he came in. I couldn't refuse a child so I always said, "Take" when he asked. As soon as I said "Take" Malcolm would say, "I took it already." It was a running gag with the show and "Malcolm" Kanin and I have been friends ever since. He called to say that he had heard other actresses were being considered for the part of Mrs. Jacobi and wasn't I going to take it. I said that I had heard some people felt I was going to remind an audience too much of Molly. There was a pause on the other end of the phone and then Garson said, "What's wrong with that? They might even sell a few tickets."

That possibility must have crossed somebody's mind also because a few hours later the Guild called to ask me if I would do the play. They said that Sir Cedric Hardwicke had agreed to play the Japanese industrialist and that Dore Schary was producing and directing. I said "Yes!" before the voice on the other end had even stopped. Sir Cedric was, in my opinion, an extraordinary actor, a man I had always admired but only from the audience. Dore Schary had a "track record" that couldn't be equaled, and the whole production was under the aegis of the Theatre Guild.

We went into rehearsal in the fall of 1958 and after the first five minutes I was wishing I had never started. Reading a play with all the actors sitting around a table is a terrible experience. The words sound wrong, the basic idea seems weak, and everything you've imagined the play could be reading it at home seems to have evaporated. At those first readings a finished production on the stage and in front of an audience seems as remote as getting to the moon.

I controlled myself. If all the other actors and actresses could sit there calmly messing up their lines, so could I. Out of the corner of my eye I watched Sir Cedric, the most experienced of all of us, and I caught not the slightest glimmer of a doubt from him. He read, he spoke his lines, fiddled with his glasses and fingered his tie as though he had been through this routine a million times, and the more he read the more he became the Japanese industrialist. By the time the second day had finished I was saying to myself that it was wonderful for a Japanese man to speak English so well. In no time at all he literally became the part, and it was only during breaks that he reverted to his very British self.

Sir Cedric had a view of himself. He was an actor, a performer with hundreds of years of tradition behind him. He walked with the air of a man who had a right to be proud and yet he had the humility of a sensitive human being. He was always correct and polite and treated his fellow performers as equal members in a very difficult craft. Also, when he wanted to, he could have everyone roaring with laughter. When several young, pretty girls came by to watch rehearsals, someone remarked on how decorative they were. Sir Cedric said they were indeed but to him they looked more like possible plaintiffs. Once, in a relaxed mood, he told us how he had gotten to be knighted. He said they were looking for an actor who was English and heterosexual; he happened to be the only one who fit the description.

Little by little the play began to take shape. Words were changed, scenes strengthened, and the original conception by Leonard Spiegelgass started to become an entity. The characters left the paper of the script and began to move around a bare stage almost like people. The changes were not what I'd call script changes. Words and lines here and there were altered to suit the actor or actress. Writing dialogue for actors he's never met is a job a writer does knowing that he's probably not putting down the final version. Some actors can say things in one way but not in another and between writer and actor there must be compromises. A writer must do the script the way he thinks it should be and then, during rehearsals, his ear makes the necessary changes.

It's not always the actor that determines the changes. Most of the time the director sees things on a stage that he didn't see in the script. Sometimes, as a play takes shape on stage, some scenes have to be dropped or new scenes have to be written. In *Majority of One* we had no problems with personalities or egos. Leonard Spiegelgass was always willing. Dore Schary listened to suggestions from all of us and he was a very patient man. Sir Cedric was a "pro" and "pros" don't complain, they work. As far as I was concerned I learned. I watched all the ingredients that went into a play and the more I watched and the more I worked the more I found that, finally, I was becoming Mrs. Jacobi, the widow with a married daughter and the memories of a dead husband and a son killed in the Pacific.

Mrs. Jacobi, understanding in all things, hated the Japanese because of the death of her son. Her daughter, married to a young man in the State Department, is going to Japan on a mission with her husband. They invite her to go with them, and, finally and in spite of her dislike of Japan, she agrees to leave her comfortable Bronx apartment and go. On the boat to Japan Mrs. Jacobi meets the Japanese industrialist, a man who

will be dealing with her son-in-law when he gets to Tokyo. The
two reach a certain understanding when Mrs. Jacobi finds that
the man has also lost a son in the fighting and a wife in the
bombings. They react to each other as human beings—but the
son-in-law objects to Mrs. Jacobi seeing too much of the industrialist. It may, in some way, compromise the work he is to
do there.

The solution to *A Majority of One* was highly predictable.
Mrs. Jacobi and her Japanese industrialist would solve not only
their personal problems but also the State Department's—and
the audience would be left with a feeling that East and West
would hold hands and live happily ever after if the State Department just had a few more sensible Bronx widow ladies
down in Washington.

The more we rehearsed and the more we were pushed and
pulled around the stage by Dore Schary the more we began to
feel about the people we were playing. And that meant we had
time to concentrate on other aspects of the show, the first being:
what if *A Majority of One* was a flop? To each other we pretended that there was no such possibility. The word "flop" was
never said out loud in the fear that some higher being, the God
of Percentages and SRO, would be listening and take a hint. It's
not that actors are superstitious, only careful. They live in a
world somebody made up for them and they've all played so
many outlandish parts that anything, even superstition, is possible. Actors don't whistle in dressing rooms. Actors never say
"good luck," they say "break a leg," because they know the
exact opposite of what they say is heard somewhere and too
often happens. I know an actor who loves animals but would
sooner shoot a black cat than take a chance of having it cross
in front of him during the rehearsal period.

And then, suddenly, we opened. Abruptly and as though without warning. To me it seemed that I had just gotten the script

and all of a sudden I was faced with an opening night in Philadelphia. I tried to believe this was all happening to me but it was as though I was watching a movie that didn't make sense. I was on a train, I was in a hotel room, and before I knew it I was being made up. It was only when I was on the stage waiting for the curtain to go up that the image I was looking at and myself came together and even at that moment time seemed very strange. In a few seconds before the curtain's rise, the stage manager walked around checking the props like a stranger in slow motion.

When the curtain went up I couldn't see beyond the footlights and my world was suddenly only as deep as the stage and as long as the distance between the proscenium arches. The three acts went fast and, it seemed to me, smoothly, and when it was all over we heard heavy applause and later read wonderful notices and found that we were booked solid for our stay.

We were getting seasoned "out of town" but there was a terrible black cloud staring us in the face: Broadway! In Philadelphia we could be wonderful but in New York we could still be chopped to ribbons. It's true that, on the basis of the Philadelphia reviews, we had a big advance sale in New York. But we had our pride, and we had our fears. We wanted to be a hit. That's part of what an actor lives for, and even if the show is assured a run nobody wants to be in a flop. No matter what *we* or the Philadelphians thought about the play or the performances, the critics and the audiences in New York would still make or break us.

Before going to New York we were booked in Boston. For some reason theater people approach a run in Boston as not so much out of town but out of the country altogether. Dore Schary warned us all that in Boston, a town full of blue bloods and Yankees and codfish, we shouldn't expect too many laughs—if any. He told us to play the play and not be thrown if there were no reactions. Boston has a reputation for not having a sense of humor. We went on expecting the worst and came off with only the best. Blue bloods laugh and Yankees too, it seems. They laughed as hard as the common people of Philadelphia and it only proves that the state of the Union is ticklish and in the same places.

The New York opening was scheduled for February 16, 1959, and the date started to come closer and closer, like a train that couldn't be stopped. It was as though we were all back in school and there was an examination coming, or as though we all had to go to the dentist together. Then the day came. I told myself I wasn't going to worry. I even went to a movie in the afternoon and don't think I don't remember all about it, except that it was a double feature, a western and a mystery. While I watched the western I saw Sir Cedric as a cowboy and myself as the dance-hall hostess—and when the scene shifted from the town to back at the ranch, Sir Cedric was the foreman with two guns and I was the rancher's daughter. In the mystery picture Cedric was the detective and I was the victim's wife—and so it went, on into the long afternoon.

When I left the movie house I walked back to the theater past people all walking in the wrong direction or going into restaurants. I kept wondering what was the matter with them, didn't they know there was a play opening tonight? They all ought to be backstage getting on the make-up. I walked past doughnut shops and secondhand book stores. The street lights were just going on and as I turned down the block where the theater was the marquee lights went on. My name was up there next to Sir Cedric Hardwicke's and I thought to myself, "You're on Broadway and in very good company." I turned into Schubert Alley and opened the stage door and I began to get ready for who knew what.

None of us, even Sir Cedric, knew what we were in for. Dore

Schary was going from dressing room to dressing room being kind and understanding and reassuring. He had the look of a man who needed a little comforting himself. Dore's folks had been in the hotel business just like mine. I told him to remember back to when the curtain went up for the season at the hotel. Now *that* had been a tense moment, what with empty rooms and temperamental chefs and rainy weather. If the play didn't go over in New York none of us would starve but in the old days if the hotel season wasn't a success, we would have gone hungry. There were worse things than bad reviews. I meant what I was saying but after we had hugged each other one last time and Dore went off to reassure another actor, I looked at myself in the mirror and asked myself what was worse than bad reviews? I couldn't think of a thing.

Well, what was done was done. I felt myself in the position of someone jumping from a plane—if the parachute opened, I'd live through the night. If it didn't, well, it was too late to worry.

I wish I could remember details of that first New York performance but I can't because hundreds of other nights and matinees, all with almost the same lines and expressions, laughs and gestures, have intervened. I only remember how worried I was about the critics. Now and then I would glance over the footlights to try to catch a glimpse of those austere judges (stern-faced, I imagined them)—Mr. Atkinson and Mr. Kerr and Mr. Chapman and the others. I didn't see them but I thought I could hear them growling to one another. It was probably my own nervous stomach.

We finished to wave after wave of applause. I found the tears beginning to play havoc with my make-up. Someone out front even shouted "bravo!" It was probably Lew.

After the curtain fell on the last act, backstage was mobbed. An opening night audience is made up of families, friends, actors who know everyone in the cast—and they all come back to say that everyone was wonderful and the play is a hit. What else can they say?

Then came the waiting up for the reviews. Usually there's a party someplace—Sardi's, most likely—where everyone waits and pretends he doesn't care. That kind of a party isn't for me. I like to go home and get the news in familiar surroundings. What'll be'll be which is Yiddish for "Que Sera Sera."

My family and a few friends came over to the house and we had our own nervous party. Henry Weinstein, then of the Theatre Guild, a man with connections, kept a line open to his office. He had stationed people at newsstands waiting for the first editions and every time the phone rang we lost our sophistication and jumped. When the papers came out, Henry had the reviews read to him over the phone. He repeated them line for line as they were said to him. I stayed away but Lew came running to me with each good line. By the time I had pieced everything together it dawned on me that we were a hit! I couldn't believe it and I tried to make believe that it wasn't news to me; that I knew it all along. It was only when I went to bed that night and was alone with my husband that I could relax enough to tell him how glad I was that it was all over and that there was a happy ending.

"My dear girl," Lew said, "this is just the beginning," and the more I thought about what he was saying, the better I liked it. A new beginning is much better than a happy ending.

Lew was so right. *Majority* ran on and on and it's still running.

Also out in Hollywood, business goes on as usual. That lovely lady Rosalind Russell has been cast as Mrs. Jacobi and she's taking Yiddish lessons night and day to pick up the accent. Like I said in the beginning, I was born with advantages.

5 *Through a Glass, Brightly*

I think that we all live in worlds that are part real, part unreal, sometimes wishing that the real might be touched with just a little of the unreal.

My profession has been making-believe. Almost every day I move from my real apartment to a stage apartment. I write words for characters who never were but aren't too different from people I've really known. I have enjoyed this double identity so much that I've never really asked myself "Why?"

When I put on make-up I watch myself become another person. When I take it off I watch myself becoming me again. But then I have a third image to contend with when someone from a long time ago knocks on the dressing room door, as so often happens. Then, in the mirror, I see Tillie, the daughter of Jake and Dinah.

A dressing room is like that. The past keeps walking in. I'm happy to see it, happy to know it's still there, and happy that a memory can still be reality. It's like reading Proust long ago with Lew and the title is Tillie's Way. Time hasn't moved and yesterday was just a few minutes ago. And when I look at my face in the mirror again I think that maybe I have a little too much make-up on—too much putty here and there, and I've penciled in too many lines.

Whitey, the bellboy from Fleischmanns, came to visit one night and he's still Whitey even if he's Mr. Stone and he owns oil wells and a factory in Texas. On the outside he's a stout, bald-headed man, but inside is the thin little boy with the same sense of humor and the same understanding of people. Whitey, the younger, looks out of the eyes and it's by the eyes that I know he's really Whitey. In my dressing room that night we started in where we had left off just as though thirty years ago was yesterday and Whitey had run down to the village for something and come back dressed as his rich father.

So many of the people who come backstage were friends of my parents and they say, "You don't remember me?" Could I forget people who still call my mother and father Jake and Dinah? One night "Nahrishkeit" came for a visit. That's the only name I ever knew him by. In English it means "Foolishness." My father named him. He was a Lexington Avenue bookbinder and everybody thought that if a person bound books he also must have read them. Nahrishkeit was looked on as the final authority in any argument and when he was asked a question he always came up with an answer—the wrong one. He liked to make believe that knowledge rubbed off on his hands even if he never opened a book to read it. That's why my father called him Foolishness. Still, he was lovable foolish, not nasty foolish. Poor Nahrishkeit! He came to see me after the play and he talked about it as if he had never seen it but had just looked at the billboards outside.

Where did it all begin? With a little girl named Tillie writing skits—were they bad? good? so-so? who knows? who cares?— for rainsoaked guests at a Catskill hotel. From Tillie of Fleischmanns to Molly on the air is, looking back, an easy step to follow. And from there to television and Broadway—this seems a natural progression.

Where will it all lead? I only know the next step—that's all I've ever wanted to know. From *Majority of One* I am going to a television series called *The Freshman,* about a widowed grandmother who goes to college and studies under a kindly middle-aged professor with impeccable manners. You guessed

it—Sir Cedric Hardwicke. I wanted to call the series *Hello,
Mr. Chips,* but no one would listen to me.

After that? Your guess is as good as mine. It could be off
Broadway in somebody's experiment—it could be on Broadway in somebody's sure thing. Vaudeville might even come
back. Who knows? I don't. That's what makes it so much fun.